Buddhism and Business

Contemporary Buddhism

MARK M. ROWE, SERIES EDITOR

Architects of Buddhist Leisure: Socially Disengaged Buddhism in Asia's Museums, Monuments, and Amusement Parks
Justin Thomas McDaniel

Educating Monks: Minority Buddhism on China's Southwest Border
Thomas A. Borchert

From the Mountains to the Cities: Buddhist Propagation in the History of Modern Korean Buddhism
Mark A. Nathan

From Indra's Net to Internet: Communication, Technology, and the Evolution of Buddhist Ideas
Daniel Veidlinger

Soka Gakkai's Human Revolution: The Rise of a Mimetic Nation in Modern Japan
Levi McLaughlin

Guardians of the Buddha's Home: Domestic Religion in the Contemporary Jōdo Shinshū
Jessica Starling

Morality and Monastic Revival in Post-Mao Tibet
Jane E. Caple

Buddhist Tourism in Asia
Edited by Courtney Bruntz and Brooke Schedneck

Monastic Education in Korea: Teaching Monks about Buddhism in the Modern Age
Uri Kaplan

Buddhism and Business: Merit, Material Wealth, and Morality in the Global Market Economy
Edited by Trine Brox and Elizabeth Williams-Oerberg

Buddhism and Business

Merit, Material Wealth, and Morality in the Global Market Economy

Edited by Trine Brox and Elizabeth Williams-Oerberg

UNIVERSITY OF HAWAI'I PRESS
HONOLULU

Paperback edition 2021

Printed in the United States of America

26 25 24 23 22 21 6 5 4 3 2 1

Library of Congress Cataloging-in-Publication Data

Names: Brox, Trine, editor. | Williams-Oerberg, Elizabeth, editor.
Title: Buddhism and business : merit, material wealth, and morality in the global market economy / edited by Trine Brox, Elizabeth Williams-Oerberg.
Other titles: Contemporary Buddhism.
Description: Honolulu : University of Hawai'i Press, [2020] | Series: Contemporary Buddhism | Includes bibliographical references and index.
Identifiers: LCCN 2019057906 | ISBN 9780824882730 (hardcover) | ISBN 9780824884161 (adobe pdf) | ISBN 9780824884178 (epub) | ISBN 9780824884185 (kindle edition)
Subjects: LCSH: Buddhism—Economic aspects. | Economics—Religious aspects—Buddhism.
Classification: LCC BQ4570.E25 B84 2020 | DDC 294.3/373—dc23
LC record available at https://lccn.loc.gov/2019057906

ISBN 978-0-8248-8979-1 (pbk.)

University of Hawai'i Press books are printed on acid-free paper and meet the guidelines for permanence and durability of the Council on Library Resources.

Cover photo: Buddha statues being made in a factory park, Sichuan, China. Photo by Trine Brox.

Contents

Series Editor's Preface

DUE IN PART TO WHAT GREGORY SCHOPEN famously called the "Protestant presuppositions" of Buddhist studies, scholars are only just beginning to conduct serious research into the connections between Buddhism and business. This exhilarating, multi-authored volume thus marks a crucial development in the field by using ethnographic case studies from Asia, Europe, and beyond to develop new theoretical frameworks for understanding the "economics of religion." Although critiques of Buddhist materialism have dogged the tradition for millennia, Buddhist institutions have always been embedded in market economies. Rather than offer further examples of Buddhist commoditization, the authors focus on the very processes of commodification and commercialization—how exactly are Buddhists engaging with markets, commodities, and exchange in an era of neo-liberalism? How are Buddhist semantics being deployed in economic contexts? Approaching Buddhism as both "commodity and capital," they present explorations of Buddhist branding, "prosperity Buddhism," the affective and gendered elements of Buddhist giving, the "blasphemy" of Buddhist marketing, mindfulness and self-actualization in the work place, the connection between wealth and monastic virtue, and "constellative networks" in Buddhist urbanism. The results will have far-reaching effects on how scholars approach the business of Buddhism.

Acknowledgments

THE PRESENT VOLUME IS THE RESULT OF an international, interdisciplinary, and collaborative research project, Buddhism, Business, and Believers (the BBB project), under the auspices of the Center for Contemporary Buddhist Studies at the Department of Cross-Cultural and Regional Studies, University of Copenhagen. The editors gratefully acknowledge generous financial support from the Danish Council for Independent Research | Humanities. Additionally, the Carlsberg Foundation granted funding toward several activities as well as a postdoctoral research position organized under the BBB project. We are grateful for the inspiration and insight we have gained through the discussions and presentations by participants at the conference "Buddhism, Business, and Economic Relations—in Asia and Beyond" (University of Copenhagen, October 2016), the panel "Buddhism and Business: Examining Ambiguous Religious Economic Practices from the Past to the Present" (International Association for Tibetan Studies, Bergen, 2016), and the panel "Buddhist Wealth Accumulation and Distribution: The Spiritual Politics of Wealth in the Global Economy" (Association for Asian Studies, Philadelphia, 2014), which were organized as part of the BBB project. We would like to thank Niclas Juul and Jennifer Durant, who were our student assistants and helped us copyedit the manuscript. We also want to thank Thomas Nielsen, Tabita Rosendal Ebbesen, Solvej Hyveled Nielsen, Janus Søndergaard Hjorth, Therese Fredgaard, and Renee Maria Kazimierska Andersen, who helped us organize conferences and workshops in Copenhagen. Finally, at the University of Hawai'i Press, we are grateful to our two anonymous reviewers, whose encouragement and feedback contributed to the final manuscript; Stephanie Chun, our acquisitions editor; Cheryl Loe, our managing editor; and Robert Fellman, our copy editor.

Introduction

Buddhist Encounters with the Global Market Economy and Consumer Society

Elizabeth Williams-Oerberg and Trine Brox

A VOLUME THAT FOCUSES ON BUDDHISM AND Buddhists in the global market economy brings attention to what at first glance might seem to be a paradox: For a religion that emphasizes the importance of nonattachment to materiality and money, how is it that Buddhists become involved with the global market in the first place? Buddhists are often depicted as ideally refraining from economic activities, exemplified by images of a meditating Buddhist adept sitting in the lotus position on top of a mountain, displaying their disengagement with the wider society. Associating Buddhism with asceticism and antimaterialism has been a longstanding trope in predominantly Orientalist discourses, albeit a positive one that postulates a moral, spiritual East in contrast to an immoral, materialistic West. The formulation of Buddhists as noneconomic or "economy-less" has been promoted by prominent scholars such as Max Weber (1958), with the ideal Buddhist somehow apart from economic as well as political and social engagements in their pursuit of spiritual development and "salvation" (see also Pryor 1990). In some cases Buddhism as a religious system has been interpreted as incompatible with modern economics (Lorentz 2001). These widespread understandings give prominence to ideals written in scriptural sources, a process of "textualization" in which Western scholars in particular have emphasized what is written in texts rather than what is practiced in local contexts (see Hallisey 1995). Consequently, this text-based approach has led to understanding Buddhism as prioritizing asceticism over wealth and spirituality over materiality, contributing to the image of Buddhism as a religion, philosophy, and lifestyle devoid of economic concerns and engagement.

This volume attempts to redress these understandings and assumptions about Buddhists as somehow apart from economic activity and ideally apart from the global market economy. As Reader and Tanabe (1998, 229) have pointed out, "economics, marketing, and commercialization are part of the religious process." One could even say that "Buddhism happens economically" (King 2016, 4). The chapters in this volume attest to how connections between Buddhism and the economy are in fact numerous and multifaceted. The authors take a closer look at the entanglements of Buddhists and the global market economy and present new research on contemporary Buddhist economic dynamics. The volume highlights a dual emphasis on not only the economic dimensions of religion but also the religious dimensions of economic life. In other words, the contributions in the volume bring attention to how Buddhists have engaged with the global market economy and how Buddhism has been drawn upon to expand business and consumer capitalism.

Although we focus on contemporary Buddhist-economic engagements, it is important to stress that these economic relations are a continuation of processes that have a long history (Benavides 2005). Material and economic engagements have been central aspects of Buddhist life since at least the fifth century BCE, the time of the historical Buddha (Benavides 2005; Schopen 1999, 2004), and the spread and development of Buddhism throughout Asia and globally has been largely mediated by economic relations (Bailey and Mabbett 2003; King 2016). Buddhist monastic institutions have been dependent on economic relations for the growth and sustenance of clerical livelihoods, with the financing of monasteries typically dependant upon donations (Skt.: *dāna*) of food, cash, and free labor but also upon fundraising and business ventures in which surpluses have been channeled into the monastery or temple economy (Brox and Williams-Oerberg 2017; Walsh 2007, 2010). In this manner, Buddhist individuals and institutions have always depended on economic and material resources in order to operate and expand.

More recently, the interconnectedness between the economy and Buddhism has undergone further developments with the impact of the global market economy in the contemporary world. Whether as an adoption of market logics to promote the teachings of the Buddha, as a source of semantics and technologies to maximize company profits, or as a reaction against the marketing and branding of Buddhism, Buddhism in the twenty-first century is marked by a heightened engagement with capitalism and market economics.

Buddhist Economics versus Economics of Buddhism

In response to contemporary changes in the global market economy, an entire field of study and advocacy has arisen that explores "Buddhist economics." A focus on how Buddhists engage with economics and general concern about how one *should* engage economically has led to a turn to Buddhism for insight. Schumacher (1973) coined the term "Buddhist economics" as an alternative to, and deliverance from, heedless consumerism and capitalism.[1] While the field of Buddhist economics arose with the work of Schumacher, Thai monastic scholars (e.g., Payutto 1998; Sivaraksa 2011) picked up this thread and related Schumacher's ideas to doctrinal sources. The field of Buddhist economics has since turned into a transnational movement with contributions by scholars from various Buddhist traditions and Western academics (King 2016).[2]

While this approach has benefited some scholars as well as Buddhists/non-Buddhists in their attempts to think about the economic conditions of late modernity and consumer capitalism, we take a very different approach to the field of Buddhism and economics. Instead of creating normative frameworks for how one *should* engage economically, we look toward the dynamics of how Buddhists *are* engaging with these newer market dynamics in a global age and of how Buddhism is being engaged economically by Buddhists and non-Buddhists alike. In other words, we do not focus on how Buddhism might provide a remedy for modern ailments amid a capitalist consumer society; rather, we turn to how Buddhists engage in processes of commodification and commercialization and to how these processes, while often assumed to lead to a lessening of authenticity and authority, may in some cases lead to an increase in authority and the spread of Buddhism. Thus, instead of considering Buddhist economics, we look at the economic framing of Buddhism, the inherent economic-ness of Buddhist action and engagement, and how this Buddhist economic engagement is pursued by Buddhists and non-Buddhists alike within the current modern consumer society.

Late Modernity and the New Spirit of Capitalism

The current global context within which religions are positioned has altered significantly with the rise and spread of what has been termed "late modernity" (Giddens 1991) or "second modernity" (Beck 2002). Whereas the first modernity was marked by a process of industrialization and resulting changes in the social fabric of society, with increasing urbanization and bureaucratization, the second modernity has entailed a loosening of the powers of the nation-state with the growth of free-market capitalism, advancements in technology, and globalization (Speck 2013, 27). While the first modernity was characterized by "socially integrating institutions" such as the nuclear family, class-communal relations, religious organizations, etc., the second modernity is characterized by the emphasis on the individual that can be self-realized through consumerism and spirituality (Speck 2013, 27; see also Taylor 2007). Late modernity is marked by the twin processes of globalization and commoditization in which a growing international exchange (that is, globalization)—not only economic but also social, cultural, political, and religious exchange—is accompanied by the wholesale marketing of all aspects of human life and society (that is, commoditization) (Dawson 2013, 133). Luc Boltanski and Eve Chiapello (2005, 162) have analyzed this contemporary economic condition as the advent of a "new spirit of capitalism." This new spirit involves "a major re-organisation in dominant value systems," in which recent transitions in capitalist dynamics have entailed ideological changes (162). With the rise and spread of neoliberalism, which professes the efficiency and rationality of markets and the positioning of all social aspects as marketable, a "new spirit of capitalism" has arisen, leading to an "element of profit into every service" (Gauthier, Woodhead, and Martikainen 2013, 2). Within this context, economics has affected all aspects of social, cultural, and religious life.

These socioeconomic transitions have led to the rise of the "consumer society," in which consumerism has become a powerful cultural vector and where marketization works to position consumerism and consumption as a "desirable ethos" (Gauthier, Woodhead, and Martikainen 2013, 16). The rise of the consumer society coincided with late modernity within a context of postindustrialization, where the emphasis has turned from production to consumption (Koch 2016, 357).[3] Within this new spirit of capitalism and the consumer society, the market has become a primary site as not only a place for the exchange of goods but also for creating extended networks of persons, companies, and organizations (Koch 2016, 358). In this sense, "markets are marketplaces: loci for complex social interactions and social reformations. They are socially instituted and socially embedded institutions that are best described as networked and hyper-mediatised arenas of mutual exposure" (Gauthier, Woodhead, and Martikainen 2013, 18). The consumer market has thus become a central institution shaping social interaction and global religious formations in this context of late modernity.

Furthermore, with the growth and spread of neoliberalism accompanying these processes, society has become increasingly organized through a management ethos that emphasizes self-realization, especially through consumption. Consumption, in this sense, is a social fact, not just an economic one. Through the functions of meaning, value, and communication, consumer goods become markers of social relations and socially constructed meanings (Gauthier, Woodhead, and Martikainen 2013, 11). In this way, consumer capitalism entails a process in which social life becomes mediated through global market relations. With the fundamental processes of marketization, commoditization, advertising, and branding affecting the choice and consumption of commodities, individuals increasingly define themselves through consumption practices.

The effect that consumer culture and commodification has had on religion has often been framed as destructive, leading to the debasement of the spiritual and aesthetic ethos of religion (McKenzie 2013, 159; Obadia, this volume). Carrette and King (2005), in their book *Selling Spirituality*, paint a dark portrait of not only the state of religions but the state of humanity, in which big business has "taken over" religion and promoted spirituality in its place in order to promote a market-oriented value system (28). It is not surprising that economic engagement has invoked moral trepidation since, as Koch (2016, 362) astutely points out: "ethics and economics are two evaluative perspectives on human actions." The relation between economy and religion highlights these moral quandaries, according to Koch, since religious organizations are often in a field of material as well as symbolic exchange.

The new spirit of capitalism and relatively recent changes in the global market economy have indeed resulted in "a major re-organisation in dominant value systems" (Boltanski and Chiapello 2005, 162). However, in contrast to the work of Carrette and King, we argue that, while issues can be raised as to the moral and ethical practice of commoditizing religion, in which market dynamics are the pervasive exchange relation regarding religion, this context is not only unavoidable but also more complex than merely "positive" or "negative." Within this current consumer society, for example, Buddhists participate and orchestrate the accumulation of material wealth and capital. The consumption of associated Buddhist goods and services offered on the global marketplace allows access to and fosters the spread of Buddhism. It also aids in the establishment of "constellative networks" (Smyer Yü, this volume) that strengthen the position of especially charismatic and entrepreneurial monks, nuns, and lay Buddhist leaders. Buddhist networks thus are often facilitated by the global market economy in which consumption practices also carry and express values. In this way, rather than emphasizing the corroborative impact of consumer capitalism on Buddhism, we argue it is necessary to take into consideration the possibilities and complexities that this consumer society has had on contemporary Buddhist practices in Asia and beyond.

Theoretical Approaches to Buddhism and Economy

The twentieth century brought a wave of theories as to the position of religion within late modernity. The predominant assumption underlining these theories has been that of secularization: religion would decline and become increasingly relegated to the private sphere, apart from social, economic, and political spheres of activity—a process that Casanova (2006) refers to as "differentiation." However, these theories of secularization have since been largely reevaluated and discarded (Berger 2012; Bubandt and van Beek 2012; Stark 1999). Religion in many contexts has simply not disappeared from the public sphere as presumed, nor does it seem likely that this will happen in the future.

Economists, on the other hand, have tended to analyze the market economy as somehow apart from social, political, and religious aspects, even though it has been well documented that the economy is indeed embedded in social relations (Douglas and Isherwood 1979). While Karl Polanyi's (1944) concept of embeddedness has been drawn upon widely in these discussions, Polanyi went to great lengths to show how the economy was embedded in pre-capitalist societies. According to Polanyi, with the rise of capitalism and the market economy, the economy would somehow become dis-embedded. While this process has perhaps not occurred as Polanyi predicted, we can return to Polanyi to analyze how the global market economy is embedded in religious contexts and how religions are embedded in economic contexts in global capitalist societies—in sum, how religion and economy are interdependent (Koch 2016, 355–356; see also King 2016, 4; Martikainen and Gauthier 2013, 16).

In considering how to approach the complex entwinement of Buddhism and economics, Lionel Obadia discusses in this volume whether an economic model that has been framed after the vagaries of Christianity in a Euro-American context can apply to studies of Buddhism in Asian contexts. He argues that we must scrutinize two parallel conceptual repertoires: economy in an analogical perspective (via Max Weber) and an ontological perspective (via Walter Benjamin). These two perspectives use similar language, but they aim to describe different realities. Other studies employ the vocabulary of economics in their analysis, such as "market," "consumers," "entrepreneurs," "competition," and "capital," in order to describe religious dynamics. Examples include how Buddhist organizations compete for shares in a "spiritual marketplace" (Kitiarsa 2010) or "religious market" (Taylor 2008) and how economic capital can be exchanged for spiritual and cultural capital (Bao 2005). The chapters in this volume point out the limitations of economic metaphors and economistic readings of Buddhism, although they do indeed talk about economic relations. They highlight how affective measures alter market-driven appraisals and show us that it is not all about *Homo economicus*, that is, about the rational calculation of how to maximize self-interest (see, for example, Caple and McLaughlin, this volume). However, some Buddhists apply a similar economic lexicon to describe Buddhist dynamics, for instance when one interlocutor described to Borup (this volume) the workings of religious meritocracy, where devotion and rituals were investments in a "karmic savings account." This merely brings attention to the need for more studies into the emic workings and understandings of the relationship between economy and religion, especially within the changing dynamics of the global market economy.

Buddhism in the Global Market Economy

The contributing authors in this volume take a closer look at this complex religio-economic embeddedness and examine particular instances of how Buddhists engage with and how Buddhism is engaged in the global market economy. Within this new spirit of capitalism and the consumer society, which further entails a heightened commoditization and consumption of Buddhism (and religion more generally), meaning and values are produced through the circulation of not only commoditized religious goods but also symbols associated with Buddhism. In this sense, Buddhist-related goods, services, and symbols are not only for sale; they are for sale for profit. These produced and commoditized goods and symbols are further spread by the global media landscape and in turn affect social relations.

In the contemporary world of consumer capitalism and global Buddhism, Buddhism is inescapable. Rituals, icons, symbols, practices, and ideas associated with Buddhism are produced and packaged for consumption, mass produced, marketed, and made into a profitable business (Kitiarsa 2008, 2012; Levine 2017; McKenzie 2013; Scott 2009). Individual monks, monastic institutions, and lay Buddhist organizations market these commodities, but so do entrepreneurs with no previous connection with Buddhism except for its exchange value, which is mediated by the capitalist market. In focusing more clearly on the consumer-society ethos and the prevalence of Buddhist commodities within this consumer market, we find that Buddhist-related goods and services are marketed to a wider, and at times mostly non-Buddhist, consumer base.

However, this is by no means a new phenomenon. Investigations into the economy of monks and monasteries, lay Buddhists and their organizations, and non-Buddhists have historically involved economic exchange relations and entrepreneurship. Monasteries and monks earn cash income and collect offerings from the ritual services they provide (divination, funeral services), engage patronage networks, operate money-lending schemes, and run businesses, which include not only the production and distribution of Buddhist goods (scriptures, incense, medicine, etc.) but also supplemental goods and services. Today these Buddhist-run services might include running gas stations, convenience stores, tourist facilities, and e-commerce sites. Nonmonastic agents market and sell the goods and services produced and offered by monastic agents and create their own products and organizations to disseminate Buddhist-related commodities. People not only consume these goods and services (no matter how vaguely or strongly they relate to Buddhism) but also produce their own Buddhist-related goods, drawing on the positive connotations, aesthetics, and branding power Buddhism currently holds (see Borup 2016a; Jerryson and Prohl, this volume; Williams-Oerberg 2020). Within these many fields, a variety of agents operate for whom Buddhism entails something different. In the economic life of Buddhism, we see how the positioning of Buddhism—as a religion, spirituality, and nonreligion; as an identification, a tradition, or culture; a source of values, morals, and ethics; a worldview or way of life; and as a philosophy, science, even an economy, brand, and commodity—highlights the flexible and shifting qualities of how Buddhism can be utilized and situated within the context of consumer capitalism.

The commerce in Buddhist products is, of course, nothing new. The changes that are noticeable in this "new spirit of capitalism" are mostly attributable to the scale and extent to which Buddhist-related commodities are sold on the global market. Mass production offers consumers a seemingly endless supply of a variety of Buddhist products (Brox 2019). While statistics on the amount of profit amassed in the selling of Buddhist-related commodities are difficult to come across, a Google search reveals a flourishing market (see Prohl, this volume). Commerce conducted via the internet, or what Levine (2017, 260) has called "ecommerce click consumption," expands not only the reach and market for these Buddhist commodities but also the kinds of commodities produced. In this way, the spread and reach of Buddhist commodities allows for a wide array of consumption practices in which Buddhist commodities are bought and sold by Buddhists and non-Buddhists alike.

Responses to the Commodification of Buddhism

There is no religious or ethical guideline embedded in the new spirit of capitalism that restrains using Buddhist technologies to maximize company profits or using Buddhist images and semantics in unexpected places. Nevertheless, it has not gone without notice or protest. In some cases, as Michael Jerryson relates in his chapter, Buddhists have deemed products utilizing the image of the Buddha as blasphemous. For instance, the Buddhist governments of Myanmar, Thailand, and Sri Lanka have enforced strict regulations to safeguard that Buddhist objects and symbols are treated with respect, resulting in imprisonment and expulsion of foreign nationals for acts that have been interpreted as offensive.

Jerryson in his chapter illuminates how the transnational movement Knowing Buddha Organization (KBO) works worldwide to protect Buddha images from being disrespected and misused, such as when Buddha heads are used as bar stools or Buddhist symbols appear on toilet seats, bikinis, and beer bottles. Many of the companies that have been targeted by KBO for employing symbols and imagery from Buddhism in ways perceived to be offensive have been forced to pull their goods off the market. Jerryson reports that online petitions initiated by KBO have mainly framed the inappropriate usage of Buddhist imagery within a context of infringing on the feelings of Buddhists, where these acts occur out of ignorance. While efforts by the KBO have led to boycotts or pressure placed on businesses so as to prevent disrespect, at the same time these efforts help spread awareness about Buddhism. In order to show respect, knowledge is necessary, hence the name Knowing Buddha Organization. Nonetheless, while certain uses of Buddhist images in branding have been interpreted as blasphemy by some Buddhist organizations and governments, further research is needed to assess how widespread this opposition and resistance is within Buddhist communities as well as to examine whether there are certain ways in which Buddhism is used in commercial contexts that are broadly accepted or not.

The consumption of Buddhism has entailed the disembedding of Buddhist goods from Buddhist institutions and their related economies. Buddhist semantics have aided this disembedding in that Buddhist-related goods are no longer necessarily associated with Buddhism as religion but more with Buddhism as a brand relying on effective marketing strategies and affect (see Prohl, this volume). Buddhist-related products are not merely placed on the consumer market but are advertised and marketed by employing the tools of branding. Brands[4] can be understood as "creating economic value" (otherwise referred to as brand equity) and involving "meaning-based activities" that draw upon preexisting meanings or imaginings and also create new meanings (Usunier 2014, 30). Religions are particularly strong brands in that the ideas and images of religions are recognizable by a large population. Some religions, such as Buddhism, work better as brands, since they carry more positive connotations than others (Tweed 2008). Where religion is another marketable commodity and individuals are able to choose "packaged meaning systems" (Digance 2006, 38), Buddhism fares well in today's consumer society (see also Brox and Williams-Oerberg 2017; Prohl, this volume; Borup 2016a; Obadia 2011).

As Inken Prohl highlights in her chapter, "Buddhism Sells," the association with Buddhism helps add an ethos, provenance, and meaning to the product through recognizable symbols. The values associated with Buddhism, such as peace and spirituality, are intangible assets used in marketing strategies to acquire or increase the value of a product or a place (Schedneck 2014; Williams-Oerberg 2020). In this respect, Buddhism's symbols and iconography appear to have an exclusively positive image that seem to be able to sell just about anything (cars, computers, mobile phones, packed foods, face cream, beer, etc.). Prohl argues in this volume how Buddhist semantics, images, and designs are effective marketing and branding tools given their ability to appeal to the senses. The simple meditating Buddha invokes a sense of not only calm but also that of striving for a better life, of self-management and self-improvement.

In this sense, it is not only the Buddhist message and material culture that are for sale but also a lifestyle, image, or ambience of Buddhism, which people are willing to pay for. Buddhist semantics have frequently been used as tools for branding non-Buddhist goods, services, firms, organizations, and ideas in spheres typically considered to be nonreligious. Buddhist images and aesthetics are used by designers and manufacturers to brand products, drawing on the value that Buddhism as a meaning system adds to these products—what we otherwise can think of as capital. Buddhism, in this way, is both a commodity and capital (Brox and Williams-Oerberg 2017). The consequence of this mediatization is what Prohl in this volume terms the "triple religion effect": how religious semantics, popular religion, and branding imbued with religion have in turn led to "an oversaturation of religion." Religion is everywhere.

Even in the workplace, Buddhist semantics and technologies can be located in management efforts to produce productive employees (see Hedegaard, this volume). Corporate businesses have adopted Buddhist concepts such as mindfulness and mind training: Buddhist meditation techniques become part of the labor that the mindful employee performs. In order to become productive employees, they must work on themselves first (see Hedegaard, this volume; Cook 2016). With the globalization of the economy since the 1980s, a new, legitimizing narrative has arisen that has led to the pervasiveness of the neoliberal ethic emphasizing self-management and self-creation. In other words, "Neoliberalism-as-ideology gave way to neoliberalism-as-governmentality," and this has been set in motion by market civilization and capitalist expansion (Gauthier, Woodhead, and Martikainen 2013, 20).

Critique of the more secularized mindfulness practices finding their way into the corporate setting frames this trend as a "neoliberal tool" and an engine for furthering neoliberal mechanisms, in that it teaches people to regulate their emotions, take responsibility for their own development, and develop resilience in accordance with the management ethos of neoliberalism (for a critique of these approaches, see Cook 2016 and Purser 2018). Marianne Hedegaard (this volume) recognizes how neoliberalism as governmentality appears through the self-actualization and self-regulation narrative of her interlocutors and discussions related to mindfulness interventions in the companies that she studied in Denmark. Nonetheless, Hedegaard contends that employees involved in mindfulness interventions in the workplace are concerned about fundamentally transforming the ways in which they affect others and are being affected. She contends that this work entails "ethical engagement marked by the aspiration of attaining particular virtues" such as empathy, patience, and a calm presence. It is thus not only about performing better at work but about *better being* in this world.

Expanding Buddhism through the Global Market Economy

The marketization of Buddhist goods and consumption practices can also be framed as part of the missionary activity to spread Buddhism. The commoditization of Buddhist goods and services in some cases has helped provide financial resources for promoting Buddhism. In this sense, the global market economy and the new consumer society have been drawn upon as tools for securing the survival of Buddhism and for revitalizing and expanding the reach of Buddhism. The spread of Buddhism through capitalist market mechanisms is not only furthered by the branding and marketing of Buddhist semantics and aesthetics and by the networks that prominent and charismatic Buddhist teachers establish and expand upon but through the spread and adoption of new technologies.

The internet has become a powerful tool to propagate Buddhism and advertise Buddhist activities (Grieve and Veidlinger 2017). Not only is information about and access to Buddhist teachings and resources more accessible through the internet, but Buddhist-related goods and services also become more accessible through the online marketplace. Online consumption practices influence the development of Buddhism not only because these products are available and marketed in specific ways on the internet but because e-commerce includes the online sales of goods related to Buddhism, provides practice spaces (virtual sanghas, temples, etc.), facilitates practices (in the form of apps and games), and enables Buddhist masters to provide their services on demand on the internet (online chats and live-streamed teachings) (see Smyer Yü 2008 and this volume). Since Charles Prebish's (2004) review of Buddhism on the internet, online activities have developed from discussion forums, databases, online journals, virtual libraries, and cybersanghas to include a range of opportunities that support Buddhist charities, trade Buddhist services, the buying and selling of Buddhist-related goods, and, contrary to Prebish's predictions, engage in online Buddhist practices (Ostrowski 2006). This has helped the spread of Buddhism, although most often only among affluent elites who can afford to buy their entrance into the path of Buddhism (Padgett 2000; Smyer Yü 2008).

In this way, through engaging with the global market economy, Buddhist organizations and leaders have mobilized the resources necessary to further their religious goals (McKenzie 2013, 171). The Buddhist revivalism taking place globally is increasingly being shaped by religious consumerism and the forces of the market economy, and Buddhists are in a central position to expand this market through their extensive networks and fields of influence. We see how the Buddhist teacher or master, beyond the monastic institution or community, is frequently at the center of religious, social, and economic transactions. His, and in some instances her, individual charisma or reputation is essential, but the influence they amass is coproduced and maintained by both the master and devotees through preaching and hagiography, redistribution of capital and social welfare, and networking. The charismatic Buddhist leader is an entrepreneur and fundraiser engaged in building a supportive infrastructure and expanding this enterprise.

In relation to an urban Chinese context, Dan Smyer Yü in this volume refers to this building of influence among charismatic Buddhist leaders as forming "constellative networks." According to Smyer Yü, the organizational manifestation of Buddhist urbanism in China entails a diffusion of lineage-based teachings from their teacher-based origins in Tibetan regions, which are then spread to receivers in various cities in China. Dharma brothers and sisters (Chi.: *shixiong*) together form parallel networks radiating from the same spiritual master or guru. The spiritual master in turn is dependent upon the money and labor of the people who support him, constituting the auxiliary sangha. Similarly, donations from patrons are often pooled as a common resource that can cover the running and expansion of new institutions and religious movements as well as cover the cost of the leader's tours, rituals, and teachings, which demand travel, lodging, translation, and so forth—all of which cost money (see Borup, McLaughlin, and Smyer-Yü in this volume).

In many regards, the revitalization of Buddhism, such as with Tibetan Buddhism in urban China and the rise and expansion of new religious movements in Japan, is dependent upon mobilizing capital and free labor. The success of individual Buddhist masters to gain a following and establish a supportive economic infrastructure depends upon the labor provided by volunteers, who run businesses and temples on behalf of, or in the name of, their master (Smyer Yü; see also McLaughlin in this volume). It is because of their labor that a master's fame becomes widespread or that a monastery prospers. One Chinese professor of economics lamented how, since these Buddhist businesses do not have to pay salaries, their unfair advantage has skewed the competition, making it difficult for non-Buddhist entrepreneurs to gain a foothold in the market (Brox, personal communication). In taking a closer look at these auxiliary sanghas and their entrepreneurship and expansion, we see how the market-driven economy (that is, capitalism) works for the benefit of not only spreading the fame and power of individual masters and their affiliated monasteries but also for Buddhism in general, since these market dynamics work to drive the growth, revitalization, and expansion of Buddhism.

However, in taking a closer look at the market dynamics that have led to the expansion of Buddhist organizations and institutions, the affective dimensions of individual economic investments in these projects are also worth attending to. For example, as Levi McLaughlin highlights (this volume), it is just as important to determine why one gives as it is how much one gives. Often in scholarly literature related to religion and economics, statistics emphasizing the numeric qualities of religious expansions are highlighted. But, as McLaughlin astutely reveals through his in-depth ethnographic research of Soka Gakkai, the reasons for why people may give donations through money, materials, and labor reveal the dreams and desires for leading a better life, which at times also entails leading a more prosperous life. In paying attention to the affective dimensions of Buddhist-economic relations, nuances in religious giving are further revealed, such as how most of the donors to a religious organization such as Soka Gakkai are women.

Merit, Material Wealth, and Morality

Where Buddhism in the global market society and consumer capitalism has afforded economic opportunities and possibilities for Buddhist expansion, this has also led to dilemmas and concerns about the loss of authenticity, truthfulness, purity, and sacredness. Some Buddhists and outside observers have become outspoken in their critique of Buddhist engagement with the global market economy and the perceived effect this has had on the ethical, practical, and communal aspects related to Buddhism. Concerns about the loss of authenticity or moral value have arisen in cases where spiritual wealth becomes transacted into material wealth. Examples raised include the spiritual opportunism of self-proclaimed Buddhist specialists who make monkhood and spiritual charisma a money-spinning profession (Kitiarsa 2010; Smyer Yü 2008; Borchert 2005). The personal wealth of mercantile monks, the treasuries of charismatic masters, and the excess riches accumulated by successful monastic enterprises, which are displayed in the gold decor of temples, spectacular Buddhist festivals, and lavish accessories and lifestyles, have at times provoked public outcry (Crispin 2003). When monks are expected to live as moral exemplars, their abundant material acquisition, display, and consumption become targets of criticism.

This critique is not at all new. In the beginning of the fifth century in China, the luxury of monks and monasteries was criticized, including the "'parasitic' lives of Buddhist monks" (Ornatowski 1996, 220; Gernet 1995, 15). The "renegade clergy" of eighth-century Japan were accused of teaching "false doctrines" and for collecting alms (Goodwin 1994, 23), and Buddhist masters such as the eleventh-century Tibetan yogi Milarepa warned against spiritual corruption and materialism (see also Covell 2005, 141). The relative wealth and exploitative position of the Buddhist sangha were highly criticized by socialist and communist movements in the twentieth century. In Mongolia, where Buddhism eventually (but temporarily) was eradicated, socialist and Marxist critiques of the "economic tyranny" (Jerryson 2007, 42) of the Mongolian sangha—perceived as the feudalistic dealings with the surrounding society and the economic exploitation within its own hierarchy, in which higher-ranking monks exploited lower-ranking monks—became an imperative for its demolition (84). Contemporary perceptions of increasing materialism among monks have also become central to narratives of social and moral decline among the clergy, as exemplified in Japan (Covell 2012), Thailand (Scott 2009), and Tibet (Caple, this volume).

We have thus returned to the prevalent assumptions that opened this volume's introduction: that Buddhists should neither deal with money nor amass wealth. While the ideal of the Buddhist monk as the ascetic renunciator remains a prevalent portrayal of Buddhism, monks nonetheless often attract wealth thanks to this virtuous reputation. As pointed out by Caple in this volume, the ways in which material wealth is acquired often entail an association with virtue. The historical development of Buddhist monasteries as "normative centers of wealth accumulation" (Mills 2003, 63) and the symbolic virtue ascribed to religious specialists can be measured by the offerings that they receive from lay donors (see also Kemper 1990). In some cases, it is the charisma of these Buddhist monks that becomes materialized in the form of spectacularized modes supporting empire building, including the expensive gifts that these monks receive and distribute among their followers (Jackson 1999a). Wealth is associated with past virtuous actions, yet chasing wealth is negatively perceived as counterproductive to virtue. Hence, contemporary popular and academic interpretations of the excess wealth exhibited by monastic institutions tend to point in two disparate directions: either economic wealth is a sign of prosperity and generosity or of immoral decadence (see Scott 2009).

Regarding the acquisition of wealth, individual monks and monastic institutions are evaluated not only based on whether they have wealth but on what they do with it—whether wealth is merely accumulated or redistributed (Caple 2019). Jane Caple's research in northeastern Tibet shows how monks and lamas are not only evaluated based on their moral conduct and character but also the ways in which, when wealth is acquired, they display and redistribute it. In fact, redistributive giving as an "idiom of detachment" (Rozenberg 2004) has at times created hierarchies within the monastery by establishing the superiority of the monk who redistributes the alms given by lay donors among other monks (Caple, this volume; see also Harvey 2000). The ethics of redistribution, which Caple eloquently lays out in her chapter, underpins evaluations of monastic wealth and moral worth that are commonly shared to assess the qualities of lamas and monks.

While wealth can be seen as a sign of virtue among monastics, it can also be seen as the result of successful religious practice among lay practitioners. The relationship between wealth and virtue is thus complex, with contrasting and contradictory canonical writings and popular interpretations (Scott 2009). The connection between wealth and merit, especially informed by the concept of *dāna* (generosity, gift giving), suggests that if offerings to the sangha are performed in a correct manner, *dāna* will lead to a life that "is rich, with much wealth and with many possessions" (from the *Suppurisadana Sutta*, in Prebish and Keown 2010, 242). Within understandings of karma and merit in a Tibetan Buddhist context, there is an abundance of evidence that wealth is positively associated with virtue. Material wealth, health, and well-being in the present life are often perceived as dependent upon past actions (San.: *karma*) and accumulated merit (San.: *puṇya*). Merit making also is an important individual and communal activity in Theravāda Buddhist countries like Myanmar, Thailand, and Sri Lanka, but how merit making is popularly interpreted varies, for instance, whether the amount given is important or not (Foxeus 2017; Harvey 2000, 192ff.; Taylor 2008). The acquisition of merit is thus part of an economic system in which economic capital is exchanged for merit. In this way, merit can be considered a spiritual capital that can be maximized, produced, stored, and transacted (cf. Benavides 2005).

Historically, merit has been an essential practice for Buddhist communities across Asia (Amstutz 2012). However, when Buddhist commodities (goods and services) are purchased less out of a desire for acquiring merit, which will lead to a better rebirth in the next life, and more as a means for improving this-worldly conditions not based on merit, this has to do with a "non-merit economy" (Wilson 2019). In some cases, people engage in Buddhist practices or articulate religious practices within a Buddhist merit-economy framework with the expectation of this-worldly, immediate material gain. As suggested by Jørn Borup in his chapter, this form of merit economy as it manifests in the form of Buddhist-related new religious movements in Japan may be considered a form of "prosperity Buddhism." Similar to the prosperity cults that were formed by individuals searching for wealth, newly formed religious groups are often noninstitutionalized and individualized, modern, and urban (Jackson 1999a, b). Borup illuminates the logic of consumer capitalism that runs through prosperity Buddhism, such as in the cases of Soka Gakkai and Happy Science (Kōfuku no kagaku), where the larger the investment that the individual practitioner makes—in the form of capital, commitment, free labor, and proselytizing—the larger the gain.

What we see is a complex relationship between Buddhism and material gain. In other words, rather than assuming that the coalescence of religion and consumerism leads to the lessening of authenticity and value, in some cases there is not only a lack of a perceived contradiction between spirituality and business but an emphasis on how business has become part of the spiritual path (Bowman 2013, 220). Commoditization of Buddhist practices has in some cases provided the resources necessary to engage in Buddhist practice and pursue religious goals consistent with Buddhist philosophy (McKenzie 2013, 160). As McKenzie points out, some Buddhists proactively commoditize Buddhism in order to protect it from corrosion (168), thus highlighting the complex nexus of local strategies to engage with Buddhism and the global market economy.

Chapter Overview

A closer look at particular cases in which Buddhists have engaged within the global market economy reveals innovative and transformative approaches to positioning Buddhism as both a resource for economic growth and expansion among Buddhist institutions and the morally righteous path toward engaging in economic relations. Buddhism throughout its spread in Asia and beyond has proven to be highly adaptable and transmutable, transforming to accommodate the particular social, political, and economic environments in which it becomes embedded. As shown in the chapters of this volume, these innovative practices are not only a strategy for survival but a strategy for expansion.

Each of the chapters in this book highlights various responses and engagements with the global market economy and how the consumer society has reshaped the ways in which Buddhism is portrayed and promoted in these contemporary societies across the globe. The authors examine how Buddhists utilize global market dynamics through the expansion of goods and services offered as a means to support monasteries and Buddhist institutions as well as how Buddhism as a brand draws on aesthetics and technology to market consumer goods and services. The authors address such questions as: In which ways are Buddhists engaged with the contemporary market economy? How do actors within the global market economy utilize Buddhism and Buddhist semantics and technologies? How do contemporary consumption practices shape the message, organization, rituals, and other practices of Buddhism? What responses are there to the insertion of Buddhism as a symbolic resource in the market economy and to the commoditization of Buddhist goods and services? The overview and examples provided in this volume attest to how Buddhists, rather than being "economy-less," are necessarily embedded in the global market economy and engage various strategies for working within the consumer society and the new spirit of capitalism in late modernity.

The volume begins with a focus on institutional economic frameworks. We start in a Tibetan Buddhist monastery and take a closer look at the changes taking place within a context of economic development and greater access to the global market economy in China. In the first chapter, "The Lama's Shoes: Tibetan Perspectives on Monastic Wealth and Virtue," Jane Caple examines a Tibetan Buddhist monastery situated in northeastern Tibet. In this monastery, Buddhist monks are considered relatively affluent in a society that has experienced accelerated state-led development and an accompanying increase in wealth and inequality. Many of the author's interlocutors associate this affluence with moral decline, which seems to echo more global imaginings of wealth as antithetical to Buddhist monastic virtue. At the same time, they understand there to be a causal link between virtue and wealth; the chapter discusses this apparent contradiction. It shows that a positive association between wealth and monastic virtue is embedded in both institutionalized hierarchies of religious giving and personal patronage relationships. The chapter continues with a discussion on the specific economic and political contexts within which contemporary critiques of Tibetan Buddhist monastic wealth have emerged. Finally, it calls attention to an ethic of redistribution that has much deeper historical roots and serves as a corrective to the "economy of merit" framework. This ethic of redistribution is central to Tibetan perspectives on monastic wealth and virtue, even if there are different and changing ideas about where monastic wealth should be channeled and how it should be worn, both literally and metaphorically. Caple's chapter helps explain the apparent contradiction between criticisms of excessive monastic wealth and increasing levels of religious giving. It also helps resolve the apparent tension between ascetic ideals and the inherent materiality of monastic Buddhism, making it possible for monastic engagement with economic transactions to exemplify moral excellence, even in a globalizing consumer society.

Dan Smyer Yü extends this discussion in his chapter by taking a closer look at the charismatic leaders of Tibetan Buddhist institutions and the multiple formations of "constellative networks." In chapter 2, "A Sino-Tibetan Buddhist Modernism: Religious Marketplace, Constellative Networking, and Urbanism," Smyer Yü takes as his point of departure how Tibetan Buddhism is undergoing various transformations, especially in urban settings, as an increasing number of Tibetan lamas reach out to non-Tibetan populations in contemporary China. Based on his ethnographic work, Smyer Yü discusses how the politics, economics, and practices of Tibetan Buddhism are deeply entangled in contemporary Chinese society. In treating Tibetan Buddhism as a world religion situated in this sociopolitical context, Smyer Yü argues that a Sino-Tibetan Buddhist modernism emerges in urban China as a Buddhist urbanism possessing both transcendental orientation and worldly function regarding the Buddhist sense of enlightenment and practical techniques for human worldly well-being under the fast-changing, precarious conditions of livelihood in contemporary China. The organizational manifestation of this Sino-Tibetan Buddhist modernism is what the author calls "constellative networks," which, sustained by material resources donated from affluent Buddhist individuals and businesses, diffuse the lineage-based Buddhist teachings from Tibetan regions to its receivers in different cities of China and beyond.

In Japan, the diffusion of Buddhism is not only led by mainstream, established institutions in the form of temple Buddhism but also by new religious movements. Jørn Borup's chapter addresses both the monastic institutions and the new religious movements in Japan that focus on prosperity Buddhism, highlighting the leaders, institutions, and networks of these institutions. In the third chapter, "Prosperous Temple Buddhism and NRM Prosperity Buddhism," Borup unfolds how both economy and materiality are inherently part of Japanese Buddhism. Monasteries, temples, and Buddhist associations throughout history have been powerful and wealthy organizations, and with the emergence of different kinds of new religious movements, economy and value transactions found new domains and dimensions. Borup analyzes the economic embeddedness of contemporary Japanese Buddhism and discusses how material religion and economy are understood, expressed, and dealt with in temple Buddhism and new religious movements such as Soka Gakkai and Happy Science (Kōfuku no

Kagaku), which Borup considers to be typical representations of what he proposes to designate as "prosperity Buddhism." By comparing various forms of contemporary Japanese Buddhisms, Borup investigates similarities, differences, and changes as representations of value ideals and exchange systems.

Business and materiality in Japanese Buddhism is also the focus of Levi McLaughlin's chapter, "The Soka Gakkai Economy: Measuring Cycles of Exchange That Power Japan's Largest Buddhist Lay Organization." McLaughlin zooms in on Soka Gakkai and the affective dimensions of economic growth and giving, highlighting the role that women play in this growth and why these women donate their time and money. The lay Nichiren Buddhism–based organization Soka Gakkai, literally, "Value Creation Study Association," is Japan's largest new religious movement and arguably Japan's most successful religious export. The author provides case studies of how soliciting subscriptions for the *Seikyō shinbun,* performing pilgrimages to Gakkai headquarters at Shinanomachi in Tokyo, and a host of other quotidian activities have come to be conceived within Soka Gakkai as Buddhist practices and how they combine to generate Soka Gakkai's tremendous economic power. Through these case studies and by highlighting the affective dimensions of giving, McLaughlin provides insight into the ways in which Soka Gakkai's adherents cultivate a distinctive ethos that motivates members' material investments, paying particular attention to why especially women donate their time and money. The chapter thus sheds light on the cycles of exchange that propel the religion's economic engine.

Affect is also a key frame of analysis in Marianne Viftrup Hedegaard's chapter, "The Mindful Gardener and the Good Employee: Mindfulness Practices and Affective Labor in Danish Workplaces." Hedegaard brings the reader to companies in Denmark where mindfulness has become a popular offering as a stress-reducing tool and means to promote mental and physical well-being at work. Combining Buddhist-derived meditation practices and neuroscientific data, mindfulness invites participants to work with their thoughts, moods, and feelings by attending to their bodies and breath in specific ways intended to benefit the employee and the overall work environment. Drawing on ethnographic fieldwork among Danish employees receiving mindfulness training at work, Hedegaard describes how Sue, a gardener, pursues a mindful attitude not only to *feel* better but to *be* better. This pursuit can be understood as an ethical engagement marked by the aspiration of attaining particular virtues such as increased empathy, patience, and calm presence. Hedegaard suggests that attaining a mindful attitude is the result of a sustained effort and "affective labor" in which the practitioner works to manage affects seen as counterproductive in their working life. Mindfulness practice does not involve the mastering of a set of particular emotions to match one's job description, as Hedegaard argues. Instead, employees train in mindfulness in order to fundamentally transform their way of affecting others and of being affected.

This takes us to Inken Prohl's dynamic chapter, "Branding and/as Religion: The Case of Buddhist-Related Images, Semantics, and Designs," concerning the prominence of Buddhist semantics in contemporary branding and marketing. Prohl also highlights affect in her chapter, wherein she examines marketing campaigns for furniture, food, toys, and other goods where pictures of the Buddha are used. Prohl relates how advertisements rely on the magic of the words "Zen" or "mindful," as in "Zen Organic Cereals" or "Mindful Mayo." Buddhist-inspired designs such as temples, rock gardens, or silently meditating monks (though not nuns) appear to have a powerful influence over consumers. In short: Buddhism sells. In a mediatized society, modern media technologies enable individuals, social groups, and institutions to get a hold of religious semantics and materialities. They can interpret, mix, and arrange them in new ways and are able to redistribute these creative arrangements with the help of the media. As a result, modern marketing and branding use semantics imbued with religion. Based on theories of branding and marketing, and taking into account recent analytical approaches to the relationship between religion and popular culture, the chapter sheds light on how and why Buddhist semantics have become such powerful tools of branding in conditions of mediatization. Furthermore, Prohl raises the questions of what this transformation means for what we consider to be "Buddhism" as well as for "religion." Finally, the chapter discusses the consequences of the widespread infusion of Buddhist-inspired semantics and designs into the fields of marketing: Have Buddhists—or people who are drawn to the allure of Buddhist semantics—simply become prisoners of the current system of neoliberalism? Or are we to discern innovative dynamics of "consumed religion"?

Response to the pervasive presence of Buddhist goods in the consumer marketplace is then addressed by Michael Jerryson in his chapter, "Marketing the Buddha and Its Blasphemy." Jerryson unfolds the concept of blasphemy and how it has become transnationally relevant. The author observes how for centuries Buddhist institutions have marketed and branded the Buddha image; in this mode of marketing, the Buddhist doctrine identifies Buddha images as Buddhist relics: *uddesika*. Within this historical framework, Buddha images are branded as much more than materiality; they have a life of their own. However, over the last century, global consumer markets have begun to make use of religious images and icons, in particular Buddha images. Buddhist organizations like Knowing Buddha Organization (KBO) have confronted this new form of marketing and branding, arguing that neoliberal marketing and branding of Buddha images are acts of blasphemy. While globalization offers promises, it also produces problems. One of these problems is the clash between two styles of marketing and branding Buddha images, and Buddhist institutions at times find themselves at odds with the global commercialization of the Buddha image; in Thailand, Acharavadee's

KBO seeks to redress this form of marketing and branding, which it views as a desecration of the sacred.

Having examined economy and Buddhism from the perspective of traditional institutions and constellative networks, turning toward prosperity Buddhism and new religious movements, and then moving on to affective dimensions of economic growth, marketing, and work life as well as the responses to these developments in the form of activism and censorship, the concluding chapter discusses how contemporary scholarship can frame and challenge the research field of economics and religion more generally. Lionel Obadia, in "Economies of Religion, Buddhism and Economy, Buddhist Economics: Challenges and Perspectives," sets out from the observation that the social sciences and the humanities, including religious studies, have undergone different turns in the last decades—linguistic, cognitive, spatial, global, and, more recently, an "economic turn." Since the early 1990s, religious beliefs, behaviors, and organizations have been heavily interpreted in economic terms. The lexical surface has been extended and positioned in theoretical debates, and economic concepts have become more central throughout the last three decades. Departing from the classic (but still vividly questioned) examination of the relationships between religion and economy, this new approach, variously expressed as "economics of religion," is a paradigmatic and epistemological shift from "economic transactions in religion" to "consuming religion as a good." According to Obadia, this has been a shift from ontology to analogy, from economy to economics. Among other critiques, this approach is meant to apply to every religion in every region and especially to modernist movements searching for adaptations in the context of global capitalism and the global expansion of consumer culture. Nevertheless, Obadia argues, religion has been reframed after the vicissitudes of Western Christianity, in the intellectual background of a primarily North American inclination to use an economic approach to perceive religious history (in contrast to a European political history of secularization). To what extent and under which conditions do these models apply to Asian religious contexts, especially in the case of Buddhism, which is moreover torn between the humanistic project of Buddhist economics and the classical study of economy in Buddhism? Is there a place in between for an emerging genre of "economics of Buddhism"? These are questions that open up for new and continuing research, toward which this volume aims to inspire.

Notes

We wish to thank Jane Caple for her close reading and insightful comments on an earlier draft of this introduction. Moreover, this introduction benefited greatly from the comments and suggestions received by Eric Haynie, Erick White, and Benjamin Brose during a "New Works in Buddhist Studies" seminar at the University of Michigan, December 12, 2019.

1 See, for instance, Sivaraksa (2011), Schumacher (1973), Zsolnai and Ims (2006), Lennerfors (2015), Ariyaratne (1999), Tideman (2011), and Zsolnai (2011).

2 Scholars include Badiner (2002), Bubna-Litic (2000), Norberg-Hodge (2002), Schumacher (1973), Simmer-Brown (2002), Zsolnai and Ims (2006), Uprety (1996), Alexandrin (1993), Weber (1999), Zsolnai (2007, 2011), Lennerfors (2015), and Magnuson (2016).

3 According to the *Oxford English Dictionary*, consumption in the economic sense is "the purchase and use of goods, services, materials, or energy. Frequently opposed to production."

4 Here the term brand is defined as "that which is signified by a brand name: the characteristics (both physical and connotational) associated with a particular company, product, or service that distinguish it from others" (Chandler and Munday 2011).

1

The Lama's Shoes

Tibetan Perspectives on Monastic Wealth and Virtue

Jane Caple

TWENTY YEARS AGO, RUPERT MURDOCH STATED IN an interview with *Vanity Fair* that he had "heard cynics" say that the Dalai Lama is "a very political old monk shuffling around in Gucci shoes" (BBC 1999). The moral force of this comment, widely reported in the Western press and subsequently recycled in Chinese state media, suggests an underlying assumption that conspicuous wealth is antithetical to virtue. By contrast, previous accounts of the Dalai Lama appearing in Western media had written of "the sturdiness of his 'well-worn leather Oxfords'" (Barnett 2001, 300), suggesting not only modesty but also frugality. Although there is no evidence that the Dalai Lama has ever worn Gucci, this focus on his shoes as a measure of his moral worth raises an interesting question. How would the same idea be viewed from a Tibetan perspective? Reincarnate lamas and monks are offered food and money from the laity on a regular basis. Nowadays, some might also receive computers, iPads, and cars—even apartments—as gifts from lay sponsors, or they might use cash donations and/or income from providing religious services to purchase such goods themselves. Why not a pair of Gucci shoes? Does the possession and public display of such symbols of wealth and status reflect on their virtue? Is wealth antithetical to Tibetan Buddhist monastic virtue?

In the West—as indeed in China—Buddhism and Tibetan culture are often imagined to be other-worldly and eschewing of materialism, representing the antithesis of today's "global" consumer society, dominated by market values. "Buddhism" as it appears in the global economy as both commodity and brand can reinforce, rather than undermine, such ideas (see Williams-Oerberg and Brox's and Prohl's chapters in this volume). The prevalence of monks and monasteries is, alongside the natural environment and landscape, central to the aesthetics of Tibet as a spiritual other to the "modern" world.[1] Popular imagination—and the disappointment some people feel when confronted with the economic and social realities of Buddhism in practice—perhaps owes something to academic discourse and its emphasis on the Buddhist monk as an ascetic renouncer, not least as a legacy of Weber's ideas.[2] The historical development of Buddhist monasteries as centers of wealth accumulation has, within Buddhist studies, been viewed as contradictory to this ideal (Kemper 1990, 157).

Yet wealth is positively associated with virtue in Buddhist teachings and emic understandings of the workings of karma and merit. Both posit a causal link between virtuous action and prosperity, social status, and, in the Tibetan context, personal efficacy and power (*wangtang* [*dbang thang*]).[3] As Kim Gutschow (2004, 2) notes, "social difference implies moral difference." In his analysis of "prosperity Buddhism" in this volume, Jørn Borup is careful to emphasize that a prosperity orientation is not new to Buddhism, even if it is considerably more pronounced in organizations like Happy Science. Buddhist discourse on generosity, one of the main virtuous merit-making practices for lay people, is explicit about its material benefits in this life and the next (Ohnuma 2005, 110; Heim 2004, 40; Rotman 2009, 269–270), and in everyday contexts my interlocutors have been open about their interests, including wealth and status, in making religious donations (Caple 2015, 2017). As we will see, there is a moral-economic logic to the flow of wealth "upward" to Buddhist monasteries, monks, and reincarnate lamas. Moreover, monastic engagement with wealth can serve to reinforce rather than run counter to ascetic ideals. At the same time, contemporary religious and popular discourse has been critical of what is perceived to be excessive monastic wealth accumulation. This chapter considers these apparently contradictory moral positions, drawing on ethnographic fieldwork in Tibetan Buddhist monasteries of the Geluk tradition and their supporting lay communities on the northeastern edge of the Tibetan plateau. It emphasizes the importance of recognizing the specific contexts and relationships within which particular debates about, evaluations of, and attitudes toward monastic wealth unfold. However, it also argues that these reveal an underlying ethic of redistribution, central to Tibetan perspectives on monastic wealth and virtue, which helps resolve tensions and contradictions between ascetic ideals and the materiality of monastic Buddhism.

Wealth, Status, and Virtue: The "Economy of Merit and Power"

On a winter's afternoon in 2013, Trashi was taking a rest in his quarters during a break in his monastery's three-day New Year prayer festival. He was serving as the chant master at his village monastery, which houses around forty monks and is affiliated with the Repgong region's Geluk scholastic center, Rongwo Monastery. The village, characteristic of others in Repgong, acts as patron to the Geluk monastic community but also houses approximately thirty nonmonastic specialists in tantric ritual (*ngakpa* [*sngags pa*]) belonging to one of the region's collectivities of Nyingma tantrists.[4] Members of Trashi's family, necks decorated with green scarves marking them publicly as that day's sponsors, moved in and out of his quarters, which were stacked with supplies. According to Trashi, the expenses for that day ran to roughly 160,000 yuan (c. US$23,600). This included the preparation of three meals for the monks and villagers and additional gifts offered to the village's religious specialists: two or three hundred yuan for each *ngakpa* (he was unsure of the exact amount), 513 yuan and three-quarters of a kilogram of butter for each monk, and five thousand yuan for each of three reincarnate lamas.[5] They would also give money to the head (*göndak* [*dgon bdag*]) of the regional monastic center; he was in retreat but was to visit the sponsor's family the following day. Based on the local hierarchy of giving, the amount will likely have been more than that given to the other lamas, reflecting his status as the head and "protector" of the region, which had fallen under the joint political and religious authority of his reincarnation lineage before Chinese Communist Party control.

The distribution of gifts by Trashi's family at this religious event provides an illustrative example of the workings of what scholars have referred to as a Buddhist "economy of merit" in channeling wealth upward. The act of giving is potentially most fruitful when oriented upward toward the virtuous (although the results are also dependent on the motivation and state of mind of the giver). Monastics, accorded symbolic virtue as renunciates, act as a field of merit for the laity, who through their patronage are able to sow the seeds of future fruits (including wealth and status) in this and future lives. In the Tibetan context, it might be more accurately conceptualized as an "economy of merit and power," since monastics are also remunerated for their ritual efficacy.[6] They play an important role not only in performing rituals for the dead and for merit accumulation but also in summoning and pacifying nonkarmic forces and nonhuman beings understood to influence a person's or community's fortunes (for example, health and wealth).[7] The remunerations they receive for providing ritual services constitute, alongside donations (that is, gifts proper), a major source of monastic income.[8] As Smyer Yü's contribution to this volume shows, this "practical aspect" of Tibetan Buddhist patronage relations is "highly pronounced" in the contemporary Sino-Tibetan context (see also Caple 2015), but we should not underestimate its importance in the intra-Tibetan context, even if it has been "rarely studied" (Sihlé 2015, 353). Scholars have shown how this merit-and-power-based moral-economic framework has reproduced and reinforced economic and social hierarchies (e.g., Spiro 1982; Clarke 1989; Schober 1989; Gutschow 2004; Rozenburg 2004). It has ensured the existence and reproduction of monastic Buddhism, monasteries being "normative centers of wealth accumulation" (Mills 2003, 63).

As we saw in Trashi's village, different categories of person were given different levels of gift regardless of their personal qualities, from food and drink for fellow villagers to substantial cash donations for reincarnate lamas. This reflects a more general hierarchy of giving, which publicly reaffirms and reproduces the symbolic status of participants in the socioreligious hierarchy: the greater the distance from the ordinary villager, the greater the gift. In the Tibetan context, reincarnate lamas sit above ordinary monks at the apex of the economy of merit and power, their estates (properties, wealth) often accruing considerable fortune. The status of their respective lineages is reflected in local hierarchies of giving as well as being conspicuous in the size and placement of their residences in monasteries. Distribution of donations among ordinary monks during assembly gatherings is egalitarian. Senior monks, including elders and monastic degree holders, and those who have taken the full monastic vows are given the same share of gifts and/or remunerations as junior monks. The only monks given extra shares are certain monastic office holders, such as the chant master and master of discipline. This egalitarianism reflects the ethics of donation in Buddhist texts: as nonreciprocal gifts, donations should be oriented toward the monastic community as a collective field of merit rather than being personalized (see, e.g., Heim 2004). It also follows premodern norms as set out in Tibetan monastic constitutions (Jansen 2014; Sullivan 2013) and practice as recalled by elders who were monks before the disbanding of monasteries in 1958. From what I have observed, this egalitarian distribution of goods and cash also applies when monks are invited to a household to perform a ritual.[9] However, it is gendered. Although monasticism is largely a male preserve in my field area, studies have shown female monastics to be considered less virtuous and pure than monks, and therefore less worthy of gifts and less ritually efficacious, meaning they attract less wealth. Kim Gutschow (2004), for example, found in the 1990s that Zangskar's nuns received few donations and endowments and were "rarely called to perform public or household rituals" (6). Consequently, they "struggle[d] to subsist" (17). Charlene Makley (2005, 280–282) comments on a disparity in "wages" between monks and nuns providing religious services in Labrang, Amdo, in the 1990s. The division of ritual labor was also gendered: nuns had "to starve themselves in order to eat" (282) because they were largely limited to taking on physically demanding fasting rituals eschewed by monks.[10]

The prayer festival in Trashi's village shows the positioning of nonmonastic Buddhist specialists in the local hierarchy: they received a monetary gift, unlike their fellow villagers, but an amount less than monks. Geluk monks and *ngakpas* are ordinarily recipients of donations in distinct contexts, such as monastic assemblies and *ngakpa* ritual gatherings. It is therefore usually difficult to make a direct comparison. Another case from my field notes involving both monastic and nonmonastic specialists makes even more explicit the ordering of hierarchies of giving according to perceived symbolic distance from the ordinary lay person, this time in the context of remuneration for religious services. Drölma, a woman in her late thirties who lived and worked in the provincial capital, fell seriously ill in the autumn of 2013. In addition to seeking advice from a range of medical specialists from different traditions (Tibetan, Chinese, Chinese Muslim, and "Western"), she consulted a reincarnate lama and a spirit medium, who conducted divinations and prescribed certain rituals and recitations.[11] She and her husband requested services to be performed at three monasteries and invited eight monks from a respected Geluk scholastic monastery to their city apartment for three days of scripture recitation and rituals. Each day, they gave each monk 250 yuan and prepared and served four meals, assisted by family members. They also arranged accommodation, putting some of the monks up in a nearby hotel, and transportation, collecting the monks from their monastery some 150 kilometers away. However, the monks could not perform a "liberating" ritual (*sadak döndröl* [*sa bdag gdon grol*]) prescribed because Drölma's illness was understood to be caused by the disturbance of a *naga* [Tib.: *lü*], or water spirit, on her home grasslands. Hearing through word of mouth about two Nyingma *ngakpa* in the city on other business, the couple invited them to perform the ritual, which took one day.[12] They gave each *ngakpa* two hundred yuan and prepared and served three meals.

When Drölma and her husband "employed" different categories of religious specialist, they not only remunerated the Geluk monks more for their services (in both cash and food). There was also a qualitative difference in their relationship and interactions with the monks and *ngakpas*. Drölma said that the day they hosted the nonmonastic tantrists was "easier" because they had "wanted to respect the monks" and so had to be very careful about food and other arrangements. The *ngakpas*, she said, are "the same as us, so we worry less." The money given to the monks was more than a payment for services. It was part of a broader performance of respect, respecting monks (like generosity practices) being virtuous action (*gewa* [*dge ba*]). This included careful preparation of the apartment and food and other arrangements, such as accommodation and transportation, as well as giving the monks an appropriate sum of money. Having been present the day before and for the first two days, I saw how much effort went into making sure everything was "right." In this case at least, the transfer of wealth as remuneration for religious services fell under the same normative logic and hierarchy of giving as the gifts given by Trashi's family, the perceived moral distance between giver and recipient determining the amount.

Although this example reflects a generalized hierarchy of religious giving, it also shows that people make assessments about the *relative* virtue of particular institutions and individuals. It was important to Drölma and her husband that the monks they invited to their home were "good" monks. This was something they knew because of the reputation of the monastery (among the highest in Amdo) and through their personal relationship with some of the individual monks: her husband was from a village with patronage relations to this monastery and had himself previously studied there. Not every monastery, monastic, lama, practice, or action is evaluated in the same way by different individuals and communities or even by the same individuals/communities in different contexts or times. People make distinctions within and across categories, institutions, and individuals based on what Geoffrey Samuel (1993, 215) refers to as "reputation-type judgments," deriving from personal knowledge and interactions. The virtuous are identified as such through their position in the religious hierarchy but also through perceptions of their character, conduct, and actions. The former can condition perceptions of the latter—for example, a reincarnate lama's idiosyncratic actions might be explained as skillful means. Yet I have also found some people, particularly monks and younger, educated Tibetans, to emphasize the personal qualities of individuals over their position, finding certain monks (in one case, even a lay man) with whom they had a personal relationship of greater moral worth than the average reincarnate lama. There is an association between the perceived qualities of specific lamas and monasteries, their prestige/reputation, and the patronage they attract, within both Geluk monasticism (Caple 2019; see also Makley 2007) and Bönpo and Nyingma tantrist collectivities (Sihlé 2013, 178–179). In both contexts, the quality of discipline is particularly emphasized, along with erudition (in Geluk contexts at least) and, particularly among reincarnate lamas and tantrists, perceived power, which might be manifested in widely talked about signs and wonders.

In short, there is a normative logic to the flow of wealth to monastics, which makes explicit a positive association between virtue, wealth, and status, both in terms of generalized hierarchies of giving and patronage of particular monastic institutions or individuals. However, when people draw distinctions within and across categories, wealth is not necessarily a marker of virtue in their evaluations of and feelings about different institutions and individuals.

Wealth, Faith, and Virtue: "Development" and Moral Decline

> [Laughing] We have faith, but no money.
>
> —*Male Tibetan villager in his thirties*

During dinner in a village house in the summer of 2013, the conversation turned to Kumbum, a large monastic center and one of Qinghai's main tourist attractions. "The monks there have a lot of money," one middle-aged woman commented, simultaneously miming throwing a sack (presumably filled with money) over her shoulder. During the New Year celebrations in 2014, a male elder man from the same family joked that he had found a mobile phone on the ground in Senggé Shong. Senggé Shong is a nearby community divided into two parts (Lower and Upper), each with a monastery. Its villagers and monks are known for their relative affluence through their religious arts and patronage networks in inner China. The monks there, the elder said, "have lots of money, and so . . ." Laughing, he mimed picking up the phone and dropping it into his shirt pocket.

Monks are generally considered relatively affluent within a society that has experienced rising income levels and inequalities, often appearing at the forefront of new consumption practices, particularly in rural areas. This includes the ownership and use of motorbikes and cars and multimedia technologies such as the latest model of smartphone but also transformations in domestic space reflecting shifting aesthetic sensibilities, such as the use of glass (see Lengzhi Duojie 2014) and changing ideas about health and hygiene, such as the installation of "modern" bathrooms. However, monasteries and monks are far from equally wealthy (or poor). Even in the area where I worked, there was considerable disparity across and within institutions for various reasons. These included the relative prosperity of the communities with which each monastery has institutionalized patronage relations, the success of monastic business ventures, and the extent of their patronage networks beyond their patron communities, particularly in the Sinophone world. Dan Smyer Yü's chapter in this volume emphasizes the role of charismatic Nyingma lamas in the spread of Tibetan Buddhism in China and the emergence of what he refers to as a "Sino-Tibetan Buddhist modernism." However, it is important to note that many Geluk lamas and ordinary monks have also, albeit often in more modest ways, established patronage relationships with Han Chinese devotees or practitioners. As in premodern Tibet, each monastery has three distinct (although interconnected) economic layers: the livelihood and wealth of individual monks, the monastery's collective economy, and the wealth and properties of reincarnate lamas. The latter are administratively and economically separate from the monasteries to which their lineages are affiliated. The monastery as a collective is not responsible for supporting individual monks. The latter depend on family support, their share of the food and cash distributed during collective assemblies (and in some cases stipends), remuneration for religious services, personal patronage networks, and other income-generating activities such as religious arts and crafts. Even though the distribution of donations within monastic assemblies is egalitarian, there can still be considerable wealth disparity even within a single monastery.

Remarks made in everyday conversations alluding to the relative wealth of monks and lamas do not necessarily associate this affluence with virtue, whether in general or with reference to specific institutions/individuals, such as Kumbum and Senggé Shong. For the most part, the normative logic of the transfer of wealth upward to monastics and reincarnate lamas is not questioned. An increase in cash income and consumption levels for many individuals and communities over the past decade has been paralleled by an upsurge in religious giving—a key reason for rising monastic affluence. This includes sponsorship of religious events and projects (such as temple building) and remunerations for religious services, for which there is increasing demand and rising "rates." As discussed elsewhere (Caple 2017), the social and economic stakes of Buddhist patronage are recognized by participants, and its dynamics and consequences have been the subject of moral reflection and critique. However, in northeastern Tibet at least, this has largely centered on modes of donation perceived to involve an element of coercion/obligation or competitiveness and on religious fraud, rather than on the idea of giving to monastics and monasteries per se. There is a tension between the Geluk ideal of the monk-scholar and monks' role as religious service providers, including criticism of the economic dimension of the latter (Caple 2019, 107–108), but people still aspire to "hire" the "good" monks, who will be the most efficacious.

Yet increasing wealth is often associated with a decline of virtue in monastic and popular discourse. Common tropes are that monasteries have placed too much emphasis on external development and wealth creation, to the detriment of monastic education and discipline, and that individual monks (and lamas) focus more on chasing money than on studying and practicing (Caple 2019, 81, 94–99). There is concern about the prevalence of religious fraud and embezzlement, particularly among those who operate in inner China (Caple 2015). More specifically, the wealthiest monasteries and monks are not those considered the most virtuous. Kumbum and (particularly Lower) Senggé Shong are perceived to be the richest monasteries, housing the most affluent monks in Qinghai province and Repgong respectively, but neither have good reputations when it comes to standards in education and discipline. Indeed, Kumbum acted as the epitome of monastic moral decline among many of my interlocutors, its monks the subject of widespread critique and gossip (Caple 2019, 86–93). This seems to contradict the positive association between wealth and virtue underpinning the economy of merit and power. However, the temporality of karmic forces opens up a space for nonvirtuous wealth accumulation in the present, without undermining understandings of the deeper workings of a moral universe operating according to normative ideas about cause and effect (*gyündré* [*rgyu 'bras*]). Although wealth *is* associated with virtue, prosperity is not necessarily a marker of virtue in the present, and its accumulation is not necessarily a route to increased prosperity in the future (in this life or the next). This depends on the legitimacy of its accrual, how it is treated or "worn," and where it is channeled.

References to the corrupting potential of wealth, criticism of religious fraud, and concerns over the erosion of monastic discipline have a long history in Tibetan religious discourse (see, e.g., Makley 2007, 70–71; Wood 2013, 37). A distinction between wealth legitimately accrued and that which is solicited, chased, or fraudulently acquired by the less virtuous is clearly drawn in premodern monastic literature dealing with the proper receipt of donations (Wood 2013; Jansen 2014). Contemporary attitudes toward monastic wealth also reflect a more general ambivalence toward increasing wealth and the legitimacy of its accumulation in the context of accelerated state-led development and marketization. Remarks and intimations made in everyday conversations suggest that, in people's experience of contemporary society, those who act immorally and who cheat and lie tend to do well. As elsewhere in China, people are still coming to terms with a normative shift away from the collectivism of the Maoist period, and among Tibetans there also is an awareness that "development" is a "legitimising narrative for state power" (Yeh 2013, 175). I have also found people to experience tensions between, on the one hand, "development" and market rationality and, on the other hand, deeply ingrained values and aesthetic sensibilities shaped by shared understandings of Buddhist values and "Tibetan" identity. Like anthropologists working in other parts of Tibet (Yeh 2013; Tenzin Jinba 2014), I have heard Tibetans employing the trope of the economically minded ethnic "other" in their moral boundary work. This is often counterposed to the possession of faith, which marks the distinction between a moral "us" and immoral "other." In Rebgong, this "other" might be Hui Muslims (see also Fischer 2008), Chinese sponsors (Caple 2015), or the villagers and monks of Senggé Shong. One of a group of villages officially classified as belonging to a non-Tibetan nationality, the Tu (or Monguor), Senggé Shong people are renowned for knowing how to make money, even among the other Monguor villages. Other than their different language, this economic-mindedness has been the key marker of distinction when people have differentiated Senggé Shong's villagers and monks from "us" (real) Tibetans.[13]

The problem is not that monasteries are engaging in commerce. Monasteries with the highest reputations run small businesses such as shops and medical clinics, and they manufacture and sell religious products. Moreover, monastic business development as a way to reduce the burden of patronage obligations on local communities has been seen as a moral good, even if there are debates about how it should be managed (see Caple 2019). Moreover, one of the more broadly critiqued sources of monastic wealth is the *patronage* flowing from inner China. Monks are commonly viewed as agents of continuity of Tibetan culture and are "highly visible symbols of 'Tibetan' difference and moral distinction" (Caple 2019, 113). They should, ideally, be exemplars of Tibetan virtues. This politics of identity raises the stakes of wealth accrual, particularly in contexts extending beyond local lay-monastic moral communities and their merit-and-power-based moral economic framework, and/or in ways at least potentially undermining this framework. Examples might include tourism, commercial art production, and translocal and/or cross-cultural patronage, not to mention religious fraud. This is perhaps why Kumbum and Senggé Shong are the subjects of particularly intense moral critique. Kumbum, a large monastic center and important pilgrimage site as the birthplace of Tsongkhapa, has become one of the top tourist destinations in Qinghai. Lower Senggé Shong, one of five smaller village monasteries historically famous for their religious arts and crafts, now leads the production of what has been branded "Regong Art." This consists of statues and *tangkha* [*thang kha*] (painted or appliqué Buddhist pictorial scrolls), which can command high prices on the Chinese market. Both are known for their connections and patronage networks in inner China. In these contexts, monks and lamas are, to borrow from Makley (2007, 126), operating beyond or outside "participation frameworks that routinely displayed and fulfilled reciprocal obligations" and within which wealth was therefore understood to be—and could be known to be—legitimately accumulated.

The extension of monastic patronage networks in the Sinophone world—a key source of Senggé Shong's wealth—can be delicate to negotiate for these reasons. There is a greater risk of wealth being channeled to the wrong or even "fake" monks/lamas through misrecognition of status, virtue, and worthiness: the gullibility and ignorance of Chinese sponsors is a common trope in popular and academic discourse on Sino-Tibetan patronage (Caple 2015, 466–470). Moreover, the "wrong" gift might offend collective sensibilities "back home" if considered excessive or inappropriate in that particular and situated context, even though the gift might be entirely legitimate for a patron acting according to the sensibilities and standards of their own moral world. As Jeffrey Samuels (2010, 12–13) shows in the Sri Lankan context, lay-monastic relationships are negotiated and shaped through "affective bonds" between patrons and monastics, which are "deepened by common histories, similar values, shared sentiments and *collectively held aesthetic standards*" (emphasis mine). When monastics form relationships with multiple constituencies, they must also negotiate differences in such aesthetic standards—what appears, sounds, and feels to be right and appropriate.

The legitimacy of monastic wealth is not only dependent on how it is gained but also, both literally and metaphorically, how it is worn. Zhang Yinong (2014, 62–64) provides a useful example in his discussion of the rising status of a young reincarnate lama, Alak Bashed, of Kirti Monastery, Takstang Lhamo (Chi.: Langmusi) in Amdo. Invited to Shanghai by a wealthy auto dealer, Alak Bashed performed a blessing ritual for this dealer and other Chinese businessmen. On learning that the lama traveled by bus to give teachings and blessings—and feeling this to be inappropriate—they "suggested the collective donation of a four-wheel drive Toyota" (63). The idea that having a car is fitting to a reincarnate lama's status resonates with a comment made by a Tibetan friend: they "have to have a good car," he had exclaimed, as if stating the obvious. However, in this case, neither the lama nor his monk attendant-translator deemed it to be an appropriate gift. Zhang records the attendant-translator appearing shocked when recalling the incident (64). This was not because a lama should not possess a car per se but because it was not fitting given Alak Bashed's position within his local monastic hierarchy. The head lama had a car because he held an official government position. Alak Bashed was lower in status. It would therefore "be very awkward (Tib.: *ngo tscha* [*sic*]) if he was to own the same (or an even better) car" (64). Second, his virtue would be better affirmed and his status heightened if he was able to sponsor collective activities at his monastery: "It was more urgent for Alak Bashed at that time to make 'a lot of tea' (patronage) for the monk community during the ritual year than to ride in a luxury four-wheel drive." In the end, his patrons agreed that they would finance his sponsorship of monastic teas for a year. I have heard similar stories from other monks who have counseled Chinese patrons on the most appropriate gifts to offer to themselves and/or their monasteries (see Caple 2015), indicating that at least some are acutely aware of how this might be perceived by others.

Such stories and attitudes reflect ideas and debates about proper/improper materiality—what should be given, by whom, and to whom—in particular social and political contexts. However, they also reflect ideas and debates about where patronage and monastic wealth more generally should be channeled. Common to these is an ethic of redistribution.

Lamas and Monks as Patrons: The Ethic of Redistribution

Dorjé, a teacher in his thirties, was bemoaning the fact that he had seen monks from a highly reputed scholastic monastery visiting their home village (again, Senggé Shong) in a car bearing a personalized license plate. "Even these monks!" he exclaimed. Openly critical of the values and conduct of many contemporary monastics, Dorjé was not surprised; for him, this was symptomatic of a general state of monastic moral decline. He had expected better from monks belonging to a monastery renowned for its standards in discipline and education. However, the source of his disappointment and exasperation was not simply that the sight of these monks had offended his moral sensibilities about the conduct befitting them. Passionate about local education development, he was also frustrated that lamas and monks with wealth were not plowing this back into their local communities, for example by funding local schools. Instead, they were building grand religious structures to display their wealth and prestige, driving around in fancy cars, and even, he claimed, buying apartments in the provincial capital. Many people would not necessarily agree with his advocacy of greater monastic social engagement; some might also see greater value in temple construction than education projects (Caple 2017). However, the ethic of redistribution underpinning his evaluation of monastic wealth and moral worth *is* more commonly shared. This ethic is overlooked in—and serves as something of a corrective to—the economy-of-merit framework.

Since monks are not expected to reciprocate, the Buddhist gift has generally been understood to be nonreciprocated and asymmetrical, always directed upward (see, e.g., Heim 2004), the flow of wealth unidirectional, from laity to monastics. However, practices of redistributive giving are important within Tibetan monastic economies and central to conceptions of the relationship between wealth and monastic virtue. As Zhang (2014) shows, Alak Bashed's Chinese sponsors ended up playing a role in increasing his status because they made it possible for him to act as a patron to his monastery. Redistributive giving is perhaps not as important in other Buddhist monastic traditions (see, e.g., Rozenburg 2004, 499–500). In Tibet, however, the concentration of wealth and power in reincarnation lineages and their institutionalized position at the apex of the economy of merit and power seem to be balanced against a moral responsibility to care for the monasteries to which they are affiliated in both (intermeshed) mundane and spiritual arenas. This is particularly clear in the case of head lamas and their relationship to "their" monastery and its monks, which several monastics have described to me as analogous to that of a parent to a child. Reincarnate lamas and their estates played a central role in financing the revival of Tibetan monastic Buddhism in the 1980s, plowing gifts they received from the laity into monastic reconstruction and the funding of collective monastic activities. Although monastic economies have developed significantly since, reincarnate lamas can still be important sponsors of their monasteries. As noted earlier, some monks also accrue considerable wealth through their patronage networks or other income-generating activities and act as patrons, sponsoring temple building and monastic events. To give just one example: at a public debate at Rongwo Monastery, held during the fourth lunar month observance of Sagadawa (celebrating the Buddha's birth, death, and enlightenment) in 2012, monastics were visible in the line of major donors queuing to receive a certificate, statue, and blessing from a highly revered elder lama. Less wealthy monks also contribute to collectively funded events and projects and to central monastery funds.

Reincarnate lamas and monks named as sponsors of religious events and new temples are, generally speaking, either redistributing gifts and remunerations from patrons/clients or, as in the case of Alak Bashed, directing patronage from wealthy sponsors toward these events and projects (for other examples, see Caple 2015, 471–473, 476). Therefore, while the economy of merit and power provides a normative basis for the flow of wealth upward to reincarnate lamas and more generally to monastics, there is also a clear ethic of redistribution. This can lead to an inversion of the hierarchy of giving, with reincarnate lamas and sometimes monks contributing more than lay people. For example, many monasteries have capital funds, which are invested in small business operations. They use the profits to fund collective monastic activities for which there is no sponsor (Caple 2019). In many cases, these funds were kickstarted by a major contribution from the head and/or other senior reincarnate lama(s), supplemented by more modest donations from monks and lay patrons. The distribution of funding for a new protector deity temple at a village monastery provides another example. The villagers—a farming community of roughly four hundred households—pledged over four million yuan toward the construction, while the monks, numbering around ninety, contributed upward of a further one million yuan, thus contributing a larger share proportional to their number (Caple 2017).

This ethic of redistribution is evident in assessments of the personal qualities of lamas and monks and in social criticism leveled at those perceived to accumulate personal wealth rather than spending it for the collective good of their monastery. Stories of exemplary figures indicate that it is also a way of resolving the apparent tension between ascetic ideals and the materiality of monastic Buddhism. Wood (2013, 42–45) provides an example in his analysis of the biography of the fourth abbot of Zhalu Monastery (1399–1473), written in the nineteenth century by one of his successors. A narration of the abbot's "exemplarity of scrupulousness" appears among the host of "astonishing deeds" testifying to his enlightenment. This is in terms of both his receipt of donations, which he never solicits, and *in their allocation*. Donations are never "wasted"; they are redistributed for the benefit of the dharma. In the genre of monastic autobiography, "ledger-like passages" detailing financial interactions, including the receipt and allocation of donations, are common (40), serving as "'proof' of scrupulousness" (42), a monks' involvement in financial transactions becoming "a venue for the demonstration of spiritual enlightenment" (51).

Although the stories I heard usually reflected negatively on the virtues of the protagonist(s), some involved "great" monks whose exemplimentarity was shown through their ability to attract wealth and their attitude toward and handling of it. In 2015, for example, I went to see Könchok, a senior monk at a scholastic monastery, to ask about the construction of a new monastery office and guest quarters. He told me that the sponsor was a monk who had many Chinese patrons. On other occasions, Könchok had been highly critical of Chinese patronage and the monks and lamas who seek it. He had also been scathing about money being spent on construction. Yet when it came to his evaluation of this particular monk, neither of these issues seemed to matter. "He has great virtue," Könchok emphasized more than once. He cited as an example the good this monk had done for the monastery when he had previously acted as abbot, describing his conduct when collecting funds for monastic activities, another practice of which Könchok was usually highly critical:

> He went to collect things and was invited by the villagers who gave him money, rice, and butter. He did not take the income to his quarters, he gave it to the monastery. From start to finish he only had his robes and bowl. That was all he had. He is very pure (*namdak* [*rnam dag*]). Very pure.

In this case, as in the (auto)biographical texts studied by Wood, this monk's ascetic virtue was not demonstrated by a refusal to engage in economic affairs. In fact, it was *through* his engagement with economic affairs that he exhibited "scrupulousness" and nonattachment. The flow of wealth to monastics can therefore reinforce, rather than undermine, the ideal of the "simple monk" who eschews personal wealth and material things. Although beyond the scope of this chapter, this also can apply to monastic engagement in business.

Most often, emphasis is placed on redistribution oriented toward support of the dharma, a key debate being whether this is best achieved through temple building, funding monastic activities, and/or supporting monastic education, for example by paying monks stipends. Both Kumbum and Lower Senggé Shong conspicuously display their relative wealth through the construction of temples, stupas, and religious statuary. This was considered by some of my monastic and lay interlocutors to be excessive, exhibiting a focus on external development rather than on discipline, education, and practice. However, as evident in Dorjé's attitude, monasteries and individual monks and lamas have also been under at least some pressure from within and beyond their own institutions to redistribute some of their wealth downward, sponsoring, for example, education and health-care projects. I have heard some people speaking in high praise of reincarnate lamas who have engaged in social projects, and anecdotal evidence suggests that this might be becoming more common. Ideas about how monastic wealth should be spent therefore extend, for some Tibetans, beyond the maintenance and development of monastic Buddhism and the benefits this brings to communities and society more generally as a field of merit and power. Echoing debates about the role of monastics in society elsewhere, including Thailand and Burma, the debate about monastic social engagement in northeastern Tibet seems to have emerged (or at least intensified) concurrent with increased wealth and growing inequalities as well as with heightening political tensions, particularly since 2008. However, I would argue that this debate is rooted in shifting ideas about benefit rather than reciprocity. An ethic of redistribution has much deeper roots in the history of Tibetan monastic Buddhism.

The Case of Lama X

When I started collecting information about monastic development in northeastern Tibet in 2008, I heard a story circulating about a lama (whom I will call Lama X) who had an apartment at one of the most exclusive addresses in the provincial capital and had stashed large quantities of cash underneath his floorboards. Like the myth about the Dalai Lama's shoes in the global media, I take this avaricious image of Lama X hoarding money to be an urban myth, excessive in its depiction of excess to amplify its moral force. Offered as an example of the corruption of contemporary monastics and reincarnate lamas, it seems to echo the association of wealth with lack of virtue underlying Murdoch's comments. The ideal of the "simple monk," which resonates with Euro-American imaginings of Buddhist exemplary figures, does seem to be a constant in Buddhist textual and popular moral discourse. However, we have seen that for Tibetans this does not necessarily mean that monastic wealth is antithetical to virtue. There continues to be a normative logic to the flow of wealth upward to monastics as communities and individuals become more prosperous. The wealthiest monasteries, monks, and lamas are not popularly held to be the most virtuous, but those held to have relatively high standards in education and discipline are by no means the poorest. The understanding that, if a monastery (or individual) is worthy, it (or he) will continue to receive support—and therefore does not need to "chase money"—persists. In short, even as increasing wealth is associated with loss of faith, a societal shift in values, and moral decline, the flow of wealth to particular institutions and individuals continues to be associated with virtue.

Does the way that lamas and monks wear their wealth—whether literally in their choice of footwear or metaphorically through their possession and public display of, for example, an iPad or SUV—reflect on their virtue? The short answer is yes, but not necessarily in a negative way. This depends on a host of other contingent factors that shape the aesthetic-affective response of the onlooker in a given context, not least their relationship to the lama or monk(s) in question. Some of my interlocutors, particularly monks and younger, educated lay people, have been critical of what they consider to be the possession and display of excess wealth, whether in the form of personalized license plates, renovated monastic quarters, or new stupas and temples. Yet to the patron who gives a monk an iPad or an SUV or who funds the renovation of his quarters, these might be considered gifts entirely appropriate to his status, just as my friend felt that reincarnate lamas "have to have a good car" and Alak Bashed's patrons were appalled at the idea of him traveling by bus.

The moral force of images such as those of the Dalai Lama wearing Gucci and Lama X hoarding cash in his exclusive city apartment are thus dependent on moral sensibilities and aesthetic standards embedded in a constellation of broader social, political, and economic forces and systems of value. The politics of the "Tibet Question" and Euro-American imaginings of Tibet and Buddhism, for example, underpin the moral force of an image of the Dalai Lama wearing a pair of designer shoes. For readers familiar with Chinese state discourse, this image resonates with representations of the feudal privileges and inequalities of "Old Tibet" under the Dalai Lama's theocracy (itself reflecting modernist normative assumptions about the proper differentiation of religious and political/secular spheres of action). For others, it might jar with aesthetic sensibilities shaped by imaginings of the Dalai Lama, Buddhism, or Tibet as the antithesis of "modern" consumer society and its materialist values. The scandalous image of Lama X in a luxury apartment in the provincial capital might reflect a broader ambivalence among Tibetans toward—and perhaps "limited refusal" (Yeh 2013, 175) of—the terms and cultural politics of wealth accumulation in a context of accelerated and politicized state-led development. At the same time, I was to learn that Lama X was at the center of more local controversies I have yet to unravel fully (and too complex and sensitive to examine in detail here) but that seem to have centered on the politics of his recognition as a reincarnate lama. Rumors circulating about the legitimacy of his accrual of wealth were thus partly tied to his ambivalent position within the local socioreligious hierarchy. They were also intermeshed with the politics of Chinese patronage. Was he a "real" lama or a fraud, tricking gullible Chinese devotees out of their wealth? Was he engaged in practices understood to be harmful to the Dalai Lama, and thus (consciously or not) an agent of the Chinese state in its attempts to undermine Tibetan unity and Tibetan Buddhist authority?

Beyond these local and specific contexts and relationships, the image of Lama X hoarding wealth reflects a fundamental principle in emic perspectives on monastic wealth and virtue, particularly if juxtaposed to the image of Könchok's "pure" monk. These representations of the polar opposites of monastic immorality and virtue both feature monks who attract wealth, in *both* cases from Chinese sponsors. The central difference is that the "pure" monk is portrayed as redistributing whatever he received for the benefit of the dharma. As we have seen, the economy of merit and power, which channels wealth upward to monastics, operates alongside an ethic of redistribution. This makes it possible for monastic engagement with money and material things—necessary for the existence and continuity of monastic Buddhism—to *exemplify* rather than to work in opposition to the ascetic ideal of the simple monk. Ideas about how exactly this should work can differ and change, perhaps giving us some indication of wider tensions and shifting ideas about benefit and value. As well as debates about how monasteries should be financed, people disagree about how wealth can be best used for the benefit of the dharma. For some, like Dorjé, the ethic of redistribution should extend beyond the monastery to greater social engagement, creating new measures of moral worth. Having previously fed me rumors about Lama X, Dorjé's opinion of him changed when he learned that Lama X was funding (and fundraising for) education and social welfare projects as well as for religious construction. In this respect at least, Dorjé felt that Lama X should be emulated rather than criticized. Lama X's redistribution of wealth beyond the monastery had provided tangible "proof" of virtue.

Notes

This project has received funding from the European Union's Horizon 2020 research and innovation programme under the Marie Sklodowska-Curie grant agreement No. 747673. The chapter draws on materials and local knowledge accumulated during a total of two years of ethnographic fieldwork in communities and monasteries on the northeastern Tibetan plateau (Amdo/Qinghai) conducted between 2008 and 2015. I gratefully acknowledge the financial support of the Leverhulme Trust for fieldwork conducted between 2012 and 2015 and the White Rose East Asia Centre (WREAC) for fieldwork conducted in 2008 and 2009. I owe an enormous debt of gratitude to the monks and lay people who shared with me their knowledge, stories, and opinions. To protect their anonymity, I will not mention their names; I use pseudonyms for those mentioned or cited in the text. My thanks to Trine Brox and Elizabeth Williams-Oerberg for their comments on an earlier version of this chapter and to the chapter's anonymous reviewers for their feedback.

1 On the Western imagination of Tibet, see, e.g., Dodin and Räther (2001). On the Chinese imagination of Tibet and Tibetan Buddhism and its "ecoaesthetics," see Smyer Yü (2011, 2015c).

2 For critical reviews of the Buddhist studies literature and its emphasis on the monk as ascetic renouncer, see Mills (2003, 54–61) and Robson (2010, 3–8).

3 Tibetan terms are transcribed according to the "THL simplified phonetic transcription of standard Tibetan" (Germano and Tournadre 2003). Although not always reflecting the phonetics of oral Amdo Tibetan, it is the only relatively standard transcription system for Tibetan. I have privileged its legibility for a wider readership over the desirability of being faithful to local sounds. At the first occurrence of a term, I add the transliteration in square brackets, following the so-called Wylie system.

4 For a collection of papers on monastic and nonmonastic traditions in Repgong, see Dhondup, Pagel, and Samuel (2013).

5 The village's deity medium was not marked out for special treatment. Although mediums accrue respect/status if considered efficacious, they act as containers for the local mountain deity/deities when in trance. In other contexts, they are viewed as ordinary villagers.

6 My thanks to Nicolas Sihlé, whose comments on my earlier work prompted this reconsideration of the concept of the economy of merit.

7 For glosses of emic concepts related to forces that influence prosperity as well as the fuzzy boundaries between them in everyday usage and understandings, see da Col (2012) and Sa mtsho skyid and Roche (2011, 238–245).

8 By contrast to the Buddhist gift, this other key mode of lay-monastic transfer of wealth has a stronger element of reciprocity. Ideologically, there is no fixed price for religious services. The exchange is thus distanced from market logics. However, there is an understanding that religious specialists should be compensated appropriately. On different kinds of transfer between the laity and religious specialists in Buddhist contexts, including the distinction between remuneration and gift, see Sihlé (2015). On the fuzziness in practice of boundaries between these categories in the Geluk monastic context, see Caple (2015, 463–464).

9 Sihlé (2013, 174) has observed the same pattern in the distribution of donations during large-scale *ngakpa* gatherings in Repgong: each received a single share, "with the exception of the lama, who typically received three shares, and the ritual functionaries . . . who receive two."

10 For a discussion of sex and gender hierarchies in monastic Buddhism in relation to conceptions of the female in Buddhist canonical sources, see Gyatso (2008).

11 These instructions are referred to colloquially as *chawa* [*bca' ba*], synonymous with the more formal term *rimdro* [*rim 'gro*]. They can include recitation of mantras or scriptures, sponsoring of a monastic tea, making offerings, performing prostrations, giving to the poor, and setting animals free (*tsetar* [*tshe thar*]).

12 The specific term Drölma and her husband used for these tantrists was *pön* [*dpon*] or *xön*, as pronounced in Amdo. As Sihlé (2017) notes, this is a common term for tantrists in Amdo, but for the sake of legibility I have used the more common term *ngakpa*, since it is also a term used and understood locally.

13 On linguistic discrimination in Repgong, see Roche (2018).

2

A Sino-Tibetan Buddhist Modernism

Religious Marketplace, Constellative Networking, and Urbanism

Dan Smyer Yü

IN JANUARY 2014, PORTRAIT MAGAZINE (RENWU), A state-owned, widely distributed monthly periodical in China, featured thirteen individuals as the "Faces of the Year [2013]." Among the successful industrialists, entrepreneurs, and entertainment luminaries portrayed on the glossy cover, Khenpo Sodargye, of Larung Gar Buddhist Academy, stands out in his maroon robe. It is the first time ever that the magazine has featured a Tibetan lama as a national religious face along with the newly minted financial success stories. The featured article on Khenpo Sodargye begins with an epithet: "In this era of ever mesmerizing but thriving religious market, this son of the nomads from western Sichuan has built a trustworthy, personal brand [of Buddhism] comforting the hearts of his followers" (Xu 2014, 118). *Portrait Magazine* in this article favors a commercial language to bestow accolades upon Khenpo Sodargye as a successful Buddhist teacher whose outreach to non-Tibetans, especially Han Chinese, is representative of the emergence of Tibetan Buddhism in China as a new interethnic religious movement that awaits more inquiries and discussions.

The presence of Tibetan Buddhism among Han Chinese is increasingly becoming a topical interest not only of media outlets like *Portrait Magazine* but also of academic institutions, policy makers, and international organizations in Asia, Europe, and North America. As the author of *The Spread of Tibetan Buddhism in China: Charisma, Money, Enlightenment* (Smyer Yü 2011), I have also been contacted by assorted interest groups and public figures inquiring about the Chinese embrace of Tibetan Buddhism.

These inquiries come from leading Tibetan Buddhist figures inside and outside China and from politically diverse institutions and spokespersons of Tibet affairs. Regardless of their divergent religious and political perspectives, all of them express the same puzzled amazement—why Tibetan Buddhism among Han Chinese? To me, it is not a question of "why" but of "how"—because it is happening. Phenomenally speaking, the "why" question rests upon a perceptual bipolarity of Tibet and China, with each having their distinct developments of Buddhist traditions and cultural civilizations. The politics of this bipolarity is deeply ingrained in public debates about modern Tibetan affairs around the world, including China. Academic research on Tibet worldwide is profoundly entangled in this bipolar vision of modern Tibetan studies.

While I fully recognize this global condition of modern Tibetan studies, I would like to reemphasize that Buddhism in the context of modern Tibetan studies possesses two divergent functions. It is simultaneously an ethnic and civilizational marker of Tibet and a world religion (Smyer Yü 2011, 9–11). The former is concerned with the particularities of Tibetan national expressions, as shown by Jane Caple's (this volume) ethnographic narratives of Tibetan monastics' responses to monetary influxes from Han Chinese Buddhists. Tibetan Buddhism in Caple's case is a highly pronounced cultural identity marker. The latter is concerned with human universals insensitive to and positioned to overcome ethnic, cultural, and linguistic boundaries. The return of Tibetan Buddhism to the Tibetan social landscape and the subsequent Sino-Tibetan Buddhist encounters in China are part and parcel of these two divergent trends of Tibetan Buddhism in Tibet and the contemporary world. The research outcomes from the study of Tibetan Buddhism as a cultural identity marker are abundantly found in the ongoing scholarly discussions on the combined politics of religious revitalizations and cultural identity reclamations among Tibetans in both Tibetan regions and urban China (Goldstein and Kapstein 1998; Makley 2007; Barnett and Schwartz 2008; Adams 1996, 520; Barnett 2006, 38). As a world religion, Tibetan Buddhism has equally been studied among scholars as it finds its popularity in the world, especially in Europe and North America (Oldmeadow 2001; Paine 2004; Winter 2016). Since the last decade of the twentieth century, Tibetan Buddhism has steadily gained popularity in the religious landscape of contemporary China and is given a modern shape outside its home grounds through a few leading Tibetan teachers' outreach to Han Chinese Buddhists.

In this chapter, based on my ethnographic work over a decade and a half with Tibetan lamas in Kham and Amdo and their urban Chinese students, I start with a discussion of how the social context of Tibetan Buddhism in China is shaped by regionally and ethnically varied implementations of the state's religious policy as well as by the market economy as a social venue of religious practices. This social context could be seen as what some scholars call the "political ecology of religion" (X. Li 2010; H. Li 2011), referring to the state-induced political and economic conditions that affect the numerical growth or decline of a given religious community. These conditions include how the state legally and ideologically frames a religious tradition, how it appropriates its perceived expediency of a religious practice for nonreligious applications (for example, domestic social stability and international diplomacy), and how the political interstices in the state's development of a market economy become alternative social spaces of religious communities.

Situated in the context of China's politics of religion and economic development, this chapter takes an initiative to study an emerging Sino-Tibetan Buddhist modernism based on the observable social fact that Tibetan Buddhism is taking root in urban China in a modern form regarding its pedagogical approaches to its non-Tibetan audience and its cross-regional networks between Sino-Tibetan cultural borderlands and urban China. This emerging Buddhist modernism is apparently an outcome of Tibetan lamas' effort to spread Tibetan Buddhism to Han Chinese. As I have discussed Tibetan lamas' modern approach to their Han Chinese constituencies elsewhere (Smyer Yü 2011, 2015a; Sodargye and Smyer Yü 2017), here I will mostly focus on the context and structure of the Tibetan Buddhist cross-regional networks as an important material manifestation of this growing Sino-Tibetan Buddhist modernism.

Within this context, I argue that the current Sino-Tibetan Buddhist modernism is facilitated by what I call the "constellative networks" between Tibetan regions and urban China, in which this emerging Buddhist modernism is manifested as a Buddhist urbanism with both soteriological and apotropaic orientations concerning the convertibility of material wealth into both worldly and spiritual well-being. In both real and virtual senses, these constellative networks function as conduits and social spaces for the transference of material resources, the organization of religious teaching events, and Buddhist social engagements in urban China. In this regard, this Sino-Tibetan Buddhist modernism could also be understood as a Buddhist urbanism bearing some resemblance to the Buddhist urbanism that once attracted converts from the merchant class of ancient India during the time of Shakyamuni Buddha, when local commerce and transregional trade were booming. The transhistoricalness of this ancient Buddhist urbanism appears to reemerge in the current Sino-Tibetan Buddhist encounters.

To avoid as much generalization as possible, the phrase "Sino-Tibetan" in this chapter does not refer to Sino-Tibetan relations on the geopolitical scale, that is, the encounters between two different political systems, for example, the Tibetan Central Administration versus the People's Republic of China. "Sino-" in my case study mostly refers to Han Chinese. Likewise, Tibetan Buddhism in this chapter mostly refers to Nyingma, not all Tibetan Buddhist sects. As I discussed elsewhere, since the 1980s Tibetan lamas from Geluk and Nyingma have been, in distinct ways, the most active players in Tibetan cultural and religious revitalizations inside China. In the public sphere of the PRC, the former has mostly taken a political approach, in the forms of demonstrations and civil disobedience against the Chinese state's rule (Schwartz 1994), or takes a reserved position toward Sino-Tibetan Buddhist interactions, for example, the case of Lama X in Caple's chapter, while the latter has taken the directions not only to rebuild their monasteries from the destructive years of the Cultural Revolution but also to spread Tibetan Buddhism as a world religion to Han Chinese regions (Smyer Yü 2011, 2–5). I am not suggesting that Nyingma lamas who work with their Han Chinese followers do not have political agendas, as I do not have observed data to concur with the political interpretations of Nyingma made by some scholars (J. Li n.d., 2–3). Based on available ethnographic observations and given the popular visibility of Nyingma lamas in urban China, this chapter treats the presence of Nyingma in urban China as a representative case of how current Sino-Tibetan Buddhist networking is taking place.

An Inchoate Sino-Tibetan Buddhist Modernism

As Tibetan Buddhism becomes a familiar scene in urban China, it enters into deeper relationships with Han Chinese Buddhists not only in the matter of dharma teachings but also in social and economic aspects of their religious collaboration. With more leading Tibetan Buddhist teachers having public engagements with issues, such as social morality and environmental conservation in China (Gayley 2017, 29–57; Sodargye and Smyer Yü 2017, 5–8), the formation of Sino-Tibetan Buddhist alliances could be understood as an inchoate Buddhist modernism. This Buddhist modernism is interethnically forged on the basis of Han Chinese Buddhists' high demand for Tibetan Buddhist teachings, Tibetan lamas' lineage-based systematic dharma instructions, the availability of material resources from urban China, and both Tibetan and Chinese Buddhists' common interest in the public debates concerning national issues.

This interethnic Buddhist modernism shares similarities with its previous counterparts in early modern Sri Lanka and the Republic of China, notably Anagarika Dharmapala's Protestant Buddhism and Master Taixu's *renjian fojiao*, or humanistic Buddhism (Taixu 2005, 431–456). Dharmapala's Protestant Buddhism could be said to be the earliest form of Asian Buddhist modernism advocated as a native response to British colonialism and Christianity in nineteenth-century Sri Lanka. It emphasized the role of the laity rather than the monastic establishment in revitalizing Buddhism as an embodied tradition in the individual person's daily routines. It was regarded as a modern Buddhist movement because of its resistance to British colonial rule and the spread of Christianity and its simultaneous adoption of a Christian structure (Obeyesekere 1970, 43–63) and modern science to reconstruct Theravada Buddhism in Sri Lanka (McMahan 2004, 901).

Taixu's humanistic Buddhism advocated a modern Buddhist lay movement for the same purpose as that of Dharmapala: to rescue both nation and Buddhism from the expansion of external colonialism and internal corruptions. It was an active political engagement with both domestic and international politics. It should be noted here that Taixu was one of the instrumental historical figures who initiated the modern Sino-Tibetan Buddhist encounters (Tuttle 2005, 121). In this regard, the modern Sino-Tibetan Buddhist interactions could be traced back to the first half of the twentieth century. Although Taixu's humanistic Buddhism was not as well known as Dharmapala's Protestant Buddhism on the global scale, it nevertheless shared similar features, especially the part that "blend[s] Buddhism with science" (McMahan 2004, 901). Taixu (1995b, 378) relentlessly advocated "scientific Buddhism," intended as a lay movement with the characteristics of what he called "humanized, popularized, and scientified (*renshenghua, qunzhonghua and kexuehua*)" (Taixu 1995a, 228).

In the twenty-first century, the scientific Buddhism of Taixu and Dharmapala is being materialized in the contemporary Sino-Tibetan Buddhist encounter. The differences are that Tibetan Buddhist teachers are directly introducing their teachings to a new, broader audience without Chinese dharma teachers as intermediaries and that science is not embraced fully as a positive added feature of modern Buddhism but is instead simultaneously understood in ideological and pragmatic terms. Ideologically, it is seen as scientism, a byproduct of China's importation of modern science from Europe. It is a political ideology that treats modern science as "omniscient, omnipotent, and the bearer of man's salvation" (Hua 1995, 15). In the socialist era, science is an integral part of the state's antireligion ideology justifying the destruction of religious institutions. It thus draws criticism from leading Buddhist figures, including Tibetan lamas (Smyer Yü 2011, 126–147). At the same time, recognizing modern scientific values and practices as part and parcel of a Chinese socialist cultural ethos, Tibetan Buddhist teachers utilize science as an instrument of Buddhist conversion in the contemporary Chinese societies, which I have discussed elsewhere (Sodargye and Smyer Yü 2017).

In this social and political context, the current spread of Tibetan Buddhism in China is not socially conditioned on a popular outcry for "renewing the nation" (*xinmin*) similar to the time of Taixu and his contemporaries (Pitman 2001, 13–60). It is instead premised upon the political condition of religious practices (Yang 2008; Goossaert and Palmer 2007), the individually felt sense of existential and spiritual meaninglessness, and the affluence and resourcefulness of the growing middle class of China (Jones 2010, 204–205; Smyer Yü 2011, 99–125). In this complex social environment, the rising affluence of Han Chinese is a pivotal socioeconomic condition of Tibetan Buddhism's popularity in a gray market of religion in China, which is a lenient social space because it "comprises all religious and spiritual organizations, practitioners, and activities with ambiguous legal status" (Yang 2006, 97). It therefore affords Tibetan Buddhism admitting more converts and building new Buddhist communities. It is a Buddhist modernism at work.

To encapsulate, this Sino-Tibetan Buddhist modernism is a Tibetan lama–led, urban lay Buddhist movement with multidimensional engagements with contemporary Chinese society as a religious-spiritual practice for both personal and collective flourishing, a growing Buddhist secular force for social change, a non-Chinese system of ethics for a diagnostic reading of China's failing social morality (Sodargye and Smyer Yü 2017), a humanistic approach to critiquing the values and consequences of modern science, an advocate of Buddhist environmentalism (Woodhouse 2012), and a skillful means for translating the spiritual into the material and vice versa under the precarious conditions of modern living (Smyer Yü 2011, 99–125).

In particular, the spiritual-material nexus in this Buddhist modernism is noteworthy for us to understand that the material condition for the spread of Tibetan Buddhism in urban China does not merely refer to the wealth and resources coming from Han Chinese converts but is also a result of their practice of Tibetan Buddhist teachings concerning the necessity of harnessing, accumulating, and utilizing material resources for a hindrance-free or less hindered path toward one's spiritual enlightenment and worldly well-being. In other words, Tibetan Buddhist teachers equally deserve the credit for imparting the teachings to their urban Chinese followers, which are believed to be efficacious spiritual ways for producing and sustaining the fecundity of material wealth and resources. The mutual convertibility of spirituality and materiality in this Sino-Tibetan Buddhist modernism could be looked upon as a critical infrastructural basis for the expansion of Tibetan Buddhist networks between Tibetan regions and urban China.

Constellative Networks of a Modern Tibetan Buddhism

Based on my ethnographic work, the spread of Tibetan Buddhism in urban China is being accelerated through "constellative networks," a phrase I coin for conceptualizing the interethnic, transregional organizational pattern of Tibetan Buddhism. In astronomy, a constellation is understood as "a group of stars forming a recognizable pattern that is traditionally named after its apparent form or identified with a mythological figure" (*OED*). Phenomenally it is an asterism or a set of stars occupying a celestial sphere in identifiable patterns and boundaries. The constellative networks of Tibetan Buddhism in the social sense are a set of communities in urban China parallel to one another but centrally oriented toward their common or respective masters, who are based in Tibetan regions. The members of each community may acquaint with one another, but the modes of their daily practice and organizational structure are prescribed from a center located several thousand kilometers away. The center is often the monastic seat of the Tibetan master. Thus, each constellative network is centered on a Tibetan lama in a Tibetan region, who disseminates his lineage-based teachings to his Han Chinese followers in far-off places in urban China. If lines are drawn between the center and its multiple communities, it shows a pattern of hierarchical structure in which each community is an intended reproduction of the center's lineage. In the case of Nyingma lamas, the Great Perfection (Dzogchen [*rdzogs chen*]),[1] a tantric Buddhist system, is the primary lineage-based set of teachings transmitting from the teacher to his students. The teacher, as the center of the network, is the embodiment of his lineage. Each of the communities of his students is expected to be a reproduction of the lineage. In the Durkheimian (1915, 157) sense, the relationship between the center and its communities in urban China resembles the relationship between the whole and the parts of the sacred. They are quantitatively different in scale but qualitatively the same in principle.

At the center of a constellative network is the master. Unlike a business corporate structure with a CEO under the supervision of the board of directors, the organizational structure of a constellative network is prone to be a type of charismatic authority intended to regenerate the lineage-based teachings. Unlike the Weberian sense of sole personality-based charismatic authority, it is a combination of both personality and institution. Herein, "personality" refers to *trülkus* [*sprul sku*] (reincarnate lamas) or high lamas (Moran 2004, 17; Smyer Yü 2011, 29–50), and the institution is the given monastery as the collective body of the *trülku*. Oftentimes, it is because of the charisma of a given *trülku* or a highly learned lama that the monastery becomes widely known. In my previous studies of charismatic Tibetan lamas in Tibetan regions, the charisma of an individual high lama is inherently entwined with its affiliated monastic institution. In the intra-Tibetan context, charisma is thus both personal and institutional. Each embodies the other. It manifests itself in these characteristics: "It possesses historical records; it is institutionally discerned; it is communally sanctioned; it saturates both its ecological environment and human community; and it is materially sustained by its monastic institution and lay adherents. It is a center, but cannot exist without its dependence upon and bonding with its worldly institution and community" (Smyer Yü 2011, 12).

The charismatic authority of a constellative network in urban China inherits most of these characteristics. Through the religious personality of their charismatic master, the Chinese followers acquire Buddhist teachings from their Tibetan master, and, in turn, they offer material resources to the master's home monastery. Offerings come as both random personal donations and organized charity work for monastic construction projects, the preparation of a dharma event, purchasing and freeing wild animals from farmers' markets and slaughterhouses, or building a resource pool for Buddhist businesses circulating books and selling Buddhist ritual objects. At the turn of the century, per my initial ethnographic documentation, the cash offering from a Chinese Buddhist to a Tibetan teacher ranged from 500 to 1,000 yuan or more. Some large donors pledged for wire transfers ranging from half a million to several million yuan (Smyer Yü 2011, 112). Over a decade later, digital forms of money through Alipay, IPay, and WeChat Pay are instantaneously moving small and large cash offerings from urban China to Tibetan regions. In turn, Tibetan teachers are making their teachings ever more available through their physical travel to urban China or via online teaching sessions.

In the 1990s and at the turn of the 2000s, most Chinese Tibetan Buddhists traveled to Tibetan regions as pilgrims and long-term students to receive teachings from Tibetan teachers (Germano 1998, 53–94). Their presence at different Tibetan monastic sites was often manifested as spontaneously formed ethnic enclaves rather than organized communities. They did not yet form well-organized constituencies in their hometowns and cities. Two decades later, as the expanding constellative networks with increasingly donated resources between cultural Tibet and urban China have become a social space of the Sino-Tibetan Buddhist encounters, many new converts to Tibetan Buddhism do not necessarily consider traveling to their Tibetan masters' home monasteries as an immediate priority. To many of them, Tibetan Buddhism is another world religion in the religious landscape of China. They embrace it with a careful evaluation of its doctrine and the understanding of its requirements for personal commitments of time, material resources, and travel. In this regard, organized ways of practicing the religion become crucial to both the master and the student, with more consideration of the student's urban lifestyle. The formats of the organized teachings and dharma events are becoming ever more diverse. They are no longer limited to the physical presence of the teacher and his students or to the physical meetings of the study groups located in different parts of urban China but are also found in a variety of digital media. Thus, the constellative networks of Sino-Tibetan Buddhist teachings take both real and virtual shapes, both of which are often interfaced and, therefore, live and spontaneous.

Khenpo Sodargye's Wisdom and Compassion Association is a telling example of the constellative network. With Khenpo as the center of the entire network, it is spun together with organized Buddhist study groups located in the different cities of China as well as with formally registered participants in his online teaching sessions, which are streamed on various social media platforms.

I began to work with Khenpo Sodargye in early 2012, in the capacity of a co-researcher and co-writer on the topics of Buddhist philanthropy and Buddhist secularity; I also was the planner and delegation leader of his inaugural academic lecture tour to Europe and North America in the spring of 2013. As coauthors, we presented our paper "Empathetic Giving and the Public Good: A Han-Tibetan Buddhist Philanthropy in Practice" at the China Social Science Forum—Religion and Charity, a CASS conference held in Beijing in December 2012. In 2014, we coauthored another paper, "Revisioning Buddhism as a Science of the Mind in a Secularized China: A Tibetan Perspective." It was presented at a modern Buddhist studies conference at the University of Göttingen and subsequently published by the *Journal of Global Buddhism* (Sodargye and Smyer Yü 2017). Before our research collaboration, we were familiar with each other's publications. In addition to my working with a few of his Buddhist study groups in the Shanghai area before our meeting, it was our mutual readership that brought us together via his close monastic aides and some of his students based in North America.

For me, Khenpo Sodargye's systematic biographical documentations of Han Chinese converts to Tibetan Buddhism and social critiques of modern scientism (Sodargye 2000) are insightful works for the academic world to use to understand the sociopolitical conditions and personal psychologies of newly converted Han Chinese Tibetan Buddhists. As for him, my research angles and conceptual inquiries about the spread of Tibetan Buddhism in China reflexively reveal a range of Western academic perspectives on contemporary Tibetan religious and cultural revitalizations, for example, identity politics, interethnic conflicts, and modern religious practices. As he had already delivered numerous public lectures on prominent university campuses in China before we met, our collaboration soon led to his first lecture tour to academic institutions in Europe and America. His lecture topics, such as "Tibetan Buddhism and Inner Environmentalism" and "In Search of Humanistic Buddhism: A Contemporary Sino-Tibetan Buddhist Encounter," were the convincing expressions of a new, emerging Buddhist modernism in the context of contemporary China. At the time of his cross-continental lecture tour, the number of his Han Chinese followers reached 1.3 million, according to one of his close aides. From the perspective of my charisma studies, Khenpo Sodargye is not only a monastic scholar but also a charismatic embodiment of the Sino-Tibetan Buddhist modernism I have discussed thus far, which is systematically well organized on the fronts of transregional and international outreach, teaching, and social engagements.

Khenpo Sodargye is thus the center of a constellative network linking his Chinese Tibetan Buddhist constituencies in East Asia, America, Australia, Europe, and Southeast Asia. The primary threads of this transregional network are mainly his personal appearance, publications, social media, and Buddhist study groups. His personal appearances include public lectures, performing life-freeing rituals, dharma talks, and empowerment ceremonies. His bestselling books in Chinese include *There's Nothing We Can't Let Go* (2015a), *What Can't You Part With?* (2015b), *Living with Suffering: Khenpo Teaches You How to Stand Your Ground* (2012a), and *Accomplishing by Doing: A Shower of Blessings from Khenpo* (2012b). The readership of these bestsellers has gone beyond the Buddhist populace of the Chinese-language world: they are readily available at bookstores on university campuses, airports, bus stations, train stations, and street-corner magazine booths in urban China. In my conversation with him and visits to Larung Gar Buddhist Academy, his monastic campus, I find that his teachings could characteristically be parsed into two streams. One is intra-Buddhist specific, regarding doctrinal teachings and methods of practicing discussed in Buddhist jargons. Another is his outreach to non-Buddhist audiences, addressing personally felt, systemic issues such as social morality, the pressures of the modern lifestyle, and environmental conservation, all in a modern, scientifically prone, vernacular lingo commonly accepted in Chinese society. The non-Buddhist world is thus the secular social field where Tibetan Buddhism finds sympathetic seekers, new converts, and opponents.

Relevant to the discussion of the constellative network in this chapter, it is worth further mentioning Khenpo Sodargye's teachings specifically targeting a Han Chinese audience, which take place simultaneously in real and virtual formats. "Real" refers to his teaching sessions in the dharma lecture hall at the Han Chinese Buddhist quarter of Larung Gar Academy and the study groups scattered throughout urban China. "Virtual" refers to the digital streaming and venues that link the dharma lecture hall with study groups across China. Course schedules are published on the website of his Wisdom and Compassion Buddhist Association or predistributed by the leader of each study group to its members. Thus, each teaching session at Larung Gar and its attendees in the study groups across China are synchronized. In this sense, the real is the virtual and vice versa.

To be noted, web streaming is no longer the only digital conveyance of Khenpo's teachings. New social media, coupled with smartphones, reading pads, and other digital devices, are playing bigger roles in making Khenpo's teachings available to his students at all places and all times, such as the Wisdom and Compassion (Zhibei) app (Apple and Android), the Wisdom and Compassion Book Bank (Zhibei shuku) app, and the Sina UC and YY live-streaming software. These digital technologies and applications further tightly weave the actual and potential members of the network together. For instance, YY.com, a NASDAQ-listed digital tech giant and virtual currency platform in China, provides its 310 million users with the free YY app (current version YY7) to participate in virtual live chat rooms, concerts, professional training venues, and educational classrooms. Khenpo's students use this software on their personal computers and smartphones to access his topically specific teachings scheduled in different virtual classrooms. Each of the YY classroom IDs are listed at Khenpo's Association website. Currently, the largest class is approaching twenty thousand attendees. YY.com's current capacity could support over a hundred thousand participants in a single digital venue, for example, a virtual concert or virtual lecture hall (Geron 2012). Besides delivering his lectures, Khenpo also commissions ordained monks and nuns as teaching assistants to facilitate live in-class discussions and debates.

As more and more interest-group-based digital technologies are applied in community-building processes in China, the sense of being communal is neither real nor virtual but live and spontaneous. Tibetan Buddhism in urban China has become an integral part of the digital technologies facilitating teaching events and greater processes of social connectivity. Unlike the recent past, when web forums, blogs, and discussion threads were mostly silent, word-based postings, separating the virtual from the real, the current available visual and audio digital technologies interface the real and the virtual, making both "live." What is important about the technologies like those innovated at YY.com is that they are able to delimit the live digital space of human gatherings according to their distinct interests and orientations. In the case of Khenpo's endeavor to impart his Buddhist teachings systematically to his Chinese students, these digital venues are complimentary to the limited physical space of each of his study groups in different cities of China, hosted in private homes and businesses. The maximum number of a study group in a physical space I have seen is a few hundred, certainly not twenty thousand or more. The digital venues also provide those urban professionals with convenient access to Buddhist teachings when they are on business trips and between job assignments because the recordings of the live online gatherings can be retrieved from Khenpo's website. In the digital sense, the members of the constellative network of Khenpo Sodargye's Han Chinese Buddhist constituencies are all wired up beyond geographical locations and indifferent to temporal-spatial differences.

In the fall of 2013, when I conversed with Khenpo Sodargye during a documentary filmmaking project, I asked him about the future prospects of Larung Gar Buddhist Academy. His immediate response was that he sees the academy as a modern Buddhist university, no less than conventional universities: it too consists of different departments, including philosophy, logic, history, language (Sanskrit, Tibetan, and Chinese), and arts. In his vision, Buddhism is not merely a religion but also a human heritage deeply embodied in many cultures, nations, and personal habits. For him, Buddhist cultures have much to contribute to a sustainable future of the world in terms of global social ethics and environmental health. In my observation, if Larung Gar

Academy is a modern university, its modernity regarding social engagements and methodical application of digital technologies is clearly expressed in the contents and methods of Khenpo's teachings at Larung Gar and elsewhere, via his well-organized study groups in different Chinese cities and live online classrooms.

Khenpo Sodargye's transregional Sino-Tibetan Buddhist network is currently the most resourceful and complex system of Tibetan Buddhist teachings and social engagements in urban China. The material support comes from its Chinese Buddhist members and enthusiasts in the forms of monetary donations and volunteerism. It hosts the largest number of Chinese translations of Tibetan Buddhist texts and practicing manuals in print copies and digital forms, many of which were translated by Khenpo. Coupling with Khenpo's classes, they are redistributed to his students as reading assignments and training manuals.

Networked Sino-Tibetan Buddhist Urbanism

Not all Tibetan lamas who impart teachings to Han Chinese Buddhists have the same doctrinal and textual approach and social engagement as Khenpo Sodargye. In my cross-monastic observation, I have found that many lamas emphasize the practical aspect of Tibetan Buddhism as they field inquiries about personal health, wealth, and future prospects from their Chinese followers. The practical aspect of Buddhism is known among scholars as "apotropaic Buddhism" (Spiro 1982, 143), or a "practical religion" (Tambiah 1970, 55), which is concerned with everyday life and is therefore believed to possess utilitarian values for the this-worldly well-being of the practitioner. The practical aspect of Buddhism runs counter to the currently pervasive perception of Buddhism merely as an ascetically oriented religion (as Elizabeth Williams-Oerberg and Trine Brox discuss in the introduction to this volume). This widespread perception affords a popular image of Buddhism as a pure spiritual tradition divorced from this world, which reflects an unrealistic understanding of how Buddhism is practiced in its Asian cultural communities.

In the social and economic context of contemporary China, the practical aspect of Tibetan Buddhism is highly pronounced. On the one hand, it is a pan-Buddhist experience across Asia that has continued from the past. On the other, China-specific social and economic circumstances prompt Tibetan lamas to be selective in what Tibetan Buddhist teachings to transmit to an urban Chinese audience. These circumstances could be understood as what Anna Tsing (2015, 2) calls the "the conditions of precarity, that is, life without the promise of stability." As a fast-changing society, China is "a precarious world" built upon the "dreams of modernization and progress" (20), and, at the same time, it is generative of existential and psychological uncertainty, insecurity, vulnerability, and teleological disorientation (Smyer Yü 2008, 145–213). Tibetan Buddhism appears to possess the spiritual techniques to lessen, if not overcome, the precarious conditions of this economic superpower. In this regard, the practical aspect of Tibetan Buddhism is being particularly amplified as an effective adaptive response to the social environment and psychological conditions of urban Chinese Buddhists whose livelihoods are inextricably entangled in the force field of this precarious world.

Lungdok Rinpoché is among the lamas who teach and perform ritual techniques for the worldly affairs of their Chinese students. I have known Lungdok Rinpoché since the turn of the century, when I began my village-based ethnographic work in a tantrist (*ngakpa* [*sngags pa*]) community located in Trika (Chi.: Guide) county of Qinghai province. He is the abbot of the temple there. Like other Nyingma teachers, he also transmits Dzogchen teachings to Han Chinese students. Meanwhile, he emphasizes the material flourishing of his students through his rituals. His mastery of wealth-generating rituals has been in high demand among his Chinese students. Oftentimes he travels with a team of advanced tantrists to perform healing and wealth-generating rituals in urban China. The most frequently requested ritual performance from his Chinese students is an empowerment ceremony at a private home or business, to inaugurate a three-dimensional mandala (usually 50 cm × 50 cm × 100 cm), handmade by carpenter tantrists under the meticulous supervision of Lungdok Rinpoché. It is constructed for invoking the forces of wrathful protective deities to maintain health, attract wealth, and repel hostile hindrances in the forms of bad luck, an unfavorable work environment, and personal opponents. It has become the most desired ritual object among his urban students.

In my conversations with those who have the mandala in their homes and businesses, many of them said that they became more economically prosperous, spiritually exhilarated, and willing to give offerings to their communities after Lungdok Rinpoché and his team of tantrists performed the empowerment ritual. They attribute the increasing prosperity of their professions and businesses to the hindrance-clearing effect of the mandala and their teacher's empowerment. I find most of these testimonials prototypically to contain two phases: first, the installment of the mandala in a home or in the central space of a business and, second, the alleged prosperous transformation of the household or the business. Judging from my observation of the displays of affluence in their households and businesses, many of those who could afford large monetary donations to Lungdok Rinpoché's temple are already economically well to do. It is reasonable to suspect that they are enjoying above-average incomes while seeking a ritual empowerment to their wealth from Lungdok Rinpoché. The installation of the mandala appears to add the felt strength of their wealth.

Herein I do not mean to discredit the efficacy of the mandala among the affluent Chinese Tibetan Buddhists. Two narratives from a young advertising professional and an unemployed college graduate, respectively, appear to have the mandala work in their favor. As they could not afford large donations, they asked the same tantrist, a carpenter in the vicinity of Lungdok Rinpoché's temple, to make and install the mandala in their homes in southern China. The tantrist also performed the installation ritual at the two households. The common experience between the advertising professional and the college graduate is the last segment of the ritual, which asks the patron to write down the name of the hindrance on a slip of paper, say, a personal opponent or an object of frustration. The paper is sealed in a bull's horn by the tantrist and buried in a location north of the patron's home, approximately two to three kilometers away, preferably in woods or an open field. It is an act of exorcism.

The young professional wrote down the name of his supervisor, who allegedly had been stealing his monthly bonus for four years, ever since the number of his client accounts had begun to grow rapidly because of his hard work. According to this young advertising salesperson, less than two months after this ritual act, his supervisor was transferred to a different post. The new supervisor not only awarded him with a monthly bonus but also added him to the roster of annual company awardees. To a young urban professional, this meant that he could soon afford to buy a house and make a home in an expensive city. If he had continued to live solely on his five-digit monthly income, without the six-digit bonuses, he would be stuck in an extremely cramped "snail shelter" (Chi.: *woju*) for years, a living condition the younger Chinese generations fear.

As for the college graduate, she wrote down the name of her major: business management. She graduated from a state university in the United States. Her parents annually paid over US$50,000 for her higher education there in the hope that her business management skills would provide a good livelihood. After graduation and returning to China, she was unemployed for over three years. It was not because she could not find jobs; she had a few retail jobs. But, having grown up as a single child in a sheltered familial environment, being a salesperson was too humiliating for her. What was worse was that as soon as her peer workers found out she had an American university degree, they would ridicule her for not being able to find a "better" job. Her sense of shame, guilt, and hopelessness grew daily. She traveled with a friend to Lungdok Rinpoché's village and decided to try out this alternative way of clearing the path of her life. According to her, when she was writing down "business management" on the slip of paper, she also wrote down "hairstyle designer" in her mind. She wanted to do what she liked to do. After the ritual performance, she went through a training course and became a certified hairstyle designer. Currently she co-owns a small beauty salon. According to her, she is not making a fortune but is very happy to have a job, financial stability, and respect from her clients.

These two cases show me that the young advertising professional and the now small-business co-owner already had the intent and desire to make changes in their lives. Their own volitions and actions mattered to their current transformations. The installation of the mandala and the accompanying ritual catalyzed their wishes. As a world religion, Buddhism has both transcendental and worldly orientations. In urban China, the worldly orientation of Buddhism is as highly pronounced as its spiritual orientation and social engagements. When I asked Lungdok Rinpoché if wealth making as a worldly affair hinders the Buddhist goal toward enlightenment, he rhetorically responded:

> Why do you separate "this shore" and "the other shore"? As a social scientist, you would know better that the majority of Buddhists are not monks and tantrists but millions of people who herd livestock, till land, hold jobs, and raise families. Most of them live in fear and insecurity. Why can't we show them the efficacious and wrathful sides of wisdom and compassion that can defeat forces of harm and suffering and make their lives prosperous and happy without seeds of suffering? (field notes, Shanghai, 2017)

Phenomenally speaking, Lungdok Rinpoché's or the village tantrists' performance of the wealth-generating rituals for urban Chinese Buddhists is no different from what they do for their compatriots back home. In my observation, many Chinese Tibetan Buddhists' preference for the teachings and rituals for their worldly well-being and material prosperity is not all random. It is an index of the precarious living conditions of contemporary China. Over a decade ago, when Khenpo Sodargye documented Chinese Tibetan Buddhists' conversion narratives, nearly all his narrators pointed to modern scientism, the state ideology (atheism), and the past political campaigns destructive to cultural traditions as what finally tipped them toward Tibetan Buddhism as a spiritual tradition that could give one's life meaning (Sodargye 2002). To a large extent, these tipping points for religious conversion continue to play a contextual role in the current urban Han Chinese conversion to Tibetan Buddhism. However, as more members of the 1980s and 1990s generations take an interest in Tibetan Buddhism, the negative social forces that push them toward it are often associated with professional stresses, social stigmatization of economic failure, loneliness, and existential meaninglessness. From the Buddhist perspective, these negative forces are understood as *barché* [*bar chad*] in Tibetan, or *weiyuan* in Chinese, which means "hindrance" or "conditions of hindrance." In my ethnographic work with Chinese Tibetan Buddhists, this term frequently appears when they discuss life experiences with each other. Their claimed hindrances are not always tangible, such as a financial debt, a personal opponent, or an accident. They are also attributed to unknown forces of the modern lifestyle.

From the historical perspective, the wide spread of Tibetan Buddhism in China is not a unique case. Historically, Buddhism in its initial form thrived when it was situated in societies and regions experiencing economic and commercial growth and urbanization. This socioeconomic phenomenon of Buddhism began with Shakyamuni Buddha's time. There are many texts in the Buddhist canon, such as *Mahisaka Vinaya* (The Vinaya of five categories), *The Past and Present Causalities Sutra,* and *Upāyakauśalya sutra* (The skill in means), which record that many initial converts to Buddhism were merchants (Xu 1992, 73–75). In their sociological study of early Buddhism, Greg Bailey and Ian Mabbett (2003) find that the social environment of Shakyamuni Buddha was an economically prosperous time in many cities and kingdoms in ancient India. "Buddhism flourished essentially on account of its appeal in the urbanized society of the rising urban state" and "appealed to the nouveaux riches and found an affinity with the bourgeois ethic of thrift and diligence" (16–17). Five hundred years after the Buddha's passing, when Buddhism first went to China, its missionaries traveled there with merchants via the Silk Road (Hansen 1998). It reached a climax during the Tang Dynasty, from the seventh century to the tenth century, which is known for its historical commercial connections with its neighboring countries and beyond.

If a line is drawn to connect historical Buddhism with its thriving eras in India and elsewhere, it could be said that Buddhism is "the ideology of a mature process of urbanism" (Bailey and Mabbett 2003, 14) both in ancient times and in the contemporary world. Tibetan Buddhism happens to play a primary role in engendering an interethnically and cross-culturally formed Buddhist urbanism in China and elsewhere in the world, particularly in cosmopolitan areas of Europe and North America. The premodern Tibet is known for its abilities in cultivating transnational patron-teacher (Tib.: *chöyön* [*mchod yon*]) relationships with the Mongol and Manchu dynasties. In these historical relationships Tibet offers Buddhist spiritual guidance and blessings to the kings of these two empires and, in return, receives protection and resources from them (Goldstein 1989, 44; Powers 1995, 159; Kapstein 2009, 3). This court-to-court patron-teacher relationship ended when the Manchu dynasty collapsed in 1911. A century later, it returned not as a form of the interstate alliance of the past but is expressed in the interactions of individual Tibetan Buddhist teachers and their new students in urban China.

From an empirical perspective, Tibetan Buddhism's expansion in contemporary Chinese society is closely associated with the participation of affluent populations. If the merchants of ancient India were attracted to the

Buddha's teachings because of their demand for new social ethics for their rising economic status and because of their discontent toward the spiritually and politically limiting caste system (Bailey and Mabbett 2003, 17), Chinese Tibetan Buddhists in my ethnographic observation, especially those who are affluent, have also found a new opportunity in their masters' teachings that could ethically justify their economic activities and provide them with a skillful means to enact religious freedom in their own demarcated social niches with minimum state interference (Smyer Yü 2011, 111–116). In this regard, Tibetan Buddhism is engendering a new Buddhist urbanism in contemporary China. It emphatically regards making and sharing material wealth as a rightful means to accumulate spiritual merit for both personal and communal flourishing. It could be said that the constellative networks of Sino-Tibetan Buddhist interactions are the material expressions of this cross-ethnic Buddhist urbanism.

In this ongoing intertraditional discussion on wealth and Buddhist practice, the leading dharma masters from Chinese and Tibetan traditions resonate with each other. Dorzhi Rinpoché, based in northwestern China, regularly gives public lectures at entrepreneurial and corporate settings on Buddhism and business management (Dorzhi 2016a, 2016b). Likewise, Khenpo Sodargye reaffirms that Buddhist practice and worldly life do not oppose each other. His mentioning of the late Steve Jobs, the former Apple CEO, as an exemplary Buddhist entrepreneur is widely circulated online (Sodargye 2013). Referencing one of the issues of *New Riches Magazine* (*Xincaifu*), the website of his association informs the members of its networks and visitors that 30 percent of the world's newly wealthy practice Buddhism (Wisdom and Compassion Buddhist Web 2012). Apparently, an emphasis on worldly well-being and material prosperity are important components of their teachings.

In Tibetan teachers' formal teachings on the relationship between wealth and Buddhist practice and in their students' peer discussion of ethically accumulated wealth, I find that this urbanism is intertextual and intertraditional, meaning that they reference textual sources and teachings not merely from Tibetan Buddhism but also from Chinese Buddhist traditions and masters. Among non-Tibetan sources, the Taiwanese dharma master Hsing Yun and Bhikkhu Jiqun, the director of Suzhou Jiechuang Buddhist Studies Institute, are the most familiar names among urban Chinese Tibetan Buddhists. Both dharma teachers directly point out the existential pressure the modern economic system puts on people. Hsing Yun (2011) begins his prayer, "Great compassionate Buddha! I invoke you to empower me with worldly wealth. When economics is more important than anything else in our society, if I do not have money and wealth, life will become terribly harsh. When I pledge to have compassionate deeds for others, I need wealth." In the same manner, Bhikkhu Jiqun also emphasizes that self-worth in contemporary Chinese society is increasingly measured by one's material wealth and that seeking wealth and maintaining morality are not contradictory (Jiqun 2010, 6, 18) if ethically pursued.

The ongoing Sino-Tibetan Buddhist teachings concerning ethical living and ethical wealth have doctrinal bases and interpretive understandings. In their teachings, both Tibetan and Han Chinese dharma teachers present wealth simultaneously as a hindrance and a resource (Sodargye 2012c; Yinshun 2010, 243–266; Jiqun 2010, 7–11) contingent upon how it is acquired. Its common textual basis comes from *Ornament of the Mahayana Sutras, The Skill in Means,* and *Samyuktagama Sutra,* which emphasize livelihoods that accord with the five precepts for lay practitioners, namely, not harming living beings, not taking what is not given, not engaging in sexual misconduct, not lying, and not taking intoxicating substances. At the same time, understanding the nature of wealth is essential for the practitioner to foresee its ephemerality. The commonly quoted passage by both Tibetan and Chinese dharma masters to emphasize the paradox of wealth comes from Nagarjuna's *Great Treatise on the Perfection of Wisdom,* which says, "Wealth is a property simultaneously possessed by five families: the king legally possesses it; the thief illegally robs it; the careless later generation ruins it; water and fire drown or burn it; and the society or the heaven confiscates it" (Sodargye 2012c). At the same time, regardless of its ephemerality, the ethically earned wealth in Khenpo's teachings is a type of merit that leads to seven types of spiritual wealth, namely, confidence in dharma, precepts that keep one's path clear, humiliation from admitting one's wrongdoing in public, the sense of shame when reflecting on one's guilt in private, knowledge of dharma, generosity, and wisdom (Sodargye 2017). In this sense, material wealth and spiritual merit are interfaced and mutually interchangeable. This is a characteristic of Sino-Tibetan Buddhist urbanism coupled with its engagements with social discourses.

Tibetan Buddhist modernism as shown in the Sino-Tibetan Buddhist constellative networks is emphatically a Buddhist urbanism at work, in which one finds the acquisition of material wealth as a critical condition for Buddhist practice in an economically vibrant, precarious, and politically confining society. Scholars of modern Buddhist studies commonly recognize the late nineteenth century and early twentieth century as the starting point of Buddhist modernism, as shown in the cases of Dharmapala and Taixu. However, if we take a closer historical look at how merchants in ancient Indian cities and kingdoms became the chief patrons of Shakyamuni Buddha, it is not too difficult to see Buddhism as a modernism to start with, which is transhistorical in nature if we do not look at "being modern" as a linear, temporal scale and as if it only originated from the West. If we see modernity as a variety of new forms of human expression, Buddhism was modern at its inception and continues to be modern in the contemporary world. On this point, I share the same assessment as Marilyn Ivy (2005, 313), who emphasizes, "Buddhism as a transhistorical religion comprising transcendent technologies of liberation, thus intrinsically empty of historical signification or cultural baggage: the way it is, when- and wherever." In this sense, Dharmapala's Protestant Buddhism, Taixu's humanist Buddhism, and the variety of socially engaged Buddhism across the world are the variations of the initial Buddhist modernism starting from Shakyamuni Buddha to address spiritual enlightenment under complex but universally sensed sentient conditions regarding living and dying. The current variation of the historical Buddhist modernism in Sino-Tibetan Buddhist encounters responds to systemically and politically induced personal issues as a networked urbanism. Its urban manifestation shows that Tibetan Buddhism is both a spiritual path for enlightenment and a practical means for personal and communal flourishing. Both are inextricably entwined in the ongoing Sino-Tibetan Buddhist encounters.

Notes

The research contents of this chapter are supported by the China Social Sciences Fund (15BMZ070) and a Qianren Grant of Qinghai Minzu University.

1 Tibetan terms are transcribed according to the "THL simplified phonetic transcription of standard Tibetan" (Germano and Tournadre 2003), with the exception of familiar terms for which alternative spellings have become standard (e.g., Dzogchen). At the first occurrence of a term, the transliteration is added in square brackets following the so-called Wylie system.

3

Prosperous Temple Buddhism and NRM Prosperity Buddhism

Jørn Borup

THE IMPRESSIVE BUILDINGS IN AN UPSCALE PART of downtown Tokyo reveal a taste for pompous architecture, far from postmodern minimalism but well suited for the headquarters of Japan's perhaps wealthiest organization: Soka Gakkai (SG). The interior of the SG headquarters is equally appointed with abundant style, broadcasting a narrative of success. This style is also present in other SG buildings, such as its aspirational culture center, its art museum, and its offices containing the country's third-largest newspaper, and in the many shops around its headquarters selling religious paraphernalia, books, and souvenirs. And apart from "Soka Gakkai Town" in Tokyo, 1,200 community centers are scattered around the country to serve its roughly ten million devoted members, some of whom also use the SG schools or the SG university and most of whom vote for their close ally, the political party Komeito. Wealth is seen by many SG members as a symbol of religious success, and only critics would call this new religious movement a "business cult."

Happy Science (hereafter HS) is another modern Japanese religious group and a haven for prosperity-seeking Japanese. Entering the doors of its buildings, one encounters modern interpretations of Greco-Roman architecture and soft New Age music, shelves with books and commodities, and lists of products referencing and blending a range of mythologies. Both its main center in Tokyo and the temples in Biwako and Osaka seem unimpressed with minimalist Japanese aesthetics and join the sense of cultural blending with a story of abundance. Gold figurines of the main deity illuminate the prayer hall, and the voice of the founder, the "living Buddha," is present everywhere, through loudspeakers and TV screens showing him preaching. Display cases sell his 2,500 books and religious paraphernalia: amulets, jewelry, figurines, DVDs, etc. Lists with prayers for concrete wishes to come true are also to be found, whether for curing cancer, passing an exam, or securing prosperity in this life. Suggested donations for such prayers are negotiable, but a staff member pointed out that a donation should be seen in relation to the nature of the wish. Big changes ought to be worth a larger donation. It is not inappropriate to justify the logic of religious investment. After all, even happiness has its price.

Experiencing the world of the many new religious movements (NRMs) in Japan leaves the impression that the economy rules in a much more visible way than in the sometimes equally prosperous traditional temple Buddhism. Media narratives of corrupt, scandalous, greedy, and commodified religion naturally help in explicating the images of what George Ritzer (1999) called "cathedrals of consumption," where pompous buildings tempt with salvation and consumption in order to enchant customers to buy more. The self-presentation of these new(er) religious groups is that of a dynamic response to a traditionalist, declining, and out-of-step temple Buddhism. In that sense, the postwar generation's emphasis on neoclassical economic values of self-determination and self-responsibility (Watts and Okano 2012, 357) fits well with a more individualized religiosity beyond the limits of communal traditionalism. Japan is one of the most economically developed Buddhist countries in the world, having experienced both the blessings and curses of material and economic progress. Therefore, it is also typical of what Ronald Inglehart (1999, 223) calls "postmaterialist values": a focus on quality of life, environmental protection, and self-expression, "even when these goals conflict with maximizing economic growth." Coping with the challenges of (post) modernity and value ideals among different kinds of Japanese Buddhisms is one analytical aim of this chapter. As such, materiality and economy as value and capital are part of the general exchange patterns investigated.

Buddhism, Temple Buddhism, and NRM Buddhism

Is NRM Buddhism *really* Buddhism? Scriptural investigations can easily reveal that asceticism is quintessentially Buddhist, with its rejection of materiality, economic transactions, and this-worldly benefits. The paradigmatic parting from economic and material wealth in favor of spiritual power is not only a key plot in the Buddha legend but also a main symbolic event legitimizing the ritual process for young Buddhists in Asia going forth to monastic life. Scholarly traditions have reinforced such antimaterialistic images with Weberian classifications and textbook Buddhisms. Such ideals of puritan renunciation from a doctrinal paradigm, however, need supplementary models where the "Protestant" (and to a large extent also Eurocentric) understanding of religion is correlated with a broader lived-religion paradigm. Economy has always been part of any religion, and both materiality and economy are fields of inquiry within both classical anthropology, sociology, and the study of religion. Turning to fashionable "turns" ("material turn," "economic turn," etc.) in a way is an act of redundant performativity, but sometimes shifts of gaze are both natural and timely. This seems to be the case with the study of Buddhism.[1]

An etic gaze is never objective or neutral. But neither is an emic view. "This is authentic Buddhism; that is not" is a descriptive articulation but also a rhetorical prescription entangled in power struggles of representation. Authority and authenticity claims legitimizing classificatory exclusivity have been part of sectarian strife throughout Buddhist history, and dividing "true" and "false" Buddhism or hierarchizing between "higher" and "lower" forms of Buddhism is as reductionist as the older ("Protestant") paradigms within the study of religion. While defining and categorizing religion entirely "from the inside" can thus easily be a convenient escape with methodological challenges more serious than expected, analytical intervention is, at least as a complementary tool, necessary for the scholarly study of religion and Buddhism (which, after all, are analytical concepts, too). An inclusive understanding of what realistically could be characterized as Buddhism will not only include the doctrinal understanding and meditation practices of self-identifying Buddhists but also consumer Buddhism, folk Buddhism, ancestor-worship Buddhism, culture Buddhism, NRM Buddhism, and indeed the kind of materially and economically based transactions that are often neglected or misrecognized as belonging to the category of "Buddhism." Classifications of different kinds of religion and Buddhism (monastic Buddhism, lay Buddhism, Western meditation Buddhism, NRM Buddhism, etc.) are, of course, based on broad generalizations and empirical overlap as lived religion. Whether using analytical models based on types or Wittgensteinian family resemblances—or a combination of both—a broader, inclusivist understanding of Buddhism accepts the relevance of comparing differences and similarities in practices, discourses, and value systems, including temple Buddhism, NRM Buddhism, economy, and materiality.[2]

Temple Buddhism in this chapter is understood, taking inspiration from Stephen Covell (2005, 4), as the mainstream "Buddhism as lived by the members of those sects of Japanese Buddhism that were founded before the 1600s."[3] This kind of Buddhism is sometimes also referred to as "traditional" or "established," as opposed to the "new" Buddhist groups evolving in different waves from the late-Tokugawa period (mainly after the Meiji Restoration in 1868, after World War II, and from the 1970s).[4] That materiality and business is also very much part of this prototypical kind of Japanese Buddhism, which I will describe in what follows, before analyzing two different kinds of Buddhist

NRM.[5] While SG is typical of the postwar wave of NRMs and the "born-again Buddhists," HS is typical of a more recent wave of "new new religions" mainly beginning during the bubble-economy period of the 1980s. Both kinds share the characteristics typical of Japanese NRMs: a charismatic, idealized leader and an engaged member-based lay religiosity participating in social activities and rituals aimed at this-worldly gains.

From a different comparative perspective, they also share characteristic elements of Buddhism. Although not considered so by temple Buddhists, SG members self-identify as Buddhist. HS members do so only indirectly, but HS terminology, teachings, rituals, symbols, architecture, members' own understanding, and the fact that the leader, Ōkawa, is seen as a reincarnated Buddha justifies inclusion of this group as Buddhist.[6] They are both, however, in many ways distinctively different from mainstream temple Buddhism. As Buddhist NRMs they can also both be described as "prosperity Buddhism," a concept adopted from some Christian traditions, where "prosperity theology" designates a belief in success and material wealth as signs of blessing from God.[7] Both "soft prosperity" and "hard prosperity" (Bowler 2013, 56) are typical for most religions, to varying degrees, where material requests are part of the religiosity. Such is also the case for the common religion of Japan, which in part is focused on this-worldly benefits (Reader and Tanabe 1998). However, compared to temple Buddhism, the tenets of prosperity religion is much more pronounced in the NRMs. These not only accept religious wealth production but also encourage and sacralize it, placing it in religious worldviews to be engaged with actively by committed members who are strongly encouraged not to practice or be affiliated with temple Buddhism or other NRMs.

The focus of the present chapter is to analyze and discuss how material religion and economy is understood, expressed, and dealt with in traditional temple Buddhism and in the Buddhism of the Japanese NRMs, which I propose to designate "prosperity Buddhism." By comparing these two kinds of contemporary Japanese Buddhisms, similarities, differences, and changes are investigated as representations of value ideals and exchange systems.

Temple Buddhist Economies

Money has always played an important role in Japanese temple Buddhism, and "material objects of various types are essential parts of Buddhist practice and important constituents of the sense of what 'being a Buddhist' means" (Rambelli 2017, 3). Quintessentially, Japanese religion (including Buddhism) is focused on *genze riyaku,* "this-worldly benefits" (Reader and Tanabe 1998), rather than "other-worldly" aims such as soteriological progress toward nirvana. As in all Buddhism, karma is the driving force triggering individual effort, though institutionally sanctioned by social and doctrinal restrictions (or even taboos) of misrecognition to keep individualism and egoistic desire on guard. At the institutional level, monasteries and temples have been powerful driving forces in gaining a foothold on Japanese soil in a dialectic partnership with material and economic development.

Early in Japanese history (from the third to the eighth century), the strait between China, Korea, and Japan was a channel of exchange of material goods and culture. In the political power negotiations, Buddhism was "one of the many things that were exchanged as tribute" (Deal and Ruppert 2015, 24). Buddhist temples became powerful centers already during the Nara and Heian periods (710–1185), not least because of their role in the ritual securing of national well-being and prosperity, and from the Kamakura period (1185–1333) onward, temples became wealthy and "constituted the leading sector of economic growth" (Collins 1997, 852). The religious economy was mixed with secular society, and monasteries and market towns were generating surpluses. There was a "capitalist production emerging in the Japanese monasteries" (852), with temples having accumulated wealth and goods and engaging in loans and investments. The Tokugawa period (1600–1868) was the "period of the second-wave economic boom," with the secular market overtaking and outgrowing religious capitalism (860), and although later Meiji-era (1868–1912) reforms reduced the economic power of religious institutions, the core element of the temple economy is still based on a household parishioner system (*danka seido*), where families are bound to specific temples. This system has secured the temples a stable economic foundation but has also been criticized by both lay and clerical Buddhists for being "merely" a system of the past not encouraging engaged belief or practice and, with merit, for being primarily a religious capital circulated by the priests on behalf of a mainly passive laity.

Although having experienced a decline in both numbers of temples and religious and affiliates,[8] the contemporary economy of Buddhism is quite strong. Compared to the decline in Christianity and almost status quo in Shinto, Buddhism, with its 85,000 Buddhist institutions with 344,000 priests serving its 89 million adherents (Agency for Cultural Affairs 2017), has experienced a general increase in financial income in the last decades (*Shūyō shūkan tōyō* 2018, 23). The annual billions of yen expenditure (for individual labor, administration, and education) and income (from local temples' fees, *fukakin*) differ according to the size and number of affiliated families. Contributions made by temple-affiliated families (*dankas*) in the ten largest Buddhist organizations add up to more than 300 billion yen (~US$2.7 billion) annually,[9] excluding donations for ritual services, which are part of an overall annual funeral business estimated at almost 1.8 trillion yen (~US$16 billion).[10]

The funeral service has been a major part of Japanese Buddhism since medieval times; its monopoly over the whole ritual industry is so secure that it is often pejoratively called "funeral Buddhism" (*sōshiki bukkyō*).[11] The number of *danka* and the ability to gain income from alternative sources create huge differences between individual temples, and having a side job is a realistic option for many priests. In Nishi Honganji, for instance, the average yearly income is 5,640,000 yen (around US$51,000), and for the depopulated regions only 3,970,000 yen (around US$36,000)[12] (Borup 2016c, 3). Being defined as "religious," temple rituals and services are not considered commercial and are thus by law not taxable.

The supply market outside the temple business also profits from funerals. Companies producing and selling Buddhist altars (*butsudan*) and gravestones (*haka*) generate enormous income, as do the undertaking business, producers and sellers of death-related ritual paraphernalia, and secular funeral companies that take care of the whole package. In 2006, the industry was estimated by the Japan External Trade Organization (JETRO) to be worth 1.68 trillion yen, with roughly 6,500 operators plus a string of hotels, railway companies, and agricultural/consumer cooperatives having entered the market. New suppliers of funeral businesses include massive corporations such as Aeon Co., Japan's largest retailer, which operates supermarkets and malls; Yahoo Japan Corp.; and Amazon.com (Monami 2015).[13] Religious marketization beyond Buddhist organizations challenges the ambiguous religious-commercial distinction (Horii 2018, 70–72) and the tax exemption related to privileged practices. It also challenges the Buddhist monopoly with cheaper and explicit prices and with services demanding no commitment to traditional exchange codes.

While losing ground to competitors in the funeral market, Buddhist temples still have other means of income. Buddhist organizations oversee 241 universities and schools as well as hospitals, hotels, museums, kindergartens, and retirement homes. Individual temples rent out property for parking lots, shops, restaurants, golf courses, teahouses, and kindergartens, and generally many temples derive a large part of their income from commercial businesses. Wholesale supply of religious goods, artifacts, and paraphernalia is a profitable business in itself, providing customers with sacred images and figurines, altars, amulets, rosaries, and statues. The pilgrimage industry, particularly in Shikoku, has seen another boom, providing Buddhist temples, travel companies, manufacturers of religious goods, and publishers of religious guidebooks with a substantial income. Buddhism used as a philosophy and instrument in company management has been manufactured in Zen Buddhist temples as training for new employees, and in recent years, books referring to Buddhism can be found in the "management" section of bookstores; several of these books point to Zen as a key to efficiency and business success.[14] Buddhist temples also benefit from the tourism industry, much of which is deemed religious rather than commercial and thus tax free. The Temple and Shrine Tourism Association promotes Buddhist temples as important cultural heritage sites to visit and experience,[15] and Buddhist temples and organizations themselves take part in such marketization by organizing events and providing promotional material.

Individual entrepreneurial monks are also making efforts at sparking energy and economy back into the temples. A priest from a Tokyo-based Pure Land temple is one example. With an MBA in business, he has supplemented his Buddhist training with knowledge of how to run a modern organization—such as a religious temple. "The young monks do not learn this at their university education, and most have to rely on their father's knowledge, which is maybe not updated to a contemporary world," he explained. He conducts management programs for priests, and in 2017, 130 people participated in the courses, which have spread to nine cities and a network of five hundred temples. Topics covered are the basics of management, vision and strategy, marketing, finance, leadership, and how to present a business plan. "I teach them to how to manage a temple and how to diversify their portfolio rather than just focus on rituals for *danka*. This could be cultural events, tea seminars, calligraphy, yoga classes, temple lodging. Priests need to think in alternatives, so that they can be updated to the modern world." Another young priest from a Kyoto Zen temple has restructured the basis of the temple economy by introducing temple tours with meditation classes mainly for foreign tourists at set prices (1,500 yen for one hour, and 2,500 yen including a tour of the temple). With twenty-five to thirty daily guests (at least in the high season), most of whom will also stay overnight (in 7,000-yen-a-night rooms), plus income from their own lectures and workshops on meditation and mindfulness for companies mainly in Tokyo but also abroad, he is doing very well financially. "Dependency on a *danka*-based economy is part of a dying-out culture. I don't want to rely on this, and I don't have to," he explained.[16]

The old system of circulating religious capital in a symbolic "field of merit," with merit investments being sown and circulated through rituals and a *danka*-based affiliation, is still alive, but it is being challenged by an increasingly individualized society and the challenges of rural depopulation. More than half of the priests from one of the largest Buddhist schools (Jōdo Shinshū Nishi Honganjiha) have in recent years seen a decrease in their temple's membership, and two-thirds have felt this affect their financial situation (Borup 2016c, 3). The future of traditional temple Buddhism in Japan does not look bright and will probably lead to many more temple closures, especially in the countryside. Overall, however, contemporary temple Buddhism thrives, not least because of income from a burgeoning "death business." It is also true for Japan that "in the contemporary world of consumer capitalism and global Buddhism, Buddhism is inescapable" (Williams-Oerberg and Brox, this volume). This potentially prosperous Buddhism is generally acknowledged as a mainstream-culture religion. The prosperity Buddhism of the NRMs shares some of these characteristics but is generally of a different type, not least because of their value-exchange systems and open acknowledgment of material religion and the prospects of success and wealth-generating religious capital.

Soka Gakkai and Value Creation

"Some results come instantly, some come after a long time. Many things have come true. It is a big puzzle, where each piece assembles in the correct place, and gradually the picture appears."[17] Wealth is not a pejorative word in SG. Nor is it swept under the carpet, although accusations of economic fraud are seldom responded to with candid access to open ledgers. The impressive fourteen-billion-yen (US$124 million) headquarters is in "Soka Gakkai town" in Tokyo and part of an estimated property value of almost two trillion yen (~US$20 billion) (*Shūkan daiyamondo* 2016, 44); SG is probably "Japan's richest organization" (McLaughlin 2012, 25; see also McLaughlin, this volume). Its own declaration of income was 18.115 billion yen (US$159 million) in 2004 (Sakurai 2011, 107), and income generated from donations and revenue from its daily newspaper is estimated to be at least 40 billion yen annually (US$350 million) (Carlson 2014, 182; Shimada 2008). The personal wealth of its honorary president, Ikeda Daisaku (b. 1928), is not known, but his personal gain from having sold fifty million copies in Japan alone of the bestsellers *Human Revolution* and *New Human Revolution* contributes as much to media speculation about "business religion" as it does to devotees' conviction of his status as a successful religious hero. Soka Gakkai International (hereafter SGI) is present in 192 countries and is the world's largest lay Buddhist organization. In Japan, it has 1,200 community centers as well as museums, culture centers, schools, a university, and, through its close relations with the political party Komeito, strong political power, since most of its ten million members vote for it.[18]

SG's income is based on member donations, especially from women (see McLaughlin, this volume); subscriptions to Japan's third-largest daily newspaper (*Seikyō shimbun*); SG's thirteen cemeteries; and volunteer labor from devoted members throughout the country.[19] "Expensive *butsudan* are for the rich people, and for those with space in the countryside. Our *butsudan* are much cheaper, and there are no payments for funerals or memorial services," said a salesman in one of the shops selling Soka Gakkai paraphernalia in Tokyo. SG members take pride in belonging to a lay Buddhist group without the constraints of "funeral Buddhism" and its priestly organization, and though the often-heard claim of "no payment" is clearly overstated, it is true that generally SG funerals, gravesites, and memorial services are both simpler and cheaper than those of temple Buddhism. Officially, SG has no amulets, talismans, or pilgrimage sites,[20] the main object of worship (*gohonzon*) being a painted scroll of Nichiren's mantra (*daimoku* or *shudai*) *namu myōhō rengekyō* as a devotion to the *Lotus Sutra*. One way practitioners keep account of the effect of this "happiness machine" is to tally the number of chants chanted in a chart book. A woman in her thirties told how she counted up to one thousand *daimoku* during her twice-a-day chanting periods, writing the numbers down in her chart book, each time "planting a seed." Devotion and engaged rituals contribute to a "karmic savings account" (as one member termed it) based on religious meritocracy.

Immaterial investment through voluntary work and missionary work (*shakubuku*) also plays an important role in the overall economic system and for each individual's own merit-generating practice; every year there are focused campaigns where members are instructed to have friends subscribe to Seikyō Shimbun and, in election years, to vote for Komeito. Besides earning "institutional capital" for missionary efforts, studying courses and passing exams, generating different levels of status, and a long life of committed practice can be repaid by the receipt of personal certificates from Ikeda. This-worldly symbolic capital (the value of prestige and honor) and the religious rewards (wishes coming true, spiritual development, healing of illness, solutions to financial and personal problems, etc.) are not, however, recognized outside of SG's institutional value system; that is, the achieved religious benefits are not transferable to other social or meaning systems. Sectarian identity mainly creates social boundaries along with bonding social capital.

Institutional exclusivity is a typical trait of SG. It was also an aspect of the postwar period, during which missionary activities and religious practices were aimed at providing concrete material benefits for a newly urbanized lower social class. Following Japan's general economic success, SG members have experienced economic and social upward mobility, and SG values have become more diverse. Especially now, in the Ikeda period, the new generation of members has become more accustomed to wealth and aspires to postmaterial values (Dobbelaere 2001, 31), with less consciousness of living in a parallel religious society. Focus has thus changed from material benefits to immaterial benefits, including self-development, education, and a progress "from magic to self-analysis" (52). The SG "Super Global High School" in Kansai and the many SG cultural exhibitions are expressions of the organization as a producer and disperser of cultural capital, in the Bourdieuian sense of educational resources giving status in mainstream society. SG's Fuji Art Museum owns collections of Western and Japanese art, the Min-On Culture Center at the headquarters in Tokyo mounts exhibitions of classical European musical instruments, the Min-On Concert Association holds 1,100 annual concerts and performances, and SGI prides itself on its universities abroad and exchange programs in many countries.

Continuous missionizing, voting for the group's political party, and reading Ikeda's books and articles about a spiritual and human revolution wrap the SG world into a web of significance that each member participates in as part of their personal life progress. SG has turned from a mass-conversion movement into a religious institution with ideals of cultural capital, where anyone can aspire "to join Japan's cultural elite" (McLaughlin 2012, 279), with Ikeda as role model and quintessential symbol of educational and cultural achievement. Individual meritocracy is the principle for personal achievement. Practice, faith, mission, and a strong commitment give merit in a system where, in principle, everything can be achieved, since karma and one's own efforts are generators of limitless progress. Merit and success are achieved through mission and devotion, and achieving the worldview and habitus of a successful SG member is an ideal promoted and sought after. The path of progression and success, with prosperity and happiness, is provided by SG and materialized through Ikeda. The economic, social, and cultural capital achieved constitutes part of a general "value generator" that can only be partially repaid with continued gratitude and commitment.

Happy Science and Wealth Creation

"I am a business woman myself, but I want to learn more and be better at what I am doing. That is why I come here, very often," a woman visiting the HS main temple in Tokyo explained to me, revealing an attitude quite recognizable from other visitors and HS members in their eagerness to pursue progress.[21]

If SG typically expresses "soft" prosperity Buddhism via an increased idealization of cultural and spiritual success to counterbalance the wishes for material benefits, HS resembles more typically "hard" prosperity Buddhism in its undisguised focus on material and economic prosperity. "He is a symbol and model of capitalism" was the rather unconventional explanation of the statue of the late-Tokugawa lay Buddhist preacher Ninomiya Sontoku, when I asked about its significance in one of the Osaka temples. For HS, wealth is not only a side effect of religious devotion or an aim misrecognized as secondary to "true religion." Wealth itself is a performative value signal in a religious world of prosperity.

The group Kōfuku no kagaku was established in 1986 as an exclusive club for a few elite members who had to pass qualification exams and pay high subscription fees (Astley 1995). It changed its name in 2008 to the English and international-sounding Happy Science and has become more of a "mass-oriented system" (359) and a "religious corporation" that aims at "selling happiness" (Baffelli 2011, 260). The main headquarters in Tokyo and several of its temples in other large cities are chosen strategically to display wealth, broadcasting the organization's success and adumbrating the potential achievements its members may enjoy. Apart from its head temple (Sōhonzan

Shōshinkan) in Tokyo, it has six hundred district chapters, 240 local temples, and 12,000 missionary centers. Its founder and sensei, Ōkawa Ryūhō (b. 1956), was a former businessman, and his success in transferring what critics call a "business model" to religion is, for his adherents, a true signal of his status as a charismatic role model. His public appearance is comparable to the self-presentation of American televangelists (Baffelli 2011, 128). He is the author of 2,500 books, several of which have been on bestseller lists for years and most of which are bought by HS members. HS has its own publishing company, schools, and university, and in 2009 the group formed the right-wing party Kōfuku Jitsugentō (Happiness Realization Party), through which it aims to disseminate its teachings and influence beyond its own (overstated) twelve million members in over one hundred countries (Happy Science 2015).[22]

HS is more "open" than SG, offering concrete services and products to nonmembers. It is, however, a membership-based organization with a mission and an exchange system valorizing commitment; the level of reward corresponds to the level of belief. According to one informant, "if you don't believe, it doesn't make sense." The benefits of exclusivity are earned by its strong sectarian identity and a pronounced us-them rhetoric, typically illustrated by adherence to the leader's apocalyptic visions and political statements. Certain rituals, books, and paraphernalia are available for members only, and neither photos inside the temples nor interviews with members and access to information beyond the limits of official gatekeepers are permitted. Membership is strongly encouraged in this missionary group, which combines a very eclectic religion with exclusivist bonding and the possibility of institutional, meritocracy-based upward mobility through participation in seminars (with exams) and rituals.

Prosperity and progress are key themes of Ōkawa's books and HS's seminars and rituals. Prosperity thinking and business development are intertwined with Buddhist ideas and terminology and interpreted through the master narrative of Ōkawa as both the living Buddha and successful businessman.[23] Courses and seminars are offered at the main temples, some lasting for a few hours and others stretching over two or three days. Such courses can be attended by just a few people or a group of typically ten to twenty people, with a suggested donation of 10,000 yen for one day and 30,000 to 50,000 yen for a two-day program. Prayers can also be personally conducted by purchasing envelopes with written requests, such as prayers for human relations, happiness, passing exams, fortune, and success in studies or business, all of which are also collected and explained in a book for potential buyers (Happy Science 2014). A fixed price, however, is put on the books, amulets, figurines, HS-emblem necklaces, and special HS altar. Prices are also put on the many DVDs of Ōkawa's preaching and of the films and anime based on his books and produced by HS and occasionally shown for its members in the centers or at public movie theaters. The variety of commodities can be purchased individually and independently, but each item is also part of a "total system": there are books for all occasions (seminars, education, meditation, etc.), and the books and seminars mention and encourage the purchase of the religious paraphernalia and involvement in the organization.

The principle for purchasing happiness and prosperity rests on the same value-exchange system as that of SG. Donations (*fuse,* or *hōnō*) are "happiness planting" (*shokufuku*) investments in concrete life-coping and -adjusting mechanisms (prayers, rituals, courses, teachings), which are returned via both this-worldly (success in life, healing of suffering) and other-worldly benefits (good reincarnation, salvation in utopia/Buddhaland), by means of magical objects and rituals and through personal self-improvement. I was told by several members about the naturalness of having wishes come true, including wishes for wealth. It was voiced to me more than once that HS is especially attractive to young people and business leaders who are looking for an efficient teaching and practice suitable for companies and profit-making interests. "It is an insurance for the afterlife," said another, insisting, however, that benefits are not only for oneself but should be circulated to other people and the world. In a guidebook for "secret teaching and prayers" (Happy Science 2014), comments from members having used the prayers promoted in the book praise these for their usefulness, testifying to the value of purchasing the products.

In recent years, a social and political profile of the organization has also meant a broader perspective on the various kinds of return benefits. By investing in a junior and a senior high school and a university (with departments of "Human Happiness," "Business Success," and "Future Industry"), HS participation promises mainstream cultural capital. Further, by participating in political and social activities (for example, doing missionary work for Kōfuku Jitsugentō, donating money to earthquake victims, performing charity and social work), social capital can be achieved through networks both within and outside the organization and transferred to other social domains of life. However, HS has not had success with its political party, and the university does not meet the academic standards that would give it the accreditation necessary to convert the education received there into more general cultural capital. Additionally, compared to other NRMs, HS's participation in social and cultural outreach is still limited, not least because of the negative "cult" image it has been ascribed publicly and in the media. Individual prosperity is (still) the group's main brand and core product.

Temple Buddhism has always been involved with materiality and economy, the value-exchange structure being paradigmatically displayed in gift exchange between priests conducting rituals for mainly (religious) passive lay people.

Buddhist temples and priests are central in a community-based religion associated with tradition and culture, and Buddhism as "culture religiosity" is a common denominator for most Japanese. As such, Buddhism also has been economically successful for most of Japan's history. It was a main factor in the development of premodern capitalism, and even today temples and the whole industry behind the current marketization and "death boom" give Buddhism in Japan the often realistic image of being rather prosperous. Wealth is, however, unevenly distributed, and rural areas will experience in the years to come the long-predicted "temple death," given demographic changes and continuing urbanization and general secularization. Some individual priests have challenged the traditional *danka*-based system and experimented with alternative models of engaging the laity and managing the temples, not least to boost alternative paths of circulating economic and social capital.

While meritocracy is generally a key ideal of traditional Buddhism and Japanese modern culture, it is also a tricky frame for temple Buddhism, especially if it is interpreted to be a link in the causal chain between individual effort and this-worldly rewards. Japanese NRMs, on the other hand, are based on ideals of open access to and discourse about this-worldly benefits. Materiality and economic prosperity have also been the main objects of the two groups investigated here, Soka Gakkai and Happy Science. Both of them have contributed to Japan's religious economy, and SG especially has challenged traditional temple Buddhism's authority. They have taken over some characteristics of temple Buddhism's gift-exchange economy but also transformed it with new ideas and organizational structures. As prosperity Buddhism, SG and HS openly acknowledge an exchange system with this-worldly benefits and success through investments of dedication, commitment, ritual practices, and money. Both have succeeded in creating an entire religious universe in which this-worldly and other-worldly benefits are enabled by organizational rationality (centralized and decentralized smaller units); economic self-sufficiency; education systems (kindergartens, schools, universities); a mission and communication apparatus (newspapers, books, internet); political power (one powerful party, another that is aspirational); value-creating slogans and marketing (peace, dialogue); global anchorage (international centers, networks, and NGOs); identity-creating rituals, symbolism, and terminology; and systematized socialization mechanisms. The rationality of circulating religious capital is based on the idea of aligning personal investments (financial support, strong commitment, voluntary work, mission) with perceived material and immaterial, this-worldly and other-worldly religious rewards, codified by success stories about the religious leaders and buttressed by testimonials from fellow members.

However, they are also based on the cultural and social capital resulting from human investment and participation. Temple Buddhism has traditionally been the field in which this kind of capital was produced and circulated. This was where people gathered and associated as parts of an entangled network of meaning. Temples were places to meet for social events, and they were key producers of the bonds of communal identity and facilitators of economic stability and growth. Temple Buddhism was also traditionally the site of the key narratives of education and cultural appropriation. Buddhism in many ways plays the role of being the Japanese "culture religion," with its sophisticated teachings, transnational history, aesthetic depths, and monastic settings for transmitting its knowledge and values. With urbanization and secularization, temples have lost this monopoly position. Institutional efforts at regaining this role of generating and circulating economic, cultural, and social capital is a logical undertaking but probably very idealistic. Urbanized Buddhist NRMs, on the other hand, have had more success in achieving this for its members and in transforming one kind of capital into other kinds. The SG master narrative of collective social acceleration is convincing and self-generative, even for second- and third-generation members, and the cultural capital spilling out of the education systems and culture centers has an equal self-generative effect, providing members with a sense of status elevation and organizational pride. Both SG and, to a lesser extent, HS have supplemented one kind of (material) reward with other (nonmaterial) kinds, and by attempting to supplement "charismatic authority" with "traditional authority," combine faith in the teacher and institution with personal experience. As prosperity religions, they focus on rewards for personal investments. Just as evangelical priests in Christian prosperity theology promise God's material and economic rewards for true belief and devotion, the prosperity Buddhism of the Japanese NRMs, through their charismatic leaders, promise benefits for their members. The material, social, and cultural capital circulate in a self-referential capital system for the in-group of devotees. Such a value-generating and -transforming system seems to align with both a neoliberal Japanese society honoring prosperity and social acceleration based on personal efforts and at the same time postmaterialistic values catering to especially urbanized, younger generations who look for something more than material satisfaction. NRMs thus have to cater to segments applauding the possibilities of neoliberal globalization and to a segment going beyond this, finding alternative kinds of capital more interesting. Apart from a focus on economic capital and material value, the strategy of transforming this into cultural, social, and religious capital is thus also part of the prosperity Buddhist NRMs.

However, the religious currency is not directly exchangeable beyond the sectarian domains. SG, HS, and most other Japanese Buddhist NRMs are member based and maintain pronounced demarcations toward other religious and social groups. Social networks are mainly based on in-group associations, sometimes even with the attributes of being "parallel societies." An SG or HS member gains recognition and earns religious capital through the logic of the merit systems within the group, with the hope of proportionally higher this- or other-worldly returns. Capital circulation mainly has an internal value as identity-strengthening forces. Institutional achievements through sectarian education and the symbolic capital earned by experiencing sectarian fine culture do not have the same value outside the groups. Investing into such groups carries the risk of not achieving the fruits of mainstream society as a member of a religious parallel society, because the time, energy, and capital invested can turn out to be of limited worth when "returning" to the world outside the groups. Capital circulation can potentially bridge the gap to other domains of society. This is the ideal of traditional temple Buddhism, and this seems to be a continuously developing ideal of especially SG, having softened its strict exclusiveness in recent decades. Although tendencies of overlap do occur in the dynamic changes of empirical reality, what I have proposed to call prosperity Buddhism is, however, typologically and structurally different from temple Buddhism in its ideals, practices, and organizations of value transactions and capital circulation.

Notes

Parts of this article are taken from Borup (2018), with permission from *Numen* and Brill. Empirical data was gathered during two months of fieldwork in Japan in the spring of 2016 and autumn of 2017 as part of the collaborative research project "Buddhism, Business, and Believers," funded by the Danish Council for Independent Research.

1 For a general introduction to Buddhism and the economy, see Benavides (2005), Obadia and Wood (2011b), Brox and Williams-Oerberg (2017), and Borup (2019).

2 On definitions of Buddhism and the challenges of counting Buddhists, see Borup (2015). See also Prohl (this volume) on the diversity of (understanding) Buddhism.

3 The Japanese scholar Tamura has previously used "temple Buddhism" (*garan bukkyō*) as a concept, as opposed to "household Buddhism" (*shitake bukkyō*), mentioned in Deal and Ruppert (2015, 25).

4 Temple Buddhism in Japan consists of thousands of Buddhist groups, both monastic (Zen, Tendai, Shingon, Nichiren) and nonmonastic (Pure Land Buddhist groups who have priests but no monasteries). The Agency for Cultural Affairs each year counts and categorizes these. The most recent count of the seven main lineages (Tendai, Shingo, Jōdō, Zen, Nichiren, Nara bukkyō, and "others") shows a total number of 77,336 groups, 168 of which are "comprehensive religious juridical persons" (an umbrella term for a temple or group with subtemples) and 77,168 of which are "single religious juridical persons" (individual temples) (Agency for Cultural Affairs 2017, 33).

5 There are 13,947 "others" in the Agency of Cultural Affairs' terminology, in reality meaning NRMs, thirty of which are "comprehensive religious juridical persons" and 14,380 of which are individual groups/centers (Agency for Cultural Affairs 2017, 33).

6 Several of Ōkawa's books are about Buddha and Buddhism (e.g., *Buddha Speaks* and *The Laws of Great Enlightenment—Always Walk with Buddha*), with photos of Buddha statues explicitly signifying the relation to this tradition. One of its

Japanese magazines is called *Young Buddha,* and a Buddhist prayer book is used for rituals (*Buddha's Teachings: The Dharma of the Right Mind*). Architecture and symbols (e.g., stupa, dharma wheel) are Buddhist; the term for local temple, *shōja,* is Japanese for the Sanskrit/Pali term for a Buddhist monastery (*vihara*); and some of the temples have Buddhist names or are described as centers for spreading Buddhist teaching and practice. A large part of the philosophy and terminology of the teaching is Buddhist, and rituals and seminars are focused on or have clear aspects of Buddhist practice, such as the ceremony of taking the Three Precepts with training courses on kōan meditation or seminars called "unsui," "kinhin," "Noble Eight Fold Path," and "The Way of the Bodhisattva Asceticism"—all of which are terms generally identified as Buddhist markers. At a meditation course at a main temple in Biwako, we were introduced to the "original teaching of the Buddha," with the main objective of meditation (including *zazen*) to "become one with the Buddha" and, as "bodhisattvas of light," attain satori and live in Buddhaland. Abroad, HS is even more clearly associated with Buddhism for strategic missionary reasons, since Buddhism is regarded almost exclusively positively, and Ōkawa is styled as a master by Westerners typically associated with the tropes of a Zen master.

7 On modern wealth-oriented Buddhist groups in Thailand as "prosperity cults," see Jackson (1999a), and on contemporary "prosperity Buddhism" in Myanmar, see Foxeus (2017).

8 Demographic challenges and general secularization have placed religion in Japan in crisis. In the last ten years alone, the number of religious groups has declined 12 percent (*Shūyō shūkan tōyō* 2018, 22).

9 The figures are from *Gekken jūshoku* (2017, 15–24). While Shinshū Ōtaniha has an annual expenditure of 8.5 billion yen (a decrease from 11.7 billion yen the year before), the figure for Tendaishū is 1.1 billion yen (*Gekken jūshoku* 2017, 15–24).

10 The figure is from a Yano Research report, available at https://www.yano.co.jp/press-release/show/press_id/1765.

11 Especially from the Tokugawa period (1600–1867), bestowing posthumous titles and conferring lineage charts for entrance into the Buddha's family was part of the temple business (Williams 2005, 28–29). The average cost today of a funeral service with sutra chanting, posthumous naming, and offerings is 549,000 yen (US$4,600) (Horii 2018, 72). This amount does not include all the services beyond the temple.

12 The general yearly income of the priests thus corresponds to the general yearly income of Japanese in their forties.

13 At an annual "Ceremony Japan" expo in Osaka (http://ceremonyjapan.jp/en), the temple and shrine industry bring hundreds of exhibitors showing religious equipment, services, and technologies to thousands of visitors. In 2021, the number of exhibitors is expected to be 750 and the number of visitors 40,000.

14 A title of a special magazine from Nikkei Bijinesu was "Work Efficient Zen—Zen Resolves 100% the Worries of the Businessman." The founder of the successful companies Kyocera and KDDI and chairman of Japan Airlines, Inamori Kazuo is a practicing Zen Buddhist and has written several books on how to incorporate Buddhist spirituality into business.

15 The Temple and Shrine Tourism Association's website is located at http://jisya-kk.jp. The Japan National Tourist Organization (https://www.jnto.go.jp) has specific topics on Buddhism, spirituality, and travel, and in joint ventures with hotels and Buddhist Zen temples, the Nippon Foundation makes efforts to attract both Japanese and foreign tourists to "experience the soul of Japan" (https://www.nippon-foundation.or.jp/en/what/projects/culture_support/iroha-nihon/). Books on pilgrimage and temple visits are continuously being written, published, and sold in Japanese bookstores.

16 Interview was conducted in the autumn of 2017. For other examples of "experimental Buddhism" in Japan, see Nelson (2013). See also Thomas (2015) on a Tokyo temple hiring a for-profit company to help market the temple's activities.

17 Interviews with SG members were conducted in the spring of 2016.

18 On the complex relation between SG, politics, and Komeito, see Ehrhardt et al. (2014) and McLaughlin (2015). For a comprehensive introduction and analysis of Soka Gakkai, see McLaughlin (2009, 2012, 2019). See also McLaughlin's chapter in this volume.

19 Soka Gakkai's own presentation of the organization, teaching, and activities can be seen at its website (http://www.sokanet.jp) and in its annual reports (e.g., Sōka Gakkai Kōhōshitsu 2016).

20 See, however, McLaughlin (2009) for examples of amulet versions of the *gohonzon*, talismans in the form of gifts received from Ikeda Daisaku, and a well-developed pilgrimage tradition of traveling to sites of importance within the SG tradition.

21 Interviews with HS members were conducted in the spring of 2016 and autumn of 2017.

22 Religious membership figures are always extremely difficult to confirm, and some groups (especially NRMs) sometimes see a strategic advantage in exaggerating. Rather than twelve million members, others have suggested lower figures of 400,000 and 500,000 (Wieczorek 2002, 167).

23 Examples of book titles are *The Laws of Prosperity, The Philosophy of Progress: Higher Thinking for Developing Infinite Prosperity,* and *Prosperity Thinking*. Other titles can be found at https://www.irhpress.co.jp/products/list.php?category_id=94. Titles of courses include "Mind of a Rich Person," "Business Decision," "Prosperity Realization," "The Laws of Wealth," "What Is Beneficial Leadership?," "The Law of Increasing Income," "The Spirit of Management," and "Improvement of Company Fortune."

4

The Soka Gakkai Economy

Measuring Cycles of Exchange That Power Japan's Largest Buddhist Lay Organization

Levi McLaughlin

THIS CHAPTER PROVIDES A VIEW INTO A simultaneously dispassionate and emotion-driven calculus that perpetuates the circulation of money and material goods by Soka Gakkai in Japan. Soka Gakkai (the Value Creation Study Association) is a lay Buddhist organization. It also is one of Japan's wealthiest organizations. I propose that, in order to better assess why Soka Gakkai became wealthy, researchers must appraise both market and affective values. Here, I draw on my nonmember participant observation of grassroots-level Soka Gakkai communities, along with supporting documentation, to provide an overview of member practices and institutional mechanisms that drive the organization's fundraising, outline estimations of Gakkai holdings, and survey dilemmas that persist in the absence of accessible financial records. The chapter suggests ways to look beyond gaps in empirical data to consider basic questions about Soka Gakkai's circulation of money and other goods. More important than knowing *how much* wealth Soka Gakkai possesses—a question that cannot be answered satisfactorily—is *why* Soka Gakkai members contribute so much to their religion. Who invests in Soka Gakkai, what is the nature of their investment, and what do they receive in return? What do members make of money and material goods that comprise Soka Gakkai's cycles of exchange, and how do these cycles look if we take members' valuations into account?

Purely market-based calculations prevent us from knowing who powers Soka Gakkai's economy and why they do so. Analyses motivated by "how much?" questions overlook gender, material cultural practices, and the importance of the affective values adherents place on goods that constitute their religion's material base. In this chapter, I draw on fieldwork to demonstrate how Soka Gakkai relies to a large extent on members of the Married Women's Division, the organization's most dedicated subgroup. These members carry out donations and fundraising that have seen Soka Gakkai grow into one of Japan's wealthiest groups—of any type. Ethnographic episodes show how this wealth accumulation was generated by members who affectively deflate the monetary value of their donations while they radically inflate the value of items they receive from Soka Gakkai. It is a practice that complicates pricing. Any appraisal of Soka Gakkai's wealth must calculate market values—including corporate assets, real estate, stocks and bonds, cash, and other holdings—and measure how much Gakkai goods are worth to the members who circulate them. Market assessments place monetary values on the group that are legible beyond Gakkai parameters, while members' affective measures tend to appear nonsensical to outside observers. Nonetheless, both valuations must be taken into account if we are to understand Soka Gakkai's economy.

Soka Gakkai: More Than Lay Buddhism

Soka Gakkai was founded in Japan in the 1930s and grew dramatically in the postwar years to become Japan's largest new religion.[1] Originally a lay association under the temple-based denomination Nichiren Shōshū, "Nichiren True Sect," a minority lineage stemming from the medieval Japanese Buddhist reformer Nichiren (1222–1282), Soka Gakkai split from its temple parent in 1991. Soka Gakkai maintains Nichiren's exclusive embrace of the *Lotus Sutra,* the historical Buddha Śākyamuni's putative final teachings. Other core Nichiren Buddhist elements include the chanting of sections of the *Lotus* and its "great title" (*daimoku*), the seven sacred syllables *namu-myōhō-renge-kyō,* as well as an emphasis on the Nichiren Buddhist conversion practice known as *shakubuku* and a historical rejection of other religions, including other Nichiren Buddhist sects, as heterodox. Soka Gakkai has also developed a broad range of institutions and practices that extend far beyond Nichiren Buddhism, most famously its affiliated political party Komeito (founded 1964), which operates as the junior partner in Japan's national coalition government. And while it maintains Nichiren Buddhist practices, the organization is singularly dedicated to Honorary President Ikeda Daisaku, whom its adherents revere as their unquestioned authority in all matters.[2]

Scholarship on Soka Gakkai's financial dimensions has categorized the group in terms of bureaucracy and business. Asayama Taichi proposes that a key explanation for the Gakkai's unmatched growth between the end of the Second World War and the beginning of the 1970s was its development along Japanese corporate lines. Soka Gakkai exploded from a few thousand adherents in 1950 to millions of followers twenty years later as it expanded like a large Japanese company; that is, as a comprehensive headquarter/branch system that saw to all of its employees' work and family needs. Asayama (2017) convincingly tracks Soka Gakkai's growth alongside Japan's postwar-era rapid urbanization and economic expansion and notes that, just as Japan's economy stagnated after the 1973 oil shock, the Gakkai's growth in Japan came to a halt. Shimada Hiromi (2008, 2013), in several publications that speculate about Soka Gakkai's business and real estate holdings, refers to a "Soka Kingdom" (*Sōka ōkoku*) that suggests itself as a "New Religions model" of entrepreneurship. Tsukada Hotaka's (2015) research expands our perspective on the Gakkai's initiatives to emphasize ways the group's postwar institution building capitalized on utopian Japanese nationalist sentiments that gave rise to Soka Gakkai's entry into electoral politics and drove its early doctrinal objectives.

These observations help us understand dimensions of Soka Gakkai's postwar development, but they leave unexplained its full institutional range and they do not account for the specific nature of members' financial obligations. I propose that Soka Gakkai exceeds corporate models or nationalist movements and is instead isomorphic of the modern nation-state as a whole. Soka Gakkai makes the most sense as an entity mimetic of the Japanese nation-state in which it developed.[3] In the postwar decades, Gakkai adherents constructed working equivalents of standardized education, control of sovereign territory, control and distribution of information, political engagement (through Komeito), and a thriving internal economy regulated by a mimetic version of a national taxation system. Soka Gakkai's institutions are overseen by a rationalized bureaucracy that takes its cue from a civil service. Included within these are powerful fundraising systems. These mostly remain a tantalizing yet unverifiable object of popular interest, thanks to the group's legal status as a *shūkyō hōjin,* or "religious juridical person," which renders Soka Gakkai's finances all but completely closed to outside inquiry.

Soka Gakkai claims 8.27 million households in Japan and over 1.5 million adherents in 192 countries under Soka Gakkai International (SGI). These figures are exaggerated, yet assessments from outside Soka Gakkai estimate that people who self-identify as Gakkai members may make up between 2 and 3 percent of the Japanese population (McLaughlin 2019). As this chapter demonstrates, committed Gakkai adherents are just that: *deeply* committed to the group. Their commitment translates into substantial material support for the religion and its affiliated enterprises. Soka Gakkai businesses center on publishing and extend to other media producers, advertising, memorial parks, real estate, museums, educational institutions, and estimated holdings in numerous corporations and financial instruments, not to mention support for Komeito. Some of these businesses are among Japan's most profitable and certainly most solvent.

The Gakkai's financial endeavors stem from member donations. Historically, Soka Gakkai members have largely been people of modest means, yet their individual contributions combined to build an organization worth many billions of US dollars. Members' annual payments into Soka Gakkai are overseen by what the organization labeled its Zaimubu, or "Finance Division"; in Japan, national taxation is overseen by the Zaimushō, the Ministry of Finance. As members come of age within Soka Gakkai, they are cultivated to conceive of their tax-equivalent donations as meaningful self-sacrifice for their organization's victorious expansion.[4] The Gakkai's many routinized campaigns include annual *shakubuku* (conversion) drives each January or February; regular visits to venerated Soka Gakkai sites, frequently on dates that celebrate key anniversaries in Ikeda Daisaku's biography, such as his conversion to Soka Gakkai in 1947 (August 24) and his ascension to the post of third Gakkai president in 1960 (May 3); "finances" donations each December; and mobilization in support of Komeito candidates in every election. Electioneering for Komeito and its political allies has developed within Soka Gakkai into a ritual as important to members' religious lives as chanting the *Lotus Sutra,* seeking conversions, soliciting friends and neighbors to subscribe to the daily newspaper *Seikyō shinbun,* and other faith-driven activities (see Ehrhardt et al. 2014). Indeed, thanks in large part to the fact that members are expected to mobilize votes for every Komeito electoral bid, from the smallest town assembly to the National Diet, adherents are primed to mobilize for other Gakkai campaigns, including fundraising.

To gain perspective on Soka Gakkai fundraising, I will begin with an ethnographic snapshot from over a decade ago. This view into one dedicated member's donation at Soka Gakkai headquarters exemplifies what may be considered the Gakkai's financial practices at their most robust, at a juncture when decades of bureaucratic elaboration culminated in a meticulous quantification of adherents' heartfelt devotion. In 2007, when this episode took place, Honorary President Ikeda was still a vigorous presence in Gakkai members' lives; Ikeda Daisaku's last appearance at a public Soka Gakkai meeting was in May 2010. A visit to Gakkai headquarters was conceived by his followers as a pilgrimage directly to Ikeda, an obligatory trip to a sacred site and a chance to spend time deepening their affective one-to-one bond with their beloved mentor. It was also obviously the dispatch of a routine financial responsibility that powers a massive and wealthy organization.

A Pilgrimage to Shinanomachi

Friday, September 14, 2007. "It's strange to think that Prime Minister Abe is just right across the street, isn't it?" Mrs. Itahashi takes a long drag on her cigarette and exhales over her shoulder toward the restaurant window in the direction of Keiō University Hospital.[5] Days earlier, Prime Minister Abe Shinzō, deeply unpopular and beset by pressures from the media and within his own Liberal Democratic Party, shocked the country by abruptly announcing his resignation. He has repaired to the hospital to be treated for exhaustion.

Mrs. Itahashi and I are eating lunch in a small sushi restaurant on the second floor of a building in Shinanomachi, the central Tokyo neighborhood that is dominated by Soka Gakkai's administrative headquarters. Since 1991, Shinanomachi, until then an administrative center tasked with overseeing Soka Gakkai's daily operations, has confirmed its identity as a pilgrimage site. A Young Men's Division leader at a Shinanomachi meeting I attended in the summer of 2007 proudly announced that Shinanomachi's train station boasted more non–rail pass ticket sales than any other station within central Tokyo, more even than nearby Suidōbashi station, where baseball fans pack the Tokyo Dome. Waiting at the Shinanomachi ticket gates on a weekday afternoon, one sees a constant flow of people. Some of them are men from their thirties to their sixties with almost identical appearances: perfect haircuts, dark suits, white shirts, and blue or black ties. Others are women with almost identical appearances: single-color skirt-suits and carefully coiffed hair. Many of these are Soka Gakkai's *kanbu,* or "administrators," the religion's full-time employees. A few younger people come through the gates, and there are a few visible non-Japanese here and there, most wearing Soka Gakkai International nametags. A few ill and elderly people cross Gaien Higashi Street to Keiō University Hospital, yet the majority who flow through the gates are average Gakkai members. Most are women, and while a few are younger, most are elderly Married Women's Division members. They arrive alone or in groups. Some appear confused by the large Tokyo crowds and hectic transit system, but all of them quickly find their way to the Gakkai headquarters. They join the crowd of devotees out of the gates and to the right, past shops, restaurants, and Soka Gakkai's tiny Twenty-First Century Park to form lines waiting to enter Gakkai headquarters.

The pilgrimage to Shinanomachi developed organically. Until 1991, the area was primarily residential, and Soka Gakkai's presence in the neighborhood, though pronounced, was not absolute. After the November 1991 Soka Gakkai/Nichiren Shōshū schism, member visits to Shinanomachi surged, and in the years that followed, Soka Gakkai responded by expanding its presence and pushing out many long-term residents. The Gakkai administration appears to have capitalized on plummeting real estate values following the collapse of Japan's "bubble economy" in the early 1990s to buy up Shinanomachi land. According to one journalist's estimates, in 1993 alone Soka Gakkai land purchases at its headquarters were worth over thirteen billion yen (~US$104 million). In 1995, when the Gaien Higashi thoroughfare that runs the length of the Shinanomachi neighborhood was widened from seventeen to twenty-five meters,

Soka Gakkai bought out shop owners who had previously lined its east side. The population of Shinanomachi's roughly eleven hectares dropped from 2,095 residents in 1984 to approximately one thousand people twenty years later, and Soka Gakkai constructed over thirty-five new buildings in the area during this time. It also planned construction on what would be its general headquarters (opened November 2013), which covers over 94,000 square meters.[6] Soka Gakkai now maintains over seventy large and small buildings in Shinanomachi. These changes occurred because of demands placed on its administration by adherents like Mrs. Itahashi.

The restaurant where Mrs. Itahashi and I eat lunch, like almost every shop in this vicinity, displays the *sanshoku,* the Soka Gakkai tricolor flag, which resembles a European national symbol with a stylized eight-petal lotus flower at its center. Until at least the mid-2000s, if a Shinanomachi shop belonged to the Shinanomachi Shop-Owner's Promotion Society (Shinanomachi Shōten Shinkōkai), Gakkai employees had the option of paying not with Japanese yen but with *chiketto,* or "tickets," a close equivalent to currency issued by the Gakkai administration that would be redeemed by merchants for yen. Shops that line the narrow streets around the headquarters buildings sell Gakkai goods and media products. A branch of Kongōdō, an Osaka-based Buddhist altar maker, offers tea to customers who stop in to buy accoutrements for their home altars or more major purchases of the altars themselves, the largest of which cost the equivalent of a new family car.[7] Hakubun Eikōdō, a bookstore and altar seller across the street from the train station, displays hundreds of titles from Seikyō Press, Daisan Bunmei, and other Gakkai publishing houses, most of which operate from Shinanomachi. Smaller stores also display Gakkai books as well as other media, such as piles of DVDs from the monthly series intended for screening at local study meetings, in addition to hundreds of prepackaged Shinanomachi-themed gifts of chocolates, crackers, and other items that visitors bring back as souvenirs for friends and family. Even the Shinanomachi branch of Ministop, a popular convenience store with branches across Japan, sells the latest Soka Gakkai DVDs near the cash register.[8]

Mrs. Itahashi and I talk about her experience in Soka Gakkai. Now just over fifty years old, she joined in 1962 at the age of seven, when her mother converted. Her mother raised her as a poor single parent, newly arrived in Tokyo from Niigata prefecture in northern Japan at the time of her conversion. Mrs. Itahashi is fiercely proud of surviving a childhood of desperate poverty and prevailing over hardships to realize her dream of becoming a ballet dancer. Her mother died of cancer when she was seventeen, leaving her alone in the city. Mrs. Itahashi put herself through ballet school, and she now runs her own studio, training students of all ages in Tokyo's posh Setagaya ward. The neighborhood is wealthy, but Mrs. Itahashi is not. She, her husband, who runs a modest foreign car distribution company, and their teenage daughter, who is Mrs. Itahashi's prize ballet pupil, share a tiny two-room apartment. Her son, a talented violinist, went to live with her husband's mother in an equally tiny apartment one building over when he entered his early teenage years. Her family's spare living standards are a cost she bears willingly to pursue artistic objectives. Mrs. Itahashi credits her happy family and career success to Soka Gakkai—and specifically to the guidance of Ikeda Daisaku. She visits Shinanomachi at least once a month to carry out *honbu kuyō,* "headquarters memorial donation," a practice that she and other adherents typically characterize as *ongaeshi:* "returning an obligation out of gratitude."

After lunch, we walk to a main headquarters building, past shops and numerous large buildings dedicated to different Gakkai subgroups. Security, always present, has increased in recent years, perhaps in response to a rise in warnings since 2001 in public places in Japan overall and certainly in response to heightened concerns within Soka Gakkai about the well-being of their aging leader Ikeda. In previous years, one walked past smiling young men from Sōkahan, or "Soka Team," and Gajōkai, the "Fortress Protection Society"—volunteer Young Men's Division wings. Now, the entrance to the otherwise ordinary-looking office building resembles an airport security gate. The Sōkahan and Gajōkai ranks are enhanced by numerous professional uniformed security guards who see that every person signs in. Our bags are rolled along conveyors through X-ray machines, and we pass through a metal detector before entering the main doors. The ground floor is packed with visiting Gakkai members, almost all elderly women who wait in lines to fill out forms and to consult with staff at a long table along one wall of a large central hall.

We walk up the stairs to the second floor, where a similar scene greets us. The main room on the second floor resembles, most of all, a bank. Like a bank, there is a high table in the center of the room with a plexiglass top that supplies a standard form out of cubbyholes. The form, a memo-sized sheaf of papers, is worth describing in detail. It is a six-page layer of carbon paper. Pages 1, 4, 5, and 6 bear the header *uketsukehyō* (reception form), while page 2 is labeled *kōfu kikin mōshikomisho* (registration form for a monetary donation for *kōsen rufu* [the spread of Soka Gakkai's mission]), and page 3 is *kizō mōshikomisho* (registration form for donations). All six pages provide spaces for the donor's name, address, Soka Gakkai administrative position(s), and the identities of people for whom the donation is being made. Below this, the forms call for descriptions of donations. The first box lists letters, document collections (*bunshū*), and picture albums and asks for the number of these that are being donated; it is clear that many members bring anthologies from local Gakkai communities as gifts intended directly for Ikeda Daisaku. Under this, a box asks for a description of the type of gift included (*hinmei*) and the number of items in the donation. Below this, the form asks that the donor fill in the amount of money donated, and a final box calls for the name of the subgroup or local Gakkai meeting that occasioned the donation. Page 3 includes a more detailed checklist for donated items: the name of the item(s), title of the donation, the name of the people who produced it, and its size, "motif" (*mochīfu*), provenance, and production date. The form also inquires whether the donation is being made to commemorate the construction of a Soka Gakkai Culture Center, the anniversary of an event, or another specific objective.

As thoroughly bureaucratized as this standardized form indicates Soka Gakkai has become, it still speaks to the highly personalized connection between individual members and Ikeda Daisaku. It is a relationship mediated by letters, photo albums, and other thoughtful gifts. Though every item is quantified, the categories indicate willingness on the part of the Gakkai administration to accommodate affective dimensions. After all, how would a bureaucrat quantify "motifs" or put a value on scrapbooks filled with photos and letters? The form also acknowledges the extent to which members have internalized Soka Gakkai's imperative to commemorate all events, both personal and institutional, by registering information and material goods with the headquarters. Bureaucratized iterations of the affective relationship between members and Ikeda represent a mutually reinforced commitment on the part of nonelite adherents and leaders to channel personal celebrations into institutional support. Finally, the form makes clear that the Gakkai's administration, and its Finance Division in particular, retains a meticulous, numbers-oriented record of each member's dedication.

Gakkai representatives promote Soka Gakkai as a religion that does not cost money: members are not required to pay to convert, and their income is not tithed. However, the headquarters pilgrimage makes clear that dedication is equated with *kuyō,* a term often glossed as "memorial" but that can be translated more accurately as "to cultivate through giving." *Kuyō* functions as a Japanese translation of the Sanskrit *pūjā,* a ritual offering to a transcendent being or objective, a contribution from which the giver can expect positive karmic benefits in return. Gakkai members are encouraged to carry out their *kuyō* practice in person or via bank transfer. Members report to me that the Gakkai's Finance Division will not issue a receipt for income tax purposes unless the donation exceeds ten thousand yen (~US$100), a requirement that encourages sizeable donations. In exchange, the Gakkai administration sends small gifts to generous donors, mostly of comparatively low commercial value yet always characterized as heartfelt thanks sent directly by Ikeda Daisaku. In the eyes of their most devoted recipients, these return gifts are the equivalent of contact relics to be displayed to fellow members. The Gakkai's donation practice may be modeled on government taxation, yet it transcends taxes because it inspires a cycle of exchange that binds adherents with their apotheosized honorary president, affectively and materially. It cannot be fully controlled by administrators.

The members spend the considerable time needed to fill out the six-page form, then take a special envelope marked *kuyō,* insert cash, and bring their paperwork to a table that runs across half of the large room. Ten Gakkai employees, all elderly women and men, sit at the tables, waiting to greet each visitor with a smile and an ear for their stories. They work for the Finance Division. Mrs. Itahashi takes her turn after a long wait to sit across from a Gakkai employee, to whom she speaks about herself and her family. Mrs. Itahashi has recently been promoted to the post of *fukushibufujinbuchō,* or Assistant Chapter Married Women's Division leader. The employee smiles and congratulates Mrs. Itahashi on her continuing efforts and then takes her envelope through a door behind the table, through which I glimpse a man in tie and shirtsleeves tallying donations and writing receipts. Mrs. Itahashi only brought a monetary donation today, but many of the other members around her have come with items such as vases, lamps, and other decorations; *meibutsu,* or "famed goods," from local areas in Japan (mostly food); and other presents that one may bring on a visit to a family home, such as flowers or sweets.

Several months later, on a return visit to Shinanomachi, I ask two administrators from Soka Gakkai's International Division what happens to these nonmonetary gifts. They hesitate somewhat, couching their response in thanks to the dedicated adherents, before telling me that nonperishable items will be distributed to the Gakkai's many Culture Centers across Japan, to be displayed to their fellow devotees. My visits to Culture Centers confirm that members tend to bring items that conform with a signature Gakkai aesthetic in which they remain constantly immersed: porcelain figurines, charming clocks atop doilies for the mantelpiece, tinkling music boxes, and similar objects that evoke the feel of a twentieth-century middle-class Japanese home. It is less clear where perishables end up. They are dealt with "appropriately" (*tekitō ni*), I am informed by the administrators. The members who bring these items appear to operate with the affective understanding that their carefully selected treats will end up in the Ikeda home, for him and his wife, Kaneko, to enjoy. Practical difficulties stand in the way of making this possible, not least of which being the fact that no one outside of Ikeda's innermost circle knows where the honorary president and his wife actually live.

Mrs. Itahashi and I walk up the stairs to the top floor, where the strains of *namu-myōhō-renge-kyō* grow louder as we approach. In a central hall, several hundred chairs are lined up in front of a large and beautifully adorned altar that is opened to reveal the replica calligraphic mandala that serves as Soka Gakkai's *gohonzon,* or "object of worship." Like the rest of the building, and like almost all Gakkai facilities, the walls are decorated with framed photos by Ikeda of nature scenes shot around the world. Approximately forty women and a few elderly men sit chanting. Mrs. Itahashi sits briefly, intones the *daimoku* three times in a conventional ritual greeting to the object of worship, and then gets up quickly to leave. As we head back down the stairs, Mrs. Itahashi seems a little embarrassed by her perfunctory chant. She laughingly describes herself as *shinjin gōjō ja nai,* or "not strong and pure in faith." "Not like the members from Kansai," she says, invoking, as many Japanese members do, the Osaka-area members as paragons of devotion. She tells me that she will come back again this month, this time with her husband, in order to carry out their family's monthly headquarters visit properly.

Soka Gakkai's Business Background

Toda Jōsei (1900–1958), the second Soka Gakkai president and architect of the group's postwar expansion, distinguished himself as an entrepreneur.[9] He spent two years as a teacher in Tokyo's public school system before he launched a private academy called Jishū Gakkan in 1922, and thereafter he moved beyond teaching to related business interests. He found initial success publishing exam-preparation textbooks. One of these, a primer on arithmetic published in June 1930, sold over one million copies. Toda's publishing resulted in wealth, which he funneled into new ventures. From the late 1930s, Toda diversified his business activities to include, among other enterprises, a publishing company called Nihon Shōgakkan, a money-lending business, a soy sauce factory, and a stock trading firm. By 1943, Toda controlled seventeen companies. These were seized by the Japanese government when he was arrested with his mentor Makiguchi Tsunesaburō (1871–1944) in July of that year for refusing to abide by wartime Japan's restrictions on religion. Makiguchi died of malnutrition in Tokyo's Sugamo Prison in November 1944.

After his release in July 1945, weeks before the end of the Pacific War, Toda wasted no time reestablishing Nihon Shōgakkan. Up to the end of the 1940s, Toda split his efforts between the Gakkai and his businesses, which focused largely on publishing. In July 1947, he launched the monthly magazine *Daibyaku renge* (Great White Lotus), which remains Soka Gakkai's principal study periodical. Toda's profits soon began to suffer from spikes in the cost of paper and other materials. He switched to publishing nonreligious monthly magazines in the hopes that he could keep up with inflation by raising the price of each subsequent issue. This venture met with initial success: a boy's magazine called *Bōken shōnen* (Adventure Boy) and *Ruby,* a women's magazine, sold in the tens of thousands. However, by 1949, Japan's established prewar publishing houses had recovered their operations, along with their former readerships, and many upstart enterprises folded. By October 1949, Toda closed Nihon Shōgakkan. He then opened a money-lending business, but this was closed by the Ministry of Finance in August 1950 because it was unable to meet the terms of its loan contracts. On November 12, 1950, at a general meeting convened to observe the seventh anniversary of Makiguchi Tsunesaburō's death, Toda resigned as chairman of the Gakkai's board of directors, citing his failure as a businessman.

In late 1950, Toda resolved to take the mantle of second Gakkai president as a means of fully dedicating himself as Makiguchi's disciple. His renewed dedication involved the launch of commercial enterprises that now form the core of Soka Gakkai's holdings. In March 1951, Toda organized an editorial board for Soka Gakkai's newspaper, *Seikyō shinbun,* which now claims a circulation of 5.5 million copies daily, the third largest in Japan. *Seikyō shinbun* was first published on April 20, 1951, on a single piece of broadsheet in a run of five thousand copies. The paper featured member testimonials, advice to practitioners, and the first installment of Toda's memoir *Ningen kakumei* (The Human Revolution), a serial novel that would serve as the model for Ikeda Daisaku's bestselling opus by the same title. The twelve-volume *Ningen kakumei* under Ikeda's authorship has sold in excess of fifty million copies, and Gakkai members have come to treat this book and its serialized sequel *Shin ningen kakumei* (The New Human Revolution) as de facto scripture.

Postwar Soka Gakkai's potent combination of educational, religious, political, and commercial expansion formed a crucible for Toda's disciple Ikeda Daisaku, who converted to Soka Gakkai in August 1947 at the age of nineteen. Much of Ikeda's early discipleship took the form of training within Toda's companies, including work for Nihon Shōgakkan and as a writer and editor for Toda's magazines. By the time he was twenty-two, Ikeda was responsible for Toda's corporate finance, securing loans and managing assets for Toda's businesses. Ikeda evidently applied this formative business experience to his Soka Gakkai duties. As he rose through the ranks of the Young Men's Division, Ikeda served in numerous administrative posts, including as the division's chief executive officer (*sanbōshituchō*). Toda Jōsei died in April 1958, after which Ikeda solidified his authority. On June 30, 1958, Ikeda was appointed *sōmushitsuchō,* or head of general administration, and on June 30, 1959, he became head of the Gakkai's board of directors. He took the position of third Soka Gakkai president on May 3, 1960.

Under Ikeda's presidency, Soka Gakkai dramatically expanded its publishing efforts and moved into numerous other commercial ventures. Members' donations also came to be routinized into a series of regular and, in some cases, truly massive fundraising campaigns. The largest of these was the 1965 four-day blitz for the Shōhondō, a facility that opened in 1972 at Nichiren Shōshū's head temple Taisekiji (near Mount Fuji), which housed the temple denomination's, and what was then the Gakkai's, principal object of worship. Between October 9 and 12, 1965, eight million Japanese members contributed more than 35.5 billion yen, depositing their contributions in more than 16,000 branches of the Bank of Mitsubishi in this four-day period; this was equivalent to just under US$100 million in 1965, or close to US$760 million today.

Soka Gakkai honed a campaign-oriented way of life for its membership. The results of routinized fundraising grew visible at Shinanomachi, with the construction of hundreds of Culture Centers and other facilities across Japan, and with numerous and substantial holdings overseas.

Accounting in the Absence of Accounts

Soka Gakkai looms as a financial black box. Because the group registered in 1952 as a "religious juridical person" (*shūkyō hōjin*), Soka Gakkai is protected by law from paying tax on its assets or income derived from activities that constitute religious undertakings. Tax exempt and relying to a great extent on unpaid volunteer labor by millions of members who supplement the work of its salaried employees, Soka Gakkai is in a position to retain a large percentage of the funds it receives. Changes to the 1951 Religious Juridical Persons law that were implemented from 1996 require that religions in Japan disclose their assets to the Japanese government. However, there is no provision within the law requiring that these disclosures be publicized (see Klein 2012). In addition, Soka Gakkai is registered as a religious juridical person with the Tokyo Metropolitan Government, not with the national government. In 2002, a reporter for the magazine *Sekai* informed me that the Tokyo government at that point only tasked two staff members to oversee hundreds of registered religions, including Soka Gakkai. Two overworked civil servants are most likely not capable of or willing to audit a group as bureaucratically complex, financially powerful, and politically influential as Soka Gakkai.

An absence of reliable data has not stood in the way of enthusiastic speculation about Soka Gakkai's finances. Educated guesses by journalists and academics about the value of the group's real estate and its corporate interests hint at the scale of Soka Gakkai's wealth. Additionally, between 2002 and 2004, the Ministry of Finance released information on more than seven hundred thousand profit-generating enterprises, including some religious juridical persons. This included Soka Gakkai, which ranked 170th overall for profit-making Japanese enterprises in 2003, with earnings in the neighborhood of ~US$165 million, far and away the highest of any religion in Japan (Carlson 2014; Shimada 2008). These earnings figures only took into account Soka Gakkai itself.

Media coverage of Gakkai money reveals as-yet underexplored avenues of inquiry. For example, an entity called "Soka Gakkai, Inc." appeared in the 2015 document leak of offshore accounts known as the Panama Papers, indicating that further investigation of Gakkai holdings overseas may shed light on the group's assets in Japan.[10] In addition, not a few news stories focus on hazy boundaries that persist between Soka Gakkai and the nominally separate Komeito. In the summer of 1989, for instance, newspapers reported that police turned up wads of yen extracted from a locked safe dumped in bushes in Kawasaki, a Tokyo suburb. Investigators discovered that the safe had come from the basement of a business in nearby Yokohama connected to Nakanishi Haruo, a senior Gakkai administrator who oversaw distribution of the *Seikyō shinbun* and was connected to Komeito politicians who had been embroiled in the Recruit Scandal, a 1988 insider-trading debacle that involved numerous government and opposition Diet members and resulted in the resignation of the cabinet of Prime Minister Takeshita Noboru. The approximately US$1.7 million dumped in the Kawasaki bushes was presumed to be a discarded Komeito slush fund (Sanger 1989). This incident underlined suspicions that, in spite of a constitutional divide between religion and government, laws that strictly limit political donations, and regulations maintained internally by the religion and the party, Soka Gakkai nonetheless funds Komeito and that it uses untaxed and untraceable cash donations from its devotees to do so.

Soka Gakkai evidently possesses ample means to provide these funds, given figures supplied by journalists. The most recent substantial attempt to survey Soka Gakkai's net worth was published in June 2016 as a special issue of the magazine *Shūkan daiyamondo* (Weekly Diamond).[11] The magazine characterizes Soka Gakkai as a business conglomerate that rests on three principal enterprises: religious activities, which are not taxed; publishing, which enjoys some tax deductions; and gravesites, known in Japan as "memorial parks," which occupy religious juridical person–owned land that is not subject to taxation. The total value of Soka Gakkai's direct assets estimated by the magazine's editors is staggering. Regional Culture Centers (~US$8.34 billion), public interest corporations connected to Soka Gakkai (~US$3.9 billion), memorial parks (~US$2.5 billion), main Culture Centers (~US$714 million), facilities at Shinanomachi (~US$814 million), and companies connected to Soka Gakkai (~US$280 million) were estimated to be worth approximately US$16.64 billion.[12]

Shūkan daiyamondo identified fourteen principal Gakkai corporations. The largest of these is Seikyō Shinbunsha, the company that publishes the *Seikyō shinbun,* a number of other newspapers, and numerous magazines and books; at 5.5 million copies daily, the *Seikyō shinbun* alone was estimated to bring in approximately US$1.15 billion in annual sales. Gakkai corporations enjoy unusually high capital-to-asset ratios, or capital divided by its risk-weighted assets. While companies in Japan average approximately 40 percent capital-to-asset, many Gakkai corporations exceed 80 percent; Shinano Kikaku, the Gakkai's principal visual media production company, claims 95.4 percent. This means that the companies that Soka Gakkai relies upon can absorb tremendous losses, and many of them most likely possess substantial cash assets.

The heart of Soka Gakkai's businesses remains publishing. It is well known that Soka Gakkai maintains particularly strong interests in paper producers, printing, and Japan's major newspapers and book presses. The *Seikyō shinbun* does not own its own presses. Instead, it commissions its millions of daily copies from the *Mainichi shinbun* and *Asahi shinbun,* among other Japanese dailies. Lucrative contracts with the *Seikyō shinbun* are suggested as a principal reason why coverage of Soka Gakkai and Komeito tends to be minimized and, to the extent that it appears, presented in a neutral fashion within Japan's most widely read newspapers (see *Shūkan daiyamondo* 2016; Watanabe 2000).

Soka Gakkai funnels its profits into a wide range of investments. Judging by companies that advertise regularly in the *Seikyō shinbun, Shūkan daiyamondo* posits that Soka Gakkai's financial interests extend to Japan's major banks, including Mitsubishi Tokyo UFJ, Mitsui Sumitomo, and Mizuho; large insurance providers, such as Orix Insurance Services and AIG; and a wide range of electronics manufacturers, construction, real estate, and other large and small corporations. At the start of every new year, executives from between two thousand and three thousand companies make formal visits to Soka Gakkai headquarters to pay their respects, a tradition that indicates just how important the religion is to business in Japan.

As impressive as these estimates are, they only represent a portion of Soka Gakkai's total wealth. There is reason to believe that Soka Gakkai is a major player in Japan's bond market. In September 2016, I interviewed a retired bond trader who had spent years within Mitsubishi Tokyo UFJ, a bank that has enjoyed a long relationship with Soka Gakkai. It was Mitsubishi that oversaw the Gakkai's fundraising for the Shōhondō in 1965, and it would appear that the two organizations have retained close ties since then. According to the trader, the Mitsubishi Tokyo UFJ branch at Shinanomachi maintains a dedicated Soka Gakkai desk, where traders wait to execute orders placed by Gakkai administrators tasked with managing the religion's assets. Gakkai investments reportedly focus on a financial instrument known as an *enmansai,* a structured bond, or, more formally, an "equity-linked multi-callable note" that is linked to Japan's Nikkei index and relies on AAA- and above-rated overseas issuers, mostly in Europe. Until regulations changed following the so-called Lehman Shock, the financial crisis that unfolded after the bankruptcy of Lehman Brothers in September 2008, bond traders targeted religious juridical persons, public interest corporations, and schools as customers for *enmansai* and other structured bonds. Until 2008, these entities were not required to disclose their trades. They would therefore be attracted to *enmansai* for their comparative stability, competitive rate of return, and lack of official scrutiny. The retired trader informed me that Soka Gakkai became the largest player on the *enmansai* market. Indeed, Soka Gakkai's presence was so large that it annoyed analysts because every investment by Soka Gakkai exceeded ~US$100 million, an amount large enough to shift the Nikkei index each time the religion placed an order, thereby disrupting market predictions.

The religious juridical person (*shūkyō hōjin*) Soka Gakkai, as well as Gakkai private companies (*minkan kigyō*), public interest juridical persons (*kōeki hōjin*), and schools (*gakkō hōjin*), do not open their books to the public. This makes verifying Soka Gakkai's money an impossible task. However, the former bond trader's account introduces an alluring possibility for researchers who wish to follow the money: fieldwork undertaken by religious studies scholars within the financial world may provide insights into heretofore underexplored aspects of religious organizations and their wealth.

Toward a Hybrid Assessment

Ultimately, reports on Soka Gakkai's wealth, while they provide salacious details that hint at vast resources and concealed machinations, steer us away from more promising inquiries. Rather than dwelling on *how much,* we can pursue compelling questions as to *why* Gakkai adherents invest in their organization and *who* these adherents are. Ethnography makes obvious that women are the most important players in Soka Gakkai's internal economy, while isolated attention to financial details conceals the fact that it is women members who contribute the most to the Gakkai's finances. Women's importance within Soka Gakkai is further obscured by the group's own administration. Within Soka Gakkai in Japan, women are relegated to the Young Women's and Married Women's Divisions; all other posts are occupied by men. The group has hundreds of vice presidents, not one of whom is a woman. One visit to Shinanomachi is sufficient to demonstrate that, in spite of their administrative marginality and invisibility to market-based metrics, it is women who made Soka Gakkai rich.

Attention to women indicates the need to incorporate both market-based measures and affective understandings of Soka Gakkai's cycles of exchange.[13] Following the "affective economy" concept proposed by Sarah Ahmed (2004a), it is through circulation and exchange that emotions gain coherence: "affect does not reside positively in the sign or commodity, but is produced only as an effect of its circulation" (120). Material objects enable circulation and make it tangible, and emotional connections are amplified when the objects in question operate as metonymic substitutes for the people at either end of an exchange. As Donovan Schaefer (2015, 93) puts it, "affects have their own capacity to articulate bodies to systems of power."[14] Mrs. Itahashi characterized the money she donated as her "return of obligation" (*ongaeshi*) she owed Soka Gakkai and its honorary president—an obligation she felt she performed insufficiently, despite carrying it out at least once per month. Many other members I have interviewed provided testimonials that exhibit this self-deflationary tendency as they enact themselves through the Gakkai's cycles of exchange. The most extreme example I encountered may have been one Married Women's Division member in Nagoya named Mrs. Kumano, who in 2001 donated her entire retirement bonus, the equivalent of ~US$100,000, to a scholarship fund at Soka University of America. Mrs. Kumano characterized her gift to me as the minimum she could muster as obligatory return, and she otherwise described herself as "someone who gives to Soka Gakkai."

Giving provides women in Soka Gakkai a means of articulating themselves within the organization's unequal power structures. They operate in a way that resonates with observations Helen Hardacre (1984, 216) made about women in Reiyūkai, another Nichiren Buddhism–based new religion: Gakkai women's economic clout indicates that "normative inequality does not represent the balance of power in the relationship." The convention of self-denigration and affective deflation of one's gift, and oneself, is a paradoxically self-actualizing move standard to all cycles of exchange, as eloquently described by Marcel Mauss and in subsequent analyses.[15] Complimentary to this self-deflation in the Gakkai dynamic is a corresponding inflation of value placed on return gifts. In Soka Gakkai, these return gifts are affectively understood to have come from Ikeda Daisaku. A member named Mrs. Aoki, whom I interviewed in July 2008 in the southern city of Fukuoka, spoke to me about the centrality of these objects in her life. Twice divorced, the second time from an abusive husband whose beatings she endured to continue her Gakkai practice, Mrs. Aoki spent Japan's economic boom years living hand to mouth, working menial jobs, and moving from apartment to apartment. Over years of moving around, Mrs. Aoki struggled to maintain her home as a Gakkai space. She kept relatively few material possessions, primarily her *gohonzon* (object of worship) and items "received from [Ikeda] Sensei" in return for her monetary donations. Most precious to her was a combination clock and picture frame made from crystal. She spoke to me wistfully about her last apartment, where the crystal frame would capture sunlight from a window and create two rainbows on the wall: one for Ikeda Daisaku, and one for his wife, Kaneko. "I wrote to Sensei about the light from my clock," she told me, "in a letter that I brought to the headquarters." A purely market-based appraisal of Mrs. Aoki's clock would most likely give it a very low price. It is almost certainly a comparatively inexpensive item ordered in bulk by the Gakkai administration for dispatch to adherents who have donated money over a designated amount. For Mrs. Aoki, it is priceless, as it would be for millions of other members like her. To provide a comprehensive analysis of Gakkai finances that does justice to emic and etic views, both perspectives require attention.

We are left with a dilemma: how should observers navigate between affective and market-based measures? I argue that a realistic assessment of the organization's finances must be ready to factor in member attitudes that end up distorting dispassionate evaluations. It is only through sticking with member investments in cycles of exchange that we can hope to move beyond unanswerable "how much?" questions to understand *why* adherents invest in their religion. This reevaluation of evaluations promises to do justice to aspects of economic exchange that are obscured by singular attention to money. Namely, gender roles and social inequality.

Notes

1 For a comparative view of Soka Gakkai's status as a new religion in contemporary Japan, see Jørn Borup's chapter in this volume.

2 For more detailed histories of Soka Gakkai, see McLaughlin (2012, 2019).

3 For a fuller explanation of Soka Gakkai as "mimetic nation-state," see McLaughlin (2019, esp. chap. 1).

4 In recent years, the Gakkai administration has called this bureaucratic function *kōfu kikin,* short for *kōsen rufu kikin,* or "finances (*kikin*) for the declaration [of the Dharma] far and wide (*kōsen rufu*)," employing a Nichiren Buddhist term for conversion and institutional expansion.

5 Mrs. Itahashi and the other Soka Gakkai members in this chapter's ethnographic accounts appear under pseudonyms.

6 See *Shūkan daiyamondo* (July/August 2004) for extensive statistics on changes in Shinanomachi real estate between 1984 and 2004.

7 Kongōdō's full line of goods is available at http://kongodo.co.jp.

8 More recently, Soka Gakkai media is more likely to be distributed through a video-on-demand (VOD) service available through a proprietary service. Members whose homes serve as *kyoten,* or local bases, as well as Culture Centers across Japan now screen Gakkai videos through set-top devices that exclusively broadcast a constantly updated menu provided by the Gakkai company Shinano Kikaku.

9 This section synthesizes information from Asayama (2017), Higuma (1971), Nishino (1985), Shichiri (2000), Shimada (2004), Sōka Gakkai Yonjūnenshi Hensan Iinkai (1970), Tamano (2008), and Tsukada (2015). See also McLaughlin (2012, 2019).

10 News of this finding circulated through the Asura bulletin board in April 2016 and subsequently through Japanese media sources. See http://www.asyura2.com/16/senkyo204/msg/806.html.

11 *Shūkan daiyamondo* (June 25, 2016). See also Shimada (2013) for similar yet less precise speculations.

12 *Shūkan daiyamondo* (2016, 45). Dollar values that follow are calculated on a 110 yen to 1 US dollar conversion rate.

13 For another example of "affective labor," see Marianne Viftrup Hedegaard's chapter in this volume.

14 For an overview of research on religion and affect theory, see this volume's introduction.

15 Mauss (1950 [1990]). See also Ohnuma (2006) for implications of the gift in Buddhist traditions.

5

The Mindful Gardener and the Good Employee

Mindfulness Practices and Affective Labor in Danish Workplaces

Marianne Viftrup Hedegaard

THE BOTANICAL GARDEN IN COPENHAGEN HOSTS DENMARK'S largest scientific collection of endangered plants. Located at the intersection of two main traffic arteries, the garden represents a sanctuary in the middle of the bustling city, providing a green getaway all year round. To ensure a slow-paced, tranquil atmosphere, Copenhageners must leave their bicycles outside the entrance. I arrived at the garden on a cold January day in 2017 to meet with a hothouse gardener. The gardener, a sixty-year-old woman named Sue, had recently attended a mindfulness course for employees who wished to concentrate better, reduce stress, and increase their "work-joy." Walking along the quiet pathways of the garden, I thought to myself that gardening in these surroundings would have to be a peaceful profession. Why, then, would a gardener need a mindfulness course aimed at reducing stress? Moreover, what did mindfulness have to do with work-related stress in the first place?

This chapter focuses on Sue's engagements with the body-mind techniques as well as the philosophy of mindfulness and considers the contemporary trend of using mindfulness practice as a stress-reducing tool in workplaces. My conversations with Sue are part of my research on relations between Buddhist-derived body-mind practices, work life, and well-being in Danish workplaces. Intrigued by the framing of mindfulness practice as "good" for working bodies and businesses, I have participated in and documented a series of mindfulness interventions carried out in 2016 and 2017.[1] I have focused primarily on two workplaces, the sales department of an international health-care company and a public university.[2]

In the literature on mindfulness, gardening is often foregrounded as an exemplary mindful activity, as if gardening is something that promotes calmness and well-being and keeps you grounded in the present moment. In the influential book *Mindfulness: An Eight-Week Plan for Finding Peace in a Frantic World,* Mark Williams compares the mindful meditator to the gardener. As the gardener tends to her garden, so does the meditator "renew and nourish" her mind in meditation (Williams and Penman 2011, 246–248). The mindfulness practitioner is similarly likened to a gardener weeding his garden in the bestseller *Wherever You Go, There You Are: Mindfulness Meditation for Everyday Life* (1994) by Jon Kabat-Zinn. Practicing mindfulness and maintaining a "commitment to ethical behavior" is a way to "fence one's garden" to keep out the "goats that will eat all the young shoots" (45). In fact, "if you want to practice mindfulness, the garden is the place to be," the journalist Tom Smart (2016) states in one of the many articles promoting gardening as a pathway to total connectedness with the present moment. "There is a calm in gardening which cannot be found anywhere else," he concludes.

As I was about to find out, gardening had become far from calming for Sue, who decided to sign up for a stress-reducing mindfulness course in 2016, after the Botanical Garden merged with the Natural History Museum, resulting in a reduction and restructuring of staff. The two institutions are affiliated with a public university that for a decade had been subjected to massive centralizations to make the university more "efficient" (Hyatt, Shear, and Wright 2015). Sue turned to mindfulness to cope with the institutional merge and its turbulent aftermath. She told me that she had abandoned the idea of battling the overall system: now she dedicated time to work on herself as a way to deal with the challenges at work. She was afraid of being fired, and now under increased time pressure, Sue felt that she was not able to attend properly to her plants, her "babies," as she called them. In mindfulness practice, Sue saw the possibility to "de-stress" and regain her joy of gardening.

I met Sue through the course "Mindfulness in Five Steps," offered at a public university, where the teacher generously helped me reach several generations of participants.[3] The course runs every semester and is listed in the staff course catalogue under the category "Well-Being and Personal Growth," along with other courses such as "Mental Robustness and Well-Being," "Organizing and Task-Prioritizing with Outlook," and "Manage the Time—Personal Efficiency." These courses aim at developing personal tools and resilience and help guide employees who wish to improve their work routine. Framed in highly psychologized language, "Mindfulness in Five Steps" promised Sue and her fellow participants lower levels of stress and an increased joy in working, as well as tools to attend to and change habitual behavior.

Sue referred to mindfulness as a mindset and a way of living involving a set of practices in which regular meditation is central. Thus Sue "does mindfulness" by both thinking and acting in specific ways. In the morning, Sue meditates for fifteen minutes. She sits astride a pillow on the floor with her eyes closed and her spine straight. She likens her morning meditation to other daily routines such as brushing her teeth. Sometimes Sue ends her working day with a sitting meditation as well, sitting in the Palm House after the garden's visitors have left. She often uses headphones and streams online meditation guides.

In a Danish context, the word "mindfulness" and the meanings and practices attached to it are very diverse (Borup et al. 2015). Common for Danish practitioners, though, is that they consider meditation to be the core of mindfulness. Most of my interviewees tried meditating for the first time at a mindfulness course at work. Sitting or lying down, they did "body scans" or focused on the flow of their breath. The teacher who guided Sue on the course "Mindfulness in Five Steps" explained that she was very inspired by the eight-week program of Mindfulness-Based Stress Reduction (MBSR) but that it was "too deep" for a course running over only five meetings with busy working people. The meditation practices taught for workplace mindfulness have been adapted to the rhythms and restraints of a working day and are kept short, with meditation sessions of only five to ten minutes. Even if mindfulness courses offered to workplaces are compressed into "light" meditation routines, the practitioners report an impressive list of positive results. One reason for this is a general belief among mindfulness adherents that the ability to become and stay mindful rests within everyone.

In Williams' and Kabat-Zinn's books, as in many other books on mindfulness, the practitioner is seen as having an inherent ability to become mindful by way of meditation, no matter what circumstance or life situation they find themselves in. Thich Nhat Hanh, the renowned Buddhist Zen master, often captures the practice of mindfulness with the metaphor of a seed nesting within everyone. Here he addresses the inmates from Maryland Correctional Institute in a talk about the energy of mindfulness versus the energy of anger: "Every one of us has the seed of mindfulness within. If we know how to touch that seed we can begin to generate the energy of mindfulness. . . . Those who do not practice still have the seed of mindfulness, but its energy is very weak. By practicing just three days, the energy of mindfulness will already increase" (Hanh 2008, 3). This statement illustrates two central axioms of mindfulness practice: the first is that the ability to be mindful rests "naturally" within the individual (that is, everyone has the seed of mindfulness); the second is that a mindful state of mind has to be continuously cultivated and nurtured (that is, you must cultivate the seed). Together, the two axioms present mindfulness as an inherent ability we can maintain through daily practice. In other words, the practitioner works continuously to become and to maintain what he or she already is: mindful.[4] If the inmates are filled with anger or if Sue finds herself stressed out about her job, the promise of mindfulness is that these affects can be surpassed with meditation.

Describing the practice of meditation as the cultivation of a mindfulness garden, Williams notes how "clock time is different from meditation time." Meditation does not, in fact, "have any time" (Williams and Penman 2011, 248), and the mindfulness practitioner may find that he or she has spent thirty minutes in "the garden" in effortless meditation (248). While literature on mindfulness describes meditation as an opportunity to step out of "clock time," meditation for Sue and many other employees I encountered was precisely a way to deal *with* "clock time." To "work mindfully" meant to stay calm and collected and keep stress and frustration at bay while the workday clock was ticking away.

Propelled by the discrepancy between the peaceful gardener of mindfulness literature and the real-life gardener seeking stress reduction, this chapter examines practices of work-life mindfulness to highlight the complex, lived realities at play when employees pursue mindfulness at work. Examining Sue's everyday engagements with mindfulness reveals a tension between the often idyllic image of effortless mindfulness practice and the actual effort it takes, and failures it involves, to "become mindful." I show how Sue labors to become mindful in order to care not only for her plants but also for herself and her immediate surroundings: a labor not marked by effortlessness but by a daily fight to stay well in a stressful environment by meditating. I conceptualize this labor as "affective labor," arguing that mindfulness encourages practitioners to alter fundamentally their ways of affecting others and of being affected. I problematize how mindfulness is naturalized as an inherent and always available state of mind—a garden to venture into. Processes of naturalization, I argue, run the risk of making invisible the effort and sustained commitment that goes into maintaining a mindful headspace in a stressful work environment.

Recasting Mindfulness—From Monasteries to Meeting Rooms

Interest in mindfulness has soared in Denmark over the last decade (Borup et al. 2015), and "mindfulness programs" such as MBSR have become popular across diverse spheres of the Danish society, not least in the area of business. The version of mindfulness offered in courses such as "Mindfulness in Five Steps" is highly influenced by the way Kabat-Zinn (2011) has recasted mindfulness as a "secular practice," which, although it is said to be nonreligious, nonetheless encompasses the "essence" of Buddhism or the so-called deep dharma. While scholars have pointed to the curious fact that a religious practice such as mindfulness meditation has slipped into "secular" and mainstream Western society (Arat 2017),[5] the popularity of mindfulness testifies to the numerous and multifaceted connections between Buddhism and "the global marketplace," in which Buddhist and non-Buddhist alike take part in the consumption of "Buddhist-related goods and services" (Williams-Oerberg and Brox, this volume). Buddhism works as a highly flexible frame of reference evident in the multiple enactments of Buddhism in Danish mindfulness courses, where Buddhism is sometimes referenced as the religious roots but other times as the ethical framework or set of values informing the practice.

Even when Buddhism is foregrounded, mindfulness teachers will choose to avoid words such as "religion" and accentuate the positive physical and psychological, evidence-based effects of mindfulness. Mindfulness practice in Denmark is generally understood as a therapeutic practice to achieve "mental wellness" rather than a religious path to "mental liberation" (Elsass and Lhundup 2011). This understanding of mindfulness links with a global tendency of turning to Buddhist meditative practices for "psychological benefits" (Brox and Williams-Oerberg 2017) and relief from the "stresses and strains of modern life" (McMahan and Braun 2017). As Inken Prohl (this volume) demonstrates, Buddhist semantics and images such as Zen, mindfulness, or the figure of the Buddha are associated with a therapeutic effect that remedies feelings of stress or burnout and transcends one's stressed everyday self.

Accordingly, when the magazine *Time* announced a "mindful revolution" in 2014, it introduced mindfulness as "the science of finding focus in a stressed-out, multitasking culture." Describing how one could "work mindfully, parent mindfully and learn mindfully," the journalist Kate Pickert (2014) emphasized how mindfulness practice additionally was a means to "spend mindfully" and therefore of great value to businesses. The motivation to become mindful is fueled by the notion of mindfulness being not only beneficial as individual therapeutic treatment but also suitable for maintaining healthy corporate economies. In the numerous books encouraging the implementation of mindfulness at work, mindfulness is said to have beneficial effects on workers' "emotional tone," "affective span," and "workplace functioning" (Good et al. 2016). Mindfulness practices presumably "enhance innovation and creativity" and "increase productivity and resilience" (Chaskalson 2011), to mention only a few oft-cited benefits. The founder of the Danish Center for Mindfulness has called mindfulness a "necessary" and "economically sensible solution" to the rising numbers of employees suffering from anxiety, stress, and depression (Fjorbacke 2016). It is not surprising, then, that mindfulness teachers, HR personnel, and corporate leaders refer to mindfulness interventions as a "good investment."

While the business world embraces mindfulness interventions, heated academic debates point to the instrumentalization not only of the religious tradition of mindfulness but also of the individual, who—with mindfulness—should be able to care for himself and take responsibility for stress or burnout (see, for example, Purser, Forbes, and Burke 2016). Corporate mindfulness practice, it is argued, adheres to the logic of neoliberalism and transmutes into a project of attaining the right kind of self-management (Caring-Lobel 2016). Other scholars have pointed out that even though the concept of neoliberalism helps us account for the relationship between forms of governance, self-governance, and capitalist market forces at play in mindfulness, a focus on the multiple meanings and values invested in these practices must be kept in mind (Cook 2016). Taking my cue from Joanna Cook, I will neither discuss whether mindfulness practice is adhering to "traditional" forms of Buddhist practice nor evaluate whether mindfulness interventions *should* be implemented in workplaces. Instead, I aim to complicate work-life mindfulness and show the practices and processes involved by zooming in on the labor that goes into becoming mindful.

Analytical Approach: Social Emotions and Affective Dynamics

Focusing on mindfulness as a social phenomenon as well as an affective, bodily engagement, this chapter examines the way Sue works to alter her habitual ways of feeling, thinking, and acting in order to become more mindful. It suggests that for the novice, mindfulness training involves a new way of affecting others and being affected. This means learning specific body-mind techniques and ways of articulating experience, learning to notice, name, and let go of thoughts and bodily sensations carefully in order to maintain a mindful attitude. This happens through various techniques, among which body scans and sitting or supine meditations focused on the flow of the breath are the most common. The ability to notice, name, and release bodily tension, thoughts, or even moods should then spill over into the everyday lives of the practitioners, enabling them to go through periods or situations of stress without being stressed (Kabat-Zinn 2013, 315). The ambition with mindfulness training is to move from "doing mindfulness" to "being mindful," to embody and maintain a mindful attitude in all aspects of life.

I propose that when mindfulness training is undertaken in a workplace setting, learning to cultivate mindful attitudes can be viewed as performing "affective labor" in which the practitioner manages affects that are seen as counterproductive in their working life, turning, for instance, a state of stress into a state of composure.[6] In suggesting this, I am inspired by scholars studying "affective" and "immaterial labor" (Berlant 2011; Mazzarella 2009; Muehlebach 2014; Müehlhof and Slaby 2018) as well as earlier anthropological work on emotions that define them as the "missing link capable of bridging mind and body, individual, society, and body politic" (Scheper-Hughes and Lock 1987). These studies show how emotions and affect are not private affairs but entangled with economic and political interests and social norms.

The conceptualization of mindfulness as affective labor brings attention to how workplace mindfulness is entangled with corporate economic gains (for example, keeping the employee healthy and able to work) and points to how the aim to stay mindful for a person like Sue is partly a personal ambition and partly a professional accomplishment.

I build on the concept of "emotional labor" introduced by the American sociologist Arlie Hochschild in 1979 in her groundbreaking book *The Managed Heart*. Drawing on Karl Marx's work on capitalism and alienation, Hochschild shows how the contemporary postindustrial society capitalizes on not only the worker's body but also the worker's emotions. Hochschild identifies emotional labor as a performance of specific emotions seen as fit to the particular function carried out by the employee: the flight attendant smiles to induce safety, the bill collector frowns to induce guilt. Yet I argue that the ambition of mindfulness practice reaches beyond mastering a set of particular emotions fit to one's job description. Employees train in mindfulness to transform fundamentally their way of affecting others and of being affected all together. Mindfulness practice centers on the practitioners' management of impressions left by others as well as the mediation of these impressions, the embodiment of a mindful attitude. This process of learning to manage impressions and embody mindfulness can be captured through an attention to affective dynamics.

Moving beyond Hochschild's concept of emotional labor to talk about affective labor, I seek inspiration in the burgeoning literature on affect that, according to Sara Ahmed (2004b, 28), locates emotion neither in the individual nor in the social but looks at emotionality as circulating between bodies. Emotions involve the personal with the social and the affective with the mediated. Many scholars who employ affect as an analytical concept turn to the Dutch philosopher Spinoza for a definition. For Spinoza (1990, 231), the body is characterized by its ability to be affected by and affect other bodies. Emotional states are transitional, moving between stages of greater or lesser perfection (pleasure and pain), and they are results of activities, being "modifications of the body whereby the active power of the said body is increased, diminished, aided, or constrained" (264). For instance, joy arises because of the body moving in proximity to a loved object (308–310). A fundamental claim within affect theory is, building on Spinoza, that emotions are produced between bodies and that they are *productive*, in the sense that emotions *do* something. Affects have effects. Emotions are, in this view, not seen as psychological dispositions but as social and structural, which should lead us to look at how emotions work, in concrete ways, to mediate the relationship between the psychic and the social, the individual and the collective (Ahmed 2004b, 28). Bodies are, in effect, porous rather than autonomously bounded, leaving the person open to the environment (Blackman 2012, 4, 22).

I suggest that by introducing affect theory as a framework, we get an opportunity to rethink mindfulness as a social process involving multiple bodies, social-material relations, and power hierarchies. I demonstrate through Sue's story that mindfulness practitioners pursue a stress-free work life not only to *work* better but to *be* better by relating to others more mindfully, calmly, and with presence. The affective labor they carry out is therefore targeted toward the self as well as the social world in which they are embedded.

Sue's Pursuit of Mindfulness

When I first met Sue, she gave me a tour of her "new office"—three subtropical hothouses hosting orchids, begonias, and bromeliad. For years, Sue had been working in the Palm House, a beautiful old greenhouse and the main attraction of the garden. When budget cuts resulted in a reduction of staff, Sue's workload increased significantly. She could no longer keep up and was reassigned to three smaller hothouses. Later, when I asked her to explain how she used mindfulness in her work life, she mentioned the transfer to the hothouses: "It was a big shift having to let the Palm House go. I loved working there. To accept that I could not do it anymore . . . that it was too much. It was a bitter pill to swallow. I think my mindfulness helped me with it so that I could let go. Sort of. Without screaming too much." Sue's mindfulness practice involved meditating every morning as well as observing her behavior, measuring it against the main attitudinal pillars of mindfulness, as they have been described in the MBSR program: nonjudging, patience, beginner's mind, trust, nonstriving, accepting, and letting go (Kabat-Zinn 2004, 32–39). "Mindfulness practice," Sue stated, "is above all a *behavioral* change."

Over the fourteen years Sue has worked in the Botanical Garden, the garden staff has been reduced from twenty-eight gardeners to twelve. Even though she saw herself as "flexible and willing to adapt," the personnel cuts and increased workload created what Sue called "emotional stress" and a feeling of "disillusion":

> It [emotional stress] is different from when you have a big pile of assignments, you are not going to finish them, and they pile up and pile up. That kind of stress I am able to manage. It is the *emotional* stress. The disillusion. Of the way things developed in the garden, in society. Such a regressive movement. Like we are going backward. I thought *that* was very hard. Very stressful actually. This was not the way it was supposed to go. Then you have to sit down and meditate on it.

Stating that you should "sit down and meditate on it," Sue burst into a resigned laugh. Meditation was useful but not a miracle cure, she declared.

The problem, as Sue saw it, was that she did not feel that she had the time to do her work properly, to make sure that the plants were thriving, not just surviving, and to envision new projects or exhibitions in the garden. Sue agreed that the job in itself was enjoyable. "I love my job, and I believe in what we do. But with the last round of layoffs, it became unbearable here. For some time, no one knew if you were in or out. I could not relax anywhere. I couldn't stand myself—my way of reacting to what was going on. It was destructive." For Sue, mindfulness practice was a reminder to stay positive in the changing landscape of the garden, not "scream too much."

Sue hoped that mindfulness would prove helpful in her working life, and she also hoped, and later experienced, that training mindfulness would help her relate to herself and her surroundings in new ways. She spoke of this aspect as a step toward becoming a better person: "There is always the hope that you will become a better person, right? Having more energy and patience, a greater understanding toward others, more empathy. That you will become better at dealing with conflicts, so you won't be knocked out—which happens when you are a little too sensitive, too touchy." Sue's engagement with mindfulness was an ethical endeavor in the sense that Sue pursued a way of being affected and affecting others—in her work life and private life—that was marked by particular virtues: empathy, patience, and calm presence. Being a little too sensitive and touchy had become a problem for Sue in her daily life. She got "too affected" by events happening at work and in her family. In this way, Sue engaged with mindfulness not only to sensitize herself toward others and to cultivate particular affective virtues; she also aspired to shield herself from "negative energies" and from being "too affected."

"Feeding the Good Wolf"

Sue conceptualized her mindfulness practice as a battle between the "good wolf" and the "bad wolf." She referred to the wolves as the forces inside of her. "We have these two wolves, you know, the good wolf and the bad wolf. When you are down, you want to feed the bad one much more and to avoid it, you take a meditation and then you feed the good wolf instead." Sticking to her mindfulness practice meant feeding the good wolf, nurturing qualities such as patience and empathy. Asked what it meant to feed the good wolf, Sue listed everyday situations, such as her daily bike ride to work, during which she practiced being patient with slow bikers, crazy car drivers, and red lights. She mentioned how she would work not to judge people on the street by their looks or behavior, reminding herself that there is always more to others than the first impression. Sue explained that to "take a meditation" was a way of "nudging herself" to feed the good wolf because meditation created a sense of peace in her that did not allow her to get carried away by feelings of frustration or anxiety. Sticking to her morning meditation was not an easy task, Sue admitted: "The wicked beast, the bad wolf, is so easy to feed, and it has a big appetite. This is where discipline comes in. It would be so easy to say, 'to hell with the meditations, I am busy feeding the bad wolf.'" Aside from the bike lane, Sue related how meditating helped her navigate her family life better. She was living with her teenage son as well as the sons of her partner, and balancing trying to raise his boys while also respecting her limited role, being the dad's girlfriend, not the mother, was challenging. "I deal with conflicts in the home in a more calm and balanced way. That's nice. I am happy about that. I am less jumpy, I guess. I am more like this . . ." Sue motioned with her hands as if she was smoothing out a tablecloth.

To attend mindfulness training evoked childhood memories of going to Catholic Church and feeling "uplifted" by the sermon, Sue said, and she described mindfulness as "food for the soul." After a mindfulness class she felt better. "It does help. You are sitting on your cushion listening to the words [the guiding voice of the teacher]: 'You are peace. You are centered. You are health.' It helps!" She mused over the differences between Buddhism and Christianity, mindfulness and AA, an organization she knew well after having witnessed her ex-husband's treatment for alcoholism. She compared mindfulness to AA and noted many similarities, for instance, that mindfulness offered behavioral prescripts for everyday situations. Sue also emphasized the importance of "spiritual" aspects of mindfulness. "I think people need spirituality," Sue proposed, and elaborated that living mindfully, following the seven pillars proposed by Kabat-Zinn, was probably more difficult than following the Ten Commandments, which were "concrete" and "manageable." Mindfulness was different; it was a mental challenge or a kind of "mental spiritualism."

Sue talked about mindfulness as a practice that involved reworking her inner forces more than reworking the outer environment. As shown by Cook (2017), the therapeutic programs MBSR and Mindfulness-Based Cognitive Therapy (MBCT) locate the causes of human suffering not in events and experiences but in the ways people relate to them. In these programs, practitioners learn to decenter themselves and recognize their "thoughts as thoughts" by making a distinction between appearance and reality. This supposed unveiling of how things "really are" is not so much a revelation as it is a creation of a new "reality" by aligning meditative practice with scientific protocol, Cook (2017, 116) argues. For Sue, feeding the good wolf was a way of recognizing negative thoughts about herself, her work, or people on the bike lane as "not truly real," or at least as just one version of reality, one she could choose to bracket, so as to amplify the positive sides of herself, her work, and everyday situations. She took concrete measures to decenter herself from events that she foresaw would lead to conflict or "low feelings" that would shake up her calm state of mind. She recounted how, after having begun mindfulness, she would stay silent and observant at staff meetings, "leaning back." Sue was tired of "shouting for change" in the garden and used her mindfulness practice to find the courage to take a step back. During our conversations, she maintained that mindfulness was necessary and good for her because of her habitual reaction patterns. Sue referred to her behavior before undergoing mindfulness training as sometimes "destructive," "neurotic," and "hysterical." Practicing mindfulness meant making the decision to behave well in the sense of not getting hysterical or neurotic, a mode she had learned to relate to as her "reptile stage."

> There are some situations where I can feel that I have more . . . I react in a calm way. Not hysterical. Screaming and stuff. It is a little bit calmer. I have begun to pay more attention to when something is going on in the body: "Oh! Now I am entering that reptile stage," you know. And I know that it is no good. So I can avoid it.

Mindfulness helped Sue act less hysterically and refrain from the "reptile stage." By practicing meditation, she reminded herself that she could choose which wolf to feed. She could react "hysterically" or "mindfully" when she encountered negative thoughts or had difficult confrontations at work or with her family. Sue perceived the mindful attitude as an empowering response that allowed her to tackle problems the way she would like to: calmly and considerately, instead of "riding off with hysteria."

Affects on the Market: Cultivating Valuable Assets

We have seen how Sue with her mindfulness practice tries to promote specific affective modes while dampening others. For Sue, this "behavioral change" is a way of becoming a "better" person. Becoming more mindful is also a way of coping with work: Sue turns to mindfulness as a personal as well as professional commitment to regain a good work life, in spite of structural changes. This corresponds well to the ways in which mindfulness teachers, corporate leaders, and HR managers whom I spoke with related mindfulness practice: it invites employees to work with their mind-bodies in ways that enable them to manage affects and emotions that are productive not only to the employees but to the overall workplace.

Many scholars have highlighted the connection between emotions, affects, and productivity in postindustrial economies. As stated by Karen Lisa Salamon (2002), businesses must promote themselves on their ability to manage human minds, not physical manpower. Human resources are considered a company's most important "asset" (Bovbjerg et al. 2011), and the individual employee is seen as consisting of "potentials to be realized and capacities to be fulfilled" and should be able to develop and work with herself to handle the tough competition of the market (Martin 2000, 513–514).[7] Emily Martin has convincingly shown how the imperative that the employee must "develop" herself and cultivate particular sensibilities is a result of historical changes in the conceptualization of "the person" and changes in the modes of production.[8] The shift from the early decades of mass production to the postindustrial society corresponds to the corporations' shifting perceptions of which capacities and attitudes are productive and desirable. The assembly line at the beginning of the twentieth century required a cool, restrained worker, and the entrepreneurial work environment of the 1990s required a flexible worker and favored an "unrestrained manic energy" (Martin 2007, 39, 276). Martin underscores that the domain of emotions is considered an essential starting place from where to fuel the innovation and creativity that are important for companies to sustain and develop. Crucially, not just any form of emotion or mood will do—only moods that are "optimized" and emotions that are "harnessed for culturally specific purposes" are suitable.

Thinking along similar lines already in the 1970s, Arlie Hochschild argued that what is perceived as a "good" emotion is connected to the demands of the industry. Bodies are supposed to produce value by managing their emotions, making them productive by way of "emotional labor." Emotional labor is the labor workers perform on themselves in order to accommodate the "occupational demand on feeling" (Hochschild 2012 [1979], 16). It is possible to recognize emotional labor when there is a "pinch" between a disapproved-of feeling and an idealized feeling that calls for a "coordination of mind and feeling" (7). We can recognize Sue's strategy of feeding the good wolf instead of the bad wolf as a coordination of mind and feeling that should result in the "good," mindful state of mind. This mindful state enables Sue to deal with her reassignment from the Palm House without "screaming too much," and it helps her take a step back to let changes in the garden pass more smoothly. Mindfulness also enables Sue to face the increased stress and heightened pace in the garden without succumbing to it—without being "too affected." We might say that Sue not only became a "better" person but also more economically "productive" by way of mindfulness, as it works to turn her anxiety into calm composure.

The call to work on oneself continuously—to develop one's practice—is a cornerstone in mindfulness training. In this way, mindfulness fits well with the rationale of human resource management, in which self-development and personal growth denote important soft skills in contemporary work life (Müehlhof and Slaby 2018, 11). When Sue engages in mindfulness practice as a way to deal with her anxiety of getting fired, she contributes at the same time to the production of a good workplace by promoting positivity, sustaining her own well-being, and diminishing the chances of her getting sick. In other words, "Mindfulness in Five Steps" is a good investment because it promises to teach employees how to cultivate and harness a valuable asset: a mindful attitude.

Mindfulness as Safeguard against Stress

As Cook shows, the approach in mindfulness is not to focus on circumstances that may cause states of stress but to ensure that the practitioner has the ability to relate to stress differently. Kabat-Zinn (2013, 315) makes this point clear: "We can cultivate greater resilience and well-being, and also wisdom and equanimity, in the face of stressful circumstances. . . . All it takes is practice, practice, practice. We will certainly get plenty of opportunities for that, given how much stress there is in our lives on a daily basis." As such, embodying mindful attitudes at work is a way to accommodate occupational demands on employees to navigate high-stress work environments without losing their calm and sensitivity toward themselves and others (be it coworkers or customers). An important point is that the ability to alter one's way of being affected by stress is considered an ever-present possibility through sustained practice, regardless of the "stressful circumstances." This puts pressure on the employee. I often witnessed practitioners blaming themselves for not being able to be mindful, having been taught that the mindful state of mind is always available through meditation.

Building on and moving beyond Hochschild's notion of emotional labor, I suggest that we think of mindfulness training as "affective labor," since mindfulness aims at developing a mind-body attitude—a way of being affected and affecting—that is not tied to one particular emotion but seen as a preventive embodied safeguard against stress, depression, and burnout. Employees do not practice mindfulness to enhance or downplay one particular emotion but to relate to their thoughts and reactions fundamentally differently—mindfully—apprehending the "reality" of their condition. Sue gathered that, with sustained effort, she could nudge herself to feed the good wolf. Like Sue, many of my interlocutors trusted that mindfulness practices could induce and sustain behavioral changes that rid them of "bad habits." If they had not felt any changes at the time of our conversations, they would blame themselves for their lack of a steady practice, reiterating that mindfulness practice *would* help, if they "did it right." They *would* and *should* become mindful eventually.

Hochschild's empirical base is the emotional labor of the flight attendant, whose job is to create a sense of being cared for and of being in a safe place. Instructors supervise the flight attendants to ensure that they conduct themselves properly and manage their emotions to create the most pleasant flight they can. The flight attendant *has* to smile in order to help induce a feeling of safety during violent turbulence or when handling a difficult passenger. Hochschild (1979, 7) suggests that such a smile, which is not *of* her but *on* her, can make the flight attendant feel estranged from her own sentiments. Achieving a mindful attitude is different from faking a smile, I argue, precisely because the mindful attitude is perceived as a revelation of an inherent quality—not a performance. I experienced that mindfulness courses on the one hand invite participants on a transformational journey characterized by "nonstriving" and no expectations ("this is *your* journey," as the teacher in "Mindfulness in Five Steps" would repeat). On the other hand, the courses lay the ground for a specific transformational progress (you *will* be more concentrated, experience heightened work joy, break with behavioral patterns, and so on). Unlike the instructors who understood that the smiles of the flight attendants are a performance, mindfulness teachers present mindfulness as a state of mind that emerges naturally. It will not be a performance but a "homecoming" to yourself, as teachers often articulate it. The idea that a mindful state of mind is a way of coming home to yourself naturalizes the mindful state and effectively deems other affective states unnatural.

Naturalizing the Mindful State of Mind

As we saw at the beginning of this chapter, mindfulness teachers and authors compare mindfulness practice to gardening. By talking about mindfulness as a seed that is already nested within suggests that everybody has the ability to reach a mindful state of mind. The mindfulness practitioner weeds and nurtures his garden (his mind) to make the seeds sprout, grow, and bloom. Interestingly, mindfulness practice is often described in technical terms as well, comparing the brain to a computer or illustrating meditation as a rewiring of the "system" or a recharge of the "batteries" (evident in books such as Rick Hanson's [2013] *Hardwiring Happiness: The New Brain Science of Contentment, Calm, and Confidence*). This combination creates an organic-technical vocabulary that is additionally supported by neuroscientific terminology. What does this combination do? I suggest that it generalizes and naturalizes processes of becoming mindful and shifts individual experience to universal truths. In this last section, I problematize this process of naturalization by showing how it establishes new ways to categorize and evaluate emotional reactions and behaviors.

The course "Mindfulness in Five Steps" addresses "Leaders and employees who want to establish a routine of switching off the autopilot in their everyday life and work with their behavior and thoughts with curiosity and courage." "Autopilot" is a key term in mindfulness literature, describing a state of mind where actions are performed automatically and nonreflexively. The contemplative practices trained in mindfulness are ways to deactivate the "default mode," that is, the "autopilot," and become "aware in the here and now" (personal communication with instructor). We saw earlier how Sue referred to her "hysterical" behavior as her "reptile stage." She and other practitioners would refer to themselves and their practice with expressions like "reptile stage" or "autopilot" because mindfulness courses also provide a new vocabulary for speaking about and evaluating bodily sensations, emotions, and affects. Having a word such as "autopilot" to label her everyday experience proved helpful for Sue in that she could identify her behavior better. "Oftentimes you are not aware. You walk around in your usual rhythm, everyday life, you know, that unconscious existence one is living in. With mindfulness, you get a wakeup call. You understand how some things are connected. And sometimes when things happen around you, a sentence will pop up from mindfulness: 'Ah! That's right.'" Sue connected the lessons from mindfulness courses to her everyday behavior by pointing out moments of "unconscious existence" and "reptile" behavior. In this way, the teachings of mindfulness, with their references to neuroscientific knowledge, Buddhist philosophy, and cognitive psychology (Eklöf 2016), became a new explanatory model for how certain things were connected in Sue's life.

Steven Stanley and Charlotte Longden (2016) have analyzed the dynamics in mindfulness classes, showing how individual accounts of emotional reactions and bodily sensations are often generalized by mindfulness teachers as "natural" or "human nature" that create a "universal body." Teachers reformulate personalized constructions of "my mind" to "the mind" to generate a universality of experience. Similarly, I often heard mindfulness teachers explain affective reactions with reference to neuroscientific knowledge and human nature. They explained stress and aggression as primal reactions coming from the reptile brain, the amygdala, which only knows "fight" or "flight." They presented mindfulness as a way of "dampening" these primal reactions.[9] I will not go into the discussions of the validity of such claims but rather show the consequences of using a generalized language to explain individual behavior. The move from individual accounts to general truths about "the mind" being in the "reptile stage" or on "autopilot" establishes new categories for identifying and evaluating one's own behavior. The practitioners' minds are similar to everyone else's, and like everyone else, they should be able to manage affects and become more mindful.

When mindfulness is established as a natural state in this way, other affective states or moods can be evaluated as deviant. This was in fact what Sue and other interlocutors often expressed. They evaluated mindfulness as a preferable state of mind, one natural, better than, and more agreeable than others. This is evident in Sue's explanation for why she would like to attend another mindfulness course: "One has to have a reminder sometimes. Because it is a form of behavioral change. So you got to . . . I mean . . . I am pretty neurotic.

So it is tough work. You have to be aware all the time. Be conscious. And in the moment. Without judging." When Sue shifts between the story of what "she" is and what "one" should be, she is establishing a hierarchy for evaluating her own behavior against the behavior she aspires toward. She recognizes that she is not always aware. On the contrary, she is "pretty neurotic." We understand that being aware means being able to discover that you are neurotic and possibly avoiding the consequences of a neurotic state of mind even when acting "neurotic" might be a sensible reaction to stressful events at work.

Cultivating Nature

When I visited Sue a second time in October 2017, she showed me a new collection of plants that the Botanical Garden had brought back from the former Danish colony Saint Croix. To the untrained eye, the plants looked like ordinary green, leafy ferns. The plants were extraordinary, Sue told me while breaking off a withered branch. They only grow on the island of Saint Croix (and now in Sue's greenhouse). She cultivates them carefully to ensure that they will thrive in their new, artificial environment. As with the agaves, orchids, and cactuses in the garden, these plants need the tropical environment of a greenhouse as well as a gardener's dedicated care. The Botanical Garden is indeed cultivated, tamed nature imitating "real" nature. I could not help comparing how Sue cultivated nature in her greenhouse to the cultivation work she performed on her meditation cushion every morning. A mindful attitude required affective labor and careful attendance to her thoughts and behavior. Still, it was considered "natural," in a way that made Sue evaluate her moments of not being "mindful" as deviant or problematic—as less good, less natural. This increased the pressure and guilt that she felt when mindfulness was not achieved and disillusion prevailed.

I began this chapter by wondering why a gardener would sign up for a stress-reducing mindfulness course. Sue labored to become mindful in order to care not only for her plants but also for herself and her immediate surroundings—a labor that was not marked by effortlessness but by daily decisions to continue meditating and "feed the good wolf." Sue pursued a way of being affected and of affecting others—in her work life and private life—that was marked by particular virtues: empathy, patience, and calm presence. Mindfulness was not only a means to promote an affective sensibility toward others—greater patience and empathy—it was also supposed to help Sue limit specific affective sensibilities and shield her from being "too affected." Sue's story makes clear that states of stress and mindfulness are dependent on social circumstances and not confined to individual psychological traits. I move beyond the notion of emotional labor and suggest that for the novice, mindfulness training involves committed practices and the sustained effort of attuning to emotions and behavior in new ways. Analyzing mindfulness as affective labor also brings our attention to the economic implications of the practice as well as the potential alienation of other affective states that counter the mindful state of mind. Mindfulness is naturalized by using neuroscientific vocabulary and organic metaphors that establish the mindful attitude as universally available and independent of structural conditions and everyday encounters. I argue that this naturalization renders invisible the practitioners' continuous efforts to attune to their bodies in order to sustain a mindful way of working, that is, of not being affected "too much" while remaining patient and empathic.

For Sue, meditation did not eliminate her low days or the disillusion she felt seeing the developments in the garden. She described herself as still having a long way to go before she reached the level necessary to maintain a calm and mindful state. Instead of speaking up at staff meetings, Sue had turned her gaze toward herself. She was well aware that turning toward herself and working on not being affected "too much" in some ways made her struggles invisible, since the meditations made her act well even under stressful working situations. She made people like me think that gardening must be a serene occupation. Sue asked me to use her real name because she would like people to know that the seemingly peaceful routines of gardening were a result of her continuous efforts to meditate away daily stress, combat the "bad" emotions, and choose the "good."

Notes

This chapter is based on research funded by the Danish Council for Independent Research as part of the international research project Buddhism, Business, and Believers. I am grateful to Trine Brox, Karen Lisa Salamon, Joanna Cook, Elizabeth Williams-Oerberg, and Jane Caple for their helpful and engaged feedback.

1 I spent many hours with mindfulness teachers and practitioners, in meditation and in conversations at workplaces, offices, and cafes. I conducted thirty semi-structured interviews with seven men and twenty-three women.

2 Both workplaces were offering courses in mindfulness for all members of staff, albeit on different terms and conditions. In the health-care company, mindfulness courses targeted the "company culture," and the ambition was to enroll as many people as possible, from secretaries to leaders to canteen staff. Employees were not obliged but highly encouraged to participate. Ninety people out of the total two hundred employees participated in the ten-week-long course, meditating with colleagues every Tuesday or Thursday morning. At the university, "Mindfulness in Five Steps" was offered as a staff course; the classes were held outside of campus, in teams of at most twelve people from different faculties and departments. In my forthcoming work, I will look into the implications of these different setups and discuss how particular "affective arrangements" result in different relational dynamics, expectations, and experiences for people engaged in mindfulness at work.

3 Sue and I did not take the course at the same time. I took it six months after she did.

4 In the literature on mindfulness, especially within the field of neuroscience, there is an ongoing discussion on how to define mindfulness. Is mindfulness a

trait-like quality *or* a state that is brought about and maintained only through continuous cultivation of attention, or both (Chiesa 2013)?

5 Alp Arat (2017, 167) argues that contemporary mindfulness points toward a "new modality of the secular." He explains that while the language of mindfulness operates in complete discursive isolation from the religious, its ontological foundation is nevertheless resting on a claim toward a transcendent whole.

6 I choose the term "labor" over "work," following Marx's definition of labor as an intrinsically social process embedded in social relationships (Marx, in Muehlebach 2014, 230).

7 Martin (2007, 275) looks specifically at how people living under the diagnosis of "bipolar disorder" are encouraged to eliminate depression and extreme mania, leaving only "heightened motivation," which is seen as an "asset" in the labor market.

8 Martin (2007, 39) connects this shift in the desired worker not only to means of production and capitalist developments but also to the developments of new ways of speaking about the person, mostly within psychology. For example, the term "personality" came into use in the early twentieth century, changing the ontology of the person from somebody with a (firm) character and identity to a person with personality and the potential for more flexible self-presentation.

9 Mindfulness practice is said to reduce fear, anxiety, and aggression by training the prefrontal cortex of the brain (Kabat-Zinn 2013, 313–315).

6

Branding and/as Religion

The Case of Buddhist-Related Images, Semantics, and Designs

Inken Prohl

BILLBOARDS FROM SOUTH AFRICA ADVERTISE OUTDOOR POOLS featuring elements taken from a rock garden formation popularly known as a "Zen garden."[1] An advertisement for a navigation system in Australia shows the so-called laughing Buddha in the cockpit of a car driving through heavy rain, with the message: "Directions from above."[2] Similarly, in India an ad for microwaves features the same Buddha, albeit modified to include a lean belly with six-pack abs. The ad proclaims: "To change the way you look just change the way you cook."[3] The branding strategies for a variety of products in a variety of settings rely on the magic of the words "Zen," "karma," or "mindful," as is true for products like Evoke Morning Zen Muesli, Karma Milk, or Mindful Mayo.[4] Pictures of the Buddha are used in marketing campaigns, brand names, or the packaging of furniture, food, toys, and many other kinds of goods. Consumers with no direct relationship to Buddhism are targeted with Buddhist-inspired designs of temples, rock gardens, and silently meditating monks. Ideas and images with a Buddhist "touch" appear to have a powerful influence over consumers. Otherwise, we would not see the proliferation of these kinds of brandings. In short, it seems that Buddhism sells.

Ads and branding strategies that feature Buddhist semantics, materialities, and designs run in Europe, North America, Australia, South Africa, Latin America, India, and East Asia. Buddhist-imbued ads and branding strategies from Thailand, South Korea, and other Asian countries show that Buddhist semantics are employed as a successful sales tactic in places with historically large Buddhist populations, as well.[5] Although Buddhist-related images, semantics, and designs are used in many parts of the world in branding and marketing strategies, there are few good studies about the spread of religious semantics in the field (Kelso 2006), let alone the spread of Buddhist semantics therein. A quantitative investigation by Rick Clifton Moore (2005) on religious imagery in magazine advertising found that religious semantics are present in the magazines surveyed, if in small amounts. According to this study, the amount of semantics of Eastern religions surpasses that of Western ones. A cursory investigation of the publicly available databases of large advertising agencies in the year 2016 suggests that the proportion of religious semantics in the fields of branding and marketing has increased significantly. Furthermore, it shows that Buddhist narrations, materialities, and designs make up a significant portion of that increase.[6] Additional evidence of the common use of Buddhist semantics in branding can be obtained from the online portal Amazon.com. Looking up "Zen" in the category "Grocery and Gourmet Food" yielded more than two thousand hits. The term "Zen" is, as Joshua Irizarry (2015) has shown, a powerful tool for marketing. There are other terms taken from Buddhist discourse that have shown themselves to be useful "trademarks": The term "karma" in the category "Beauty & Personal Care" yielded more than six hundred results, and the term "Buddha" more than 25,000 hits in the category "Cell Phones & Accessories." Looking up "nirvana" in "Health & Household" yielded more than four hundred hits. Even if, along with the wares using Buddhist imagery, some results contain Buddha statues and Buddhist-inspired jewelry, these search results show that Buddhist semantics are common in the branding and marketing of products that are not, in the traditional sense, related to Buddhism. The products on offer either have only Buddhist keywords in their names or, in addition to such references, offer images of Buddhist-inspired designs. Commonly found are depictions of Buddhas, bamboo leaves, round stones, Ikebana-like flower arrangements, or other seemingly Asian elements. Taken as a whole, the findings suggest that the image of a Buddha in meditation is one of the most commonly used religious symbols in branding. Other Buddhist semantics or images, like the typical Buddhist markers of "Zen" or "karma," Buddhist monks, "Eastern" architecture, and allusions to "Zen gardens"[7] may likewise rank high on any list of the most frequently used religious icons in advertising and branding around the world.[8]

This chapter will analyze some reasons for the popularity of Buddhist semantics, designs, and images in the world of branding and ponder the consequences that have already arisen or may arise from this popularity. Beginning with a general discussion of the significance of branding, marketing, and advertisement, I will debate the consequences of mediatization on the field of what is called religion and introduce a dynamic I would like to call the "triple religion effect." Afterward, I shall briefly discuss the currency of the term "Buddhism" in the modern world. Based on these theoretical considerations, this chapter will take a closer look at the world of Buddhist-imbued branding and conclude with some reflections on the consequences of my findings for "Buddhism" and "religion" alike.

Theoretical Considerations I: Branding in a Mediatized World

Consumption, consumerism, and hypermediatization can be seen as parts of a wider phenomenon that is to be understood as a consequence of the ever-increasing pull of economics on all aspects of life (Gauthier, Woodhead, and Martikainen 2013, 2). In contemporary society, this pull translates into continuous consumption, which, in turn, is fueled by marketing and branding. Therefore, marketing and branding are subjects of considerable interest, academically and otherwise.

"Branding" is usually understood to mean the creation of a concept around a product. To brand a product means to create a medial ensemble around it, containing such factors as name, logo, packaging and strategies to create unique selling points, as well as the dissemination of information about these ensembles on the market (Laird 1998, 15). The communication of this information on the market is known as marketing, and its most important strategy is advertisement, though not all marketing can be understood as such (Andree 2010, 12). According to some estimates, approximately US$950 billion is spent annually around the globe on marketing and branding (Einstein 2017, 26). By comparison, the gross domestic product of Denmark in 2013 was roughly 300 billion euros. In an age of mass media, successful marketing can be understood as the epitome of successful communication.

James B. Twitchell (1996, 16), the well-known author of numerous books on advertising, points out that advertisement is ubiquitous. A person living in a highly industrialized society is likely to be exposed to thousands of advertisements daily (Kelso 2006, 1; Einstein 2017, 1). Theoreticians point out the enormous importance of marketing for the way individuals shape their lives. Branding can be taken as a part of the domains of consumption and lifestyle.[9] What is being sold in modern markets are building blocks for personal identity and a sense of community. With the advent of the sociology of consumption, the insight prevailed that "consumption is a central site of social reproduction whose structure is crucial in understanding processes such as identity construction, social agency and key social relationships" (Slater 2005, 175). If one understands consumption as a central praxis of modern neoliberal societies, the field of branding can then be understood as its theology, and the interesting research question becomes how this theology functions regarding its use of Buddhist semantics, materialities, and designs.

An important marker of modernity is the dissolution of traditional narratives of belonging. The religious convictions, nationality, rules, and weltanschauung of one's class background decrease in importance for the ways lives are lived and identities are constructed. Increasing levels of wealth, on the other hand, lead to a continuing increase in the levels of consumption. In the tension between this dissolution of traditional frames of reference and the continual search for new anchor points for orienting the modern self, the contemporary ethos of consumption became the vehicle for the continued reification and creation of this modern self as a project in the era that can be called "second modernity."[10] Since the middle of the twentieth century, we have witnessed a transformation of marketing. The idea gained currency that one

> had to abandon the idea that consumers made rational decisions in relation to a socially given hierarchy of needs or values. Rather, in this new area of self-expression human desire was best regarded as plastic and open. Indeed people lived in a world of goods to which they were emotionally attached and to which they owed large parts of their own personality. (Arvidsson 2006, 58)[11]

In response to the realization that the search and desire for self-expression and identity had become core parts of modern ways of life, marketing experts began to rebuild their strategies. A core of these new strategies was catering to the belief that each individual is *in possession* of their unique personal identity and that this identity needs to be *expressed in their possessions* and their ways of consumption. The field of marketing and branding opened an entirely new dimension of possibility: brands became vehicles for the self-construction of the modern subject.

Key aspects of branding a product are storytelling, emotions, and experience, as well as aesthetics and the senses. According to John Grant, one of the leading voices in modern marketing, these stories, emotions, and experiences are in constant need of rebranding and innovation in the contemporary world. This, Grant says, is achieved with the help of mythologizing the new through building up continuities with old traditions, by framing the product into a story with central ideas and immaterial qualities, which appeal to consumers. With attitudes, values, feelings, and meanings attached to a product, consumers can cobble together what they perceive as their subjectivity from offers on the market. For consumers who buy products for the notions attached to products, brands are becoming an important source of their identity (Grant 2000). The leading evolutionary psychologist Geoffrey Miller (2009) argues that people purchase things to advertise themselves to others. According to Miller, most people buy and do things not for their inherent qualities but for what the things say about them. One of the "secrets" of branding is to associate a product with the particular personal qualities it signals.

Parallel with models developed within the cultural studies/*Kulturwissenschaften* turn, marketing experts posit that ideas need to be felt and experienced in order to become entrenched. Goods become integrated into the subjective realities of their consumers through aesthetic means (Illouz 2009). Products and their surrounding narrations need to be materialized in ways that elicit positive impressions in the body and for the senses. From this insight developed strategies of "emotional branding" or "sensual branding."[12] According to Daryl Travis (2013), another well-known branding expert, emotion is winning the battle of brands that decides whether a company is successful. Therefore, successful branding has to appeal to and stimulate emotions that customers associate with what they spend their money on. These techniques are designed to create customer loyalty and cater to the universal need to belong. In fact, some marketing "gurus" compare the attraction of brands to that of religious cults (Atkin 2004). In addition to eliciting positive sensations, the purpose of branding is to make the customers feel good about themselves. Further strategies of modern branding include the cultivation of authenticity, working through consensus, and staking claims to fame.

Theoretical Considerations II: Religion in a Mediatized World

As scholars of religion point out, the way that religion is reproduced, represented, and understood in our contemporary world relies on the fundamental functions of the media age (Hoover 2006). An emerging consensus suggests that, thanks to media technologies, religion is everywhere in the now:

> The field of religious symbols, practices and modes of belonging has been radically extended through the colonization of a dizzying range of genres, technologies and forms: from popular history and pop-psychology books to websites, cartoons, trading cards, posters, rock music, bumper stickers, television dramas, scientific treatises, package tours and sundry forms of public spectacle. (Stolow 2005, 123)

We can describe what we have witnessed over the last century as a democratization and a pluralization of what are commonly held to be traditional religious semantics, images, and designs. This democratization entails the creation of a broad consensus about certain ideas, practices, and materialities self-evidently being understood as "religious." These semantics and materialities are very often summarized under the term "world religion." Take Buddhism, for example: common discourse in wide parts of the globalized world holds sutras and commentaries, temples and stupas, monks and (albeit far less frequently) nuns, and the keywords "Zen," "nirvana," "karma," "reincarnation," and "mindfulness" to belong to Buddhism.

Modern media technologies enable individuals, social groups, and institutions to get hold of religious semantics and materialities, to interpret, to mix and arrange them in new ways, and then redistribute these creative arrangements with the help of media. This phenomenon is one part of what we call "mediatized religion." At the same time, the elements of this pluralistic emergence of what are supposed to be the traditional elements of the so-called world religions do not remain confined within them; people quite happily carry them over into other fields. In the case of Buddhist semantics, materialities, and aesthetics, these fields can be psychology, psychotherapy, self-help, and the like. In these fields, we find countless examples of the incorporation of Buddhist semantics, images, and designs, with the practices of mindfulness being the most popular in contemporary societies. Further examples can be found in the realms of medicine, popular culture, and entertainment.[13] Finally, Buddhist semantics are commonly found in the field of marketing and branding. One can clearly see the spread of what are held to be traditional religious semantics into other fields of society, mainly into what is known as mediatized popular culture. Marketing and branding can, in fact, be understood as a subfield of popular culture. Popular culture offers the means whereby most people in the modern world spend the majority of their time constructing the selves and the communities defining who they are. It responds to desires and offers the means to identify with people, ideas, or movements, and at the same time it offers the means to distinguish oneself from others (Morgan 2013). Hence, popular culture has assumed many of the functions and roles that religions had fulfilled in past societies. From the standpoint of cultural studies/*Kulturwissenschaft,* it is notable that discourses and practices of branding and marketing develop dynamics of relationships between individuals and their collectives within popular culture, dynamics that had earlier been governed by religion.

Looking for religion or its dynamic analogues in mediatized contemporary societies, one can discern the field of what is traditionally held as religion, on the one hand, and the function of religion fulfilled by marketing and branding as part of popular culture, on the other hand. In the field of advertisement, we encounter branding strategies imbued with religious semantics. These are the Buddhist semantics I described earlier. Symbols of other so-called world religions might also be used, but their use lies beyond the scope of this article. One can conclude that "Religion"—in a traditional, transformed, and hybrid form—is triply at play in contemporary society, which produces a dynamic I suggest to take into account as the idea of the "triple religion effect" when analyzing contemporary mediatized cultures.

Talking about "Buddhism"

What is Buddhism? As a starting point, one can assume that there are as many variations of Buddhism as there are adherents. For some adherents, Buddhism is about this-worldly and other-worldly benefits or about the therapeutic relief gained by visiting a temple or venturing on a pilgrimage. For others, it is the joy of meeting family and friends or feeling protected and supported by the Buddha Dharma. Given the historical development of religious studies and Buddhology and the manifold interdependencies of their findings with the general, increasingly mediatized discourse on religions, the social realities of Buddhist practitioners rarely find their way into the ascriptions that dominate the contemporary public global discourse on Buddhism. Since the 1940s, Buddhism has been interpreted to be individualistic and pacifist, in harmony with shared cultural values, as Thomas Tweed (2008, 91) points out with regard to the United States. Further important features within the realm of ascriptions in the dominant discourse made toward Buddhism are notions of an ascetic and salvific monasticism and soteriology, images of meditating monks, a canon of philosophical literature considered holy and concerning ancient wisdom, and extensive arrangements considered aesthetically elaborated and understood as symbols of some underlying truth. For many adherents, these general ascriptions are both true and sources of their identity.

Even though I suggest that, apart from possessing this significance in the minds of their adherents—be that as Buddhists or as members of an academic discipline—these images are nothing but fantasies of Buddhism, they are nonetheless significant. These fantasies are the result of the close methodological focus on scripture, which was the dominant area of inquiry in research on religion for many years, starting in the early days of the discipline. This close reliance on scripture led to a proportional disregard for the social realities within the Buddhist field. Interests and initiatives of and by Buddhist apologists looking to position their religion as the equal of other world religions also did their part in creating the dominance of monks, meditation, and ascetic practice prevalent in current discourses on Buddhism. Finally, the widely successful interpretations of D. T. Suzuki and his followers helped create the widespread impression of Buddhism as a religion focused on mystical and meditative personal experience. The dynamics and transcultural interactions that have shaped a large part of the discourses on modern Buddhism have been described and analyzed at length.[14] Regarding the analysis of the rise of Buddhist semantics in popular culture and branding, it is notable that a large amount of information regarding Buddhism became accessible through media. Actors with diverse intentions can refer to a large stack of floating signifiers having in common only associations with Buddhism. Although most of the ascriptions made toward Buddhism are like dream images that fade away as soon as they are subjected to inquiries into their social realities, they nonetheless exist as such. They are, therefore, real in the minds of people. These dream images are used in mediatized societies and develop lives of their own, as we can witness by looking at the world of popular culture, marketing, and branding. Hence, independently of what we can discern on the levels of historical and contemporary social realities, ascriptions to Buddhism take on a life of their own in a mediatized society, merging with the dominant dynamics of the respective society enacting the discourse. Although I am aware of the danger of overgeneralizing, I will nonetheless try to sketch an account of some of the ascriptions made toward the Buddhist field in a mediatized world: as various observers of the field have pointed out, there is a great deal of appreciation for the word "Buddhism" and its concomitant signifiers in highly industrialized societies. Scott Mitchell (2012, 311) describes the dissemination of Buddhist ideas and images as "pop-cultural Buddhism." With this term he denotes "specific, identifiable Buddhist images or ideas that are presented or expressed within various media." Catchwords like "karma," "nirvana," "enlightenment," "mindfulness," and "Zen" as well as artifacts and materialities associated with Buddhism are well represented, since the media is favorable toward Buddhist subjects. This is partly because of the pervasive idea that what is understood to be "Buddhism" is a peaceful and ethical religion (Wuthnow and Cadge 2004). According to Jørn Borup, Buddhism has gone mainstream, and the field of Buddhism can be described as "cool" and "chic" (Borup 2016a). Since the second half of the twentieth century, images and narratives of practitioners and Buddhas sitting quietly with half-closed eyes and crossed legs have become globally popular (Prohl 2017). This iconic imagery resonates with affirmations of individualism and celebrates the value and authority of the individual (Tweed 2008, 91). Very often the solitary meditator is mildly smiling or, at the very least, showing a rather content facial expression, which affirms a strong focus on the self, in turn the supposed reason for individual happiness and well-being. The prevailing images of a meditating Buddha and other figures work to reinforce ascriptions toward Buddhism as a religion or path that strives for betterment, optimization, and healing of the self. These notions fit very well with the contemporary view of the self and its responsibilities toward itself.

The icon of the silently meditating Buddha shows a strong focus on practice inherent in this narrative. It makes sense that images of Buddhas or similar figures in meditation are so often used in the world of branding. The narrations around the image suggest the existence of something one can simply *do* in order to feel better. The associated practice seems an easy and approachable technique for everybody. The iconography fascinates, even only by association, those who wish for change, betterment, and well-being. The Buddha is said to have grasped something extraordinary, a state of mind connected to truth, metaphysical insight, perhaps even the transcendental. Iconography around the Buddha and the depicted practice of sitting still, of "meditating," can be understood as leading to a good, sometimes even transformative experience transcending quotidian life. Furthermore, the practice or experience of meditation is associated with healing and curing.[15] Thus the icon promises, at least implicitly, some therapeutic effect—whether it is to remedy the feeling of stress or burnout, the feeling of entrapment in a net of conflicts in one's family or at work, or simply boredom and a sense of lack of purpose. Because the Buddhist field is associated with the terms "religion" (or "spirituality"), it also offers a promise of access to the transcendental, thereby again manifesting the possibility of leaving behind one's bored or stressed everyday self. At the same time, the semantics, images, and materialities of the Buddhist field offer a spiritual or religious alternative to a culturally dominant generic Christianity in the West. The Buddhist field can be seen as and is associated with playfulness, embodied among others by the "laughing Buddha." Alongside this playfulness, the Buddhist semantic realm is also associated with recreation, wellness, doing something for yourself, or simply fun. Conversely, the field offers a passion for the impossible, since according to a predominant view, the Buddha reached nirvana, often constructed in analogy to paradise as an impossible land or counterworld. Finally yet importantly, the Buddhist field offers the modern marketing expert a plethora of aesthetics and designs that are able to deliver the aforementioned associations to consumers. This is one of the reasons that I am not just talking about the ideas or narratives of the Buddhist field. By pointing to the aesthetics, the designs, the materialities, and the icons and images of this field, I emphasize that the popularity of the Buddhist field in a mediatized world relies very much on its ability to appeal to the senses. The figure of the meditating Buddha is simple. It evokes an idea of striving for something beyond. Disseminated through the strands of a global discourse, it retains some spiritual aspect. Some observers of pop-cultural Buddhism or religion in general express the view that decontextualized religious ideas and icons become "secularized" in the sense that they lose their religious value or meaning. Of course, if something is to have religious meaning, its power or effectiveness always lies in the eye of the beholder. Still, I want to argue that the popularity of Buddhist semantics and materialities results from their potential to refer to transcendental spheres not necessarily constructed as religious.[16] As Singhamanas, a Buddhist observer of the vibrant field of Buddhism and popular culture, says: "It is the idea that something can give people peace, ease, energy—something mysterious holy, but not religious" (Ferrier 2017). In many parts of the globalized world, silently sitting Buddhas point to something beyond this world; at the same time, the figures possess great recognitional value. The same goes for monks. They are easy to discern because of their shaven heads and the orange garments in which they are generally presented in the media. In a mediatized world, "Zen gardens" and pictures of bamboo plants in front of buildings depicted as temples are equally easy to recognize.

Of course, the ascriptions made toward the Buddhist field I have enumerated here do not automatically exist in and for all discursive participants.

They should rather be understood as having the potential to be activated to a greater or lesser degree in relation to factors like gender or age by the semantics, materialities, and designs employed in the world of branding. According to estimates, women account for 78 percent of consumer purchases globally (Einstein 2017, 76). Market research and marketing strategies need to take up perspectives on gender and sexuality as well as considerations of generational differences (Drinck and Kreienkamp 2006). Even more important to marketers than these individual characteristics are so-called psychographics. They divide consumers into groups based on their personalities, values, and lifestyle rather than their age, income, and gender (Einstein 2017, 76). The question of whether and why Buddhist semantics in marketing appeal especially to female demographics are questions of considerable import for future research.

The World of Buddhist Branding

Let us return to the ways that images and semantics drawn from the field of Buddhism are used in many contemporary societies. One can readily conclude that advertisers would be negligent if they did not rely on these attributions, for they are effective. The Buddhist field provides tools for advertisers that are eminently suitable for accomplishing their goals. The semantics and images of the Buddhist field have a distinct positive image in contemporary discourse and are elements of a generally accepted narrative tradition. They are thus highly useful for generating brands that sell. Because of their positive value, Buddhist semantics, materialities, and aesthetics are able to inscribe into consumers a positively colored self-evaluation. It is highly possible that this self-evaluation comes with no strings attached—save those of the product on offer. David Chapman, one of the so-called "Buddhist Geeks," a group of critical thinkers and bloggers on Buddhism, notes that the association with the Buddhist field can create a good personal advertisement as well. As Chapman elaborates, no one takes Buddhist ethics seriously as ethics. "When you, a selfish Westerner, gradually convert to Buddhism, Buddhist ethics never requires you to change your moral actions or ethical thinking" (Chapman 2015, 1). Indeed, as research on people who associate themselves with Buddhist ideas and practices suggests, Buddhist ethics are generally considered wonderful but very often come without any obligations attached for the believer (Prohl and Rakow 2008). Hence by buying something that has a Buddhist touch, one can align oneself with what is seen as the more ethical, thoughtful, and generally "decent" member of a community.

Advertisements for cars, medical products, or food featuring the Dalai Lama or (mostly) monks strive to connect the product on offer with the positive image of Buddhism engendered by charismatic figures, augmenting the promise of safety and reliability. An ad for Häagen-Dazs green tea ice cream shows three circles flowing into one another. The graphical design of each circle in different green hues connotes the sand from "Zen gardens," tea fields, and a scoop of ice cream. The attendant text reads "a cup of Zen."[17] The green tea ice cream melts, so goes a possible reading, the spirit of Zen with the spirit of Japan—as represented by the tea fields—and transforms into something new that consumers can buy and savor. Advertisements with allusions to the Buddhist field promise special experiences. Their message is that eating or drinking are experiences that have to be specially cherished within the stressful realm of the everyday. This promise is the reason why a particular brand should be bought. The products on offer claim a notable taste experience designed to transcend the challenges of one's daily routine. The products are so good that even monks with daily access to extraordinary experiences would choose them.

There are numerous advertising campaigns for the cosmetic line "Zen" from Shiseido, showing elegant flagons, arrangements of plants, and beautiful woman inspired by Ikebana.[18] An endless supply of beauty products marketed for their Zen-like qualities capitalize on the allusion to Zen in order to sell these products. Ads from Asia, Europe, and America feature the laughing Buddha in order to promote dieting aids, hygiene products, nutritional supplements, and wellness articles. Finally, the world of fashion has discovered the power of the Buddha to drive sales. The logo of the fashion brand True Religion features a very happy-looking laughing Buddha, guitar in one hand, the other giving the viewer a thumbs-up. Images of this Buddha greet the visitors at the chain stores of this brand, which sells pricey jeans, jackets, and T-shirts often featuring their distinctive laughing logo.[19] Associations with the Buddhist field in the realms of fashion and cosmetics capitalize on the promise of a special experience created by the addition of the word "Zen," Buddha icons, or an elaborate Eastern-looking design. More than this, these ads draw on the ascription that the Buddha reached for the impossible. Style, fashion, and care for the body are challenging and stressful in a neoliberal world, so there's no harm in relying on some Buddhist magic.

The icon of the meditating Buddha is particularly suitable for contemporary branding, as it features an individual seen as capable of bringing about his own truth, well-being, and happiness. As such, this icon and the notions attached to it constitute subjectivities and dispositions that resonate with the neoliberal demands of self-reliance and happiness in the face of one's own exploitation. The religious aura attached to Buddhist semantics and materialities helps naturalize the predominant paradigms of neoliberalism. The findings of the widespread use of Buddhist semantics, materialities, and designs show that the relationship of Buddhism and economics in terms of this relationship being a "problem" is no longer necessary (Obadia 2011, 113). In line with Rudnyckyj and Osella (2017, 4), I argue that it is more fruitful to move beyond the narrow focus on the marketing of religious goods and the profit making of religious institutions and instead focus on the religious dimensions of neoliberalism and the consequences for the morality of the individual in society.

Side Effects of Buddhist-Imbued Branding

When we look at the functions of branding strategies imbued with Buddhist semantics, materialities, and icons, we observe that they create identity, feelings of belonging, or self-reflection. These strategies offer modern subjects the impossible: their promise is to provide the means to position oneself as a decent member of the community and to positively distinguish oneself from others at the same time. They further pledge to supply effective, if not magical—that is to say religiously effective—means for solving complex problems. They promise extraordinary experiences and create spiritual feelings, thereby hinting at the possible existence of some higher purpose in life.

Buddhist marketing connections connote these functions, which one can easily recognize as functions in the religious field. So, after having looked more closely at the dynamics of Buddhist branding, the terminology of marketing magic and symbolic power espoused by marketing experts becomes intelligible. But this is only the obverse side of the coin. What is also known from the field of religion, as well as from the field of popular culture, is that religious or popular discourse and practice comes with side effects. To paraphrase Lynn Schofield Clark (2007, 9–10), popular culture reflects—as religion does—the unconscious, taken-for-granted views that one prefers not to admit to oneself. Schofield Clark emphasizes that, from the perspective of cultural studies, people are not convinced, brainwashed, or manipulated by popular culture or religion. Neither, for that matter, are they manipulated by branding. The side effect of branding and marketing is not brainwashing. People are not helpless victims forced to buy things at gunpoint. Instead, it is much more helpful to assume the entertainment value and the effectiveness of branding as resting on its ability to articulate what people believe without threatening their sense of what they are. To paraphrase Clark again: successful marketing and branding create a space in which contradiction and negotiations are constantly played out. What are these contradictions and negotiations? An ad from Nike shows a group of Tibetan monks wearing fancy sneakers while sitting and chatting. Above them, a monk jumps on the wall to kick a soccer ball in a great feat of athleticism.[20] Take the ads for navigation systems, water softeners, all sorts of gadgets, microwaves, or bookshops: they all feature monks. They all feature the Buddha—be he in silent meditation or as a laughing figure. They all, centrally, feature *men*. One hears, repeatedly and from many corners, the claim that Buddhism is a religion of gender equality. Yet women remain strangely elusive in the advertisements imbued by this seemingly egalitarian religion. "Buddhist" ads and branding campaigns are full of pictures of men, thereby casually naturalizing the social reality of male dominance around the globe.

Furthermore, the imagery of Buddhist marketing is part of a wider discourse of positive Orientalism constituting a semiotic hierarchy. In this hierarchy, Buddhism is, at least vaguely, the generically positive religion or spirituality. Thereby the fact of religion per se is confirmed in its positive while evoking as its negative other Islam, especially since the narratives and practices of Islam remain all but invisible in large parts of the realms of popular culture and marketing. Furthermore, the images of Asia used in Buddhist-imbued marketing in the West reinforce the dominant idea of an exotic Asia, which disguises far more mundane political, social, and economic realities in Asian countries.

Buddhist-imbued marketing and branding reifies the dominant paradigms espoused within many contemporary societies. Another ad from Nike features a woman for once, sitting in a yoga asana and wearing Nike clothes. The text of the advertisement says: "My idea of nirvana is . . . Until there is a land of chocolate ice cream, you'll find paradise in a yoga-course. Discover yourself on nikewoman.com."[21] This ad illustrates that in the world of popular culture and branding, supposedly different traditions—Buddhism, Hinduism, yoga, chocolate—merge with one another. Nike explicitly uses a rhetoric of well-being by portraying the body as "the other," as a vehicle capable of facilitating a discovery of one's own self. The reference to "nirvana" puts this act of self-actualization within a Buddhist context or, maybe, tries to wrap a Buddhist context and its accompanying legitimacy around the act. The terms "nirvana" and "yoga" both invoke the hope of a form of salvation and thus add to these physical practices another layer of meaning: existential importance and legitimization. Additionally, Nike's advertisement emphasizes enjoyment. "Just think of the taste of this rich chocolate ice cream."

The process of "discovering yourself"—to quote Nike's slogan—can be understood as a strategy of increasing individual responsibility. Whereas in premodern times a successful life and individual happiness were often seen as the result of harmony between man and the cosmos, the individual self and its optimization have become the underlying imperative in late modernity.[22] Self-improvement is thus often considered the only effective way of attaining sustainable happiness as well as deep and abiding satisfaction. According to Eva Illouz (2008) and others, the self, together with its will and associated qualities, is both the source and initiator of happiness *and* the only potential barrier to achieving that happiness. The British sociologist Nicolas Rose (1996) has described this development as the "regime of the self." Hence, culture and, for that matter, the world of consumption are dominated by offers for betterment, curing, and optimization of the self. Buddhist branding strengthens this imperative through strengthening the narrative of interiority and supporting it with a novel set of aesthetics, symbols, materialities, and practices. Furthermore, such support is geared specifically toward single psychographic groups by marketers, further cementing gendered divisions in social life.

Those who believe in the existence of the self and in its responsibilities to achieve happiness on its own promote the removal of liability for that happiness from government institutions, parental care, the neoliberal economy, and society.[23] Thus, structural, economic, social, or educational reasons for stress, anxiety, or mental and physical exhaustion are often not taken into account in the discourse of self-optimization. Instead, the self becomes the main focus of bringing about happiness and normality for every human being on the planet. Allusions to the Buddhist field underpin this dominant and fundamental strain of thought in postmodern society, thereby consolidating regnant neoliberalism. Hence the Buddhist infusion into marketing and branding not only helps legitimize and even sacralize consumption but also justifies mainstream "secular" ethics mainly by naturalizing the regime of the self.

The Blurring of Boundaries between the Fields of Buddhism and Branding

When discussing the dissemination of semantics, designs, practices, and materialities of what is considered traditional religion into popular culture and branding, as well as when elaborating on recent trends in the field of what we know as Buddhism, scholars often talk about the commodification or the entertainmentization of religion or of Buddhism.[24] However, as scholars of religion also tell us, religious goods have always been for sale, entertainment has always been important in and for religion, and leaders of religious traditions have always had to be good businessmen in order to finance their institutions. Thus, the commodities, the marketing of religion, and the reliance on messages and aesthetics in order to promote religions are the historical norm. This general norm also holds true for Buddhism, as numerous scholars have shown in the past decades.[25]

So is there anything new in this brave new world of branding imbued with Buddhism? This chapter would like to suggest that, yes, there is something new to be found here. What is new, however, is simply the power and effectiveness of the technologies used to spread elements from the field known as religion into society more broadly. This analysis of the world of Buddhist branding has generated insights into the similarities between what is traditionally held as religion, on the one hand, and marketing and branding as parts of popular culture, on the other hand. One particularly striking parallel between them becomes clear when one looks at the generative powers of each field: material religion's approaches to the study of religion analyze the ways otherwise inaccessible, allegedly transcendent agents, concepts, or ideas are rendered accessible via verbal and nonverbal carriers of meaning subsumed under the term "sensational forms" (Meyer 2006). A material-religion approach helps us understand how religions activate the body as well as the senses, how they initiate transformation processes and bind actors to their respective causes. Followers of this theoretical framework emphasize the continual materialization of a transcendent element. This element is usually thought to be inaccessible to human agents and has to be mediated via certain media formats (Morgan 2008; Plate 2015). As this chapter has shown, modern marketing stresses the importance of addressing the senses and evoking emotions by creating designs and using images and other aesthetic arrangements. In fact, one of the main reasons why the Buddhist field is so readily adaptable to multisensory marketing lies in the abundance of materialities this field has to offer.

The concurrent workings of what we call religions and branding convincingly illustrate in turn how what one thinks of as religion is dependent on mediatization. This concurrence shows plainly that there is no substance or essence to be actualized beyond the realm of the mediatized or signified—or, as theories of marketing point out, that there is no "something" beyond the brand (Andree 2010). What one can discern in these fields are styles, codes, or brands—modes of mediatization—that have the power to bind, to constitute belonging and identity through emulation. They are the representation of something outside ourselves, which, at the same time, continues and extends something we consider our own.[26] Branding strategies create feelings and experiences that, if viewed from the perspective of the consumers, allow them to produce their subjectivity while concurrently offering the consumers identity and the feeling of belonging. The boundaries between what is considered to be religion or Buddhism and what is considered branding become blurred. From an analytical point of view, these boundaries can no longer be sustained.

Therefore, this chapter suggests that terms like "commodification," "capitalizations," and "entertainmentization" are not only inappropriate conceptual tools for describing current developments in the field of Buddhism: one would be better off were these categories avoided altogether. These categorizations are not only negative, but they also recurrently drag us back to the idea that there is something we can grasp as religion or Buddhism. As the analysis of the impacts of mediatization in the field of "Buddhism" shows, this idea needs to be abandoned.

The Effects of Triple Religion

In conclusion, this chapter points to some recent, innovative dynamics. As I have shown, there are three types of religion discernible in the contemporary world: first, the semantics, designs, and practices belonging to the realm of what we consider traditional religions; second, popular religion and branding as religion; and third, branding and marketing imbued with religion. What this kind of triple religion brings about is what could be called a religious "supereffect," or, to put it differently, an oversaturation of religion. If allusions to the mystical, the transcendental, or the extraordinary become mainstream, if one can find and feel them everywhere, this reenchantment raises the question: What happens to religion? If people eat cereals imbued with Buddhist semantics for breakfast, see a meditating Buddha while waiting for the dentist, and deliberate in the evening whether to relax with a mindfulness app or with some film, digital game, or music perhaps imbued with Buddhist aesthetics and semantics, then what does this do to religion? If people get their sense of belonging, identity, and habitus from the things they buy, wear, or surround themselves with, these things are also imbued with religious semantics, and, furthermore, if discourses on religion make for good entertainment and if modern marketing is a supremely influential force comparable to the reach commonly ascribed to religions, then questions about the effects of emulation are also raised. The effects of emulation might dissolve in the future because objects lose their aura of being something special, particularly cherished, or extraordinary. This dissipates the effects that are known from what is called religion, that is, the effect of being connected to something outside the actors while allowing them, at the same time, to continue to be themselves. The liquidation of the effects of religion is caused by what I call the "religious hypereffect." This effect might pave the way for an even stronger orientation toward consumerism and neoliberalism, but in that scenario the question arises whether these dynamics are able to function without the religious effects described in this chapter.

Taking into account the side effects of the merging of Buddhism and marketing analyzed here, and taking into account the side effects of religion in general, I conclude with a question: Is the triple effect of religion in a mediatized society in the age of neoliberalism automatically a negative development, as is so often assumed, or could it also have some liberating effects?

Notes

1 Published by HTH Pool Care, 2012: http://adsoftheworld.com/media/print/hth_pool_care_zen_garden.

2 Shown by GPSOZ 2007: http://adsoftheworld.com/media/print/buddha.

3 Published by LG, 2012: http://de.coloribus.com/werbearchiv/printwerbung/lg-healthwave-microwaves-buddha-3278355/.

4 See, for example, https://www.amazon.com/Evoke-Morning-Gluten-Muesli-Ounce/dp/B006GKBFN4?th=1. An abundance of examples also could be found at Whole Foods Market in 2016 and 2017.

5 I have not been able to find similar ads published in the so-called Islamic world and scarcely any from Russia.

6 Databases searched are adeevee, Coloribus, and Ads of the World (spring 2016).

7 Raked sand or rock arrangements in any form are closely associated with the popular conception of "Zen gardens." These gardens are held to epitomize a presupposed higher spiritual dimension in Zen. On the problematic ascriptions made toward "Zen gardens," see Kuitert (2002) and Prohl (2009).

8 Critical voices from within Buddhism can be heard protesting the use of Buddhist semantics and iconographies in advertisements; see, for example https://www.knowingbuddha.org; see also Jerryson's chapter in this volume.

9 It is for this reason that rational choice theory approaches are not useful in the investigation of decisions to consume or not consume. The inability of rational choice theory to explain this phenomenon may also be one main reason why approaches of the so-called economics of religion have often failed in their investigations.

10 This is a development of ideas proposed first by Charles Taylor (see Gauthier, Woodhead, and Martikainen 2013, 14). On "second modernity," see the introduction to this volume.

11 Arvidsson's (2006) book *Brands: Meaning and Value in Media Culture* contains a highly informative history and analysis from the perspective of cultural studies.

12 See, for instance, Gobé (2009) and Lindstrom (2010).

13 An example is Suh (2015), on Buddhism in films.

14 See, for instance, Almond (1988), Borup (2004), and McMahan (2008).

15 Google shows more than thirty million hits for "meditation and healing"—even more than for "Jesus and healing" (accessed in October 2017).

16 On the blurred boundaries between the religious and the secular in the case of Buddhism, see Arat (2017).

17 See https://theworsthorse.wordpress.com/category/dharma-burger/page/16/.

18 For an extensive analysis of the advertisements of the company Shiseido and many other examples of Zen branding, see Irizarry (2015).

19 For instance, see http://www.truejeansdeals.com.

20 See http://spvrtxn.tumblr.com/post/86243172130.

21 The ad was being featured, as far as I can tell, in American women's magazines during the 2000s.

22 See also Hedegaard's chapter in this volume.

23 See, for instance, Rimke (2000), Rindfleisch (2005), Martin (2014), and Cederström and Spicer (2015).

24 Most prominently Carrette and King (2005); see also Shields (2015) and Borup (2016a). For an overview, see Mitchell (2012).

25 For an overview, see Brox and Williams-Oerberg (2017).

26 The powers of emulation describe in other terms what Emile Durkheim (1915) meant when he talked about religions as "social facts." I am thankful to Gill Zimmermann for pointing out that line of argument to me.

7

Marketing the Buddha and Its Blasphemy

Michael Jerryson

IN SEPTEMBER 2010, THE ENTREPRENEUR RYAN SENTZ expanded his hookah and tea bar in Boca Raton, Florida, into a brewery and renamed the establishment the Funky Buddha Lounge and Brewery. The Funky Buddha Lounge and Brewery became a test kitchen for craft beers. Three years later, the Funky Buddha Brewery was launched and quickly became the largest craft microbrewery in Florida.[1] Since its inception, the company's marketing and branding has relied upon the image of the Buddha, which appears on all of their labels. For bars and restaurants that serve its beer, the Funky Buddha Brewery provides beer taps in the shape of the Buddha. On their website, one may buy accessory items such the "Funky Buddha Floridian Towel." The religious component to their branding is not lost on the company and its marketing. The "Funky Buddha Dog Collar" is displayed on a Buddha image, and the caption next to the Buddha bracelets declares, "Much like the nature of our very existence, our Buddha bracelets are ever-changing and unique; each beaded bracelet's color, shape, and size varies."

The Funky Buddha Brewery draws upon a brand that existed long before the free market and neoliberalism. While many adherents would shudder to consider their religious institutions comparable to neoliberal markets, there are significant weak comparisons at play (Lincoln 2012, 121–130). An economic analysis of Buddhist institutions quickly reveals that Buddhists have a long history of using Buddha images for veneration and for promoting their religion. Scholars have written extensively on the Buddhist practice of creating amulets, which Stanley Tambiah (1984, 195–207) calls the "commodification of charisma." Both the Funky Buddha Brewery and traditional Buddhist institutions make use of the Buddha image to promote their interests. The differences are in the purposes behind their use. The Funky Buddha Brewery is not primarily invested in promoting Buddha; for them, the branding is a capitalistic endeavor. As Inken Prohl notes in her chapter in this volume, images and ideas with a "touch" of Buddhism sell. Thus, we find that, while both traditional Buddhists and neoliberal businesses use Buddha images for marketing and commodification, the two retain conflicting motives.

The popular commercial use of Buddha images does not necessarily conflict with the religious use of Buddha images; however, as in the case of the Funky Buddha Brewery, it can. Many Buddhist traditions place restrictions on how to use a Buddha image in order to protect its sacrality. In this vein we should consider the Buddhist morality that prescribes to its followers five moral precepts: no harm, no stealing, no sexual misconduct, no lying, and *no intoxicants that cloud the mind*. The Funky Buddha Brewery's use of the Buddha image on beer dispensers, bottles, and paraphernalia (all of which are connected to the brewery) is at odds with lay Buddhist morality.

The rise of the neoliberal market has produced a new form of commodification and commercialization of Buddha images. This includes the practice of branding. Branding is the creation of a concept around a product, and in contrast to religious institutions and their branding of religious images to promote their visions of the sacred, neoliberal markets are not constrained by moral restrictions on their branding. Rather, the only determinates in the neoliberal market are legal restrictions and the profitability of the product.[2] The Funky Buddha Brewery is a successful corporation, and one trait that makes for a successful company in a competitive market, such as beer, is its marketing and branding. Corporations, in their brand strategy, may use religious images in positive ways that are conducive with the religion's principles, or they may not, such as in the case of the Funky Buddha Brewery.

When these two different styles of branding and commodification meet, Buddhists declare the neoliberal style blasphemous. For many Buddhists, there are correct ways to treat Buddha images. In the typical classical Greek usage, *blasphēmia connotes the broader act of slandering or harming a reputation*. While the exact term might not exist in Sanskrit, the concept certainly does. Stephen Jenkins (2016) finds a virtual cornucopia of examples in Buddhist scriptures that reference disrespect and harm to Buddhism. Through these examples, Jenkins reveals that Buddhist scriptures greatly revile the slandering of the Buddha and Buddhist doctrine. The connections between Buddhism and blasphemy become clearer in contemporary Thai Buddhism. Contemporary Thai Buddhists use the term *loblū* to describe the blasphemy-like slandering of the Buddha image.

For these Thai Buddhists, the misuse of a Buddha image is not only blasphemous; it is even harmful to witness. Other Buddhists do not invoke blasphemy in their efforts but nonetheless protest what they believe are unethical treatments of Buddhist images. The vast majority of these Buddhists do not respond with violence. They view karma (Pāli: *kamma*) as the principal adjudicator and reconciler of the offense, but while karma may produce consequences for inappropriate actions, it does not prevent the inappropriate actions. To address this, some Buddhists pursue campaigns to halt corporate misappropriations of the Buddha image.

There have been important analyses concerning the relevance of the term "blasphemy" in Buddhist scriptures.[3] Various Buddhist traditions have linked the disrespect of Buddha relics, including Buddha images, to the gravest of sins. For Buddhist communities that venerate stupas (reliquaries), which can house the remains of Buddhas, the harming of a stupa is the equivalent of spilling the Buddha's blood. Jonathan Silk explains:

> Drawing the blood of a Buddha is thus understood to mean, in a Buddhaless world, the destruction or damaging of a stupa, the memorial mound which encases relics of the Buddha. This makes perfect sense from the perspective of Buddhist doctrine, once one understands the stupa as equivalent, legally and otherwise, to the Buddha, as recent scholarship has demonstrated may be the case. (Silk 2007, 261)

Moreover, Buddhist relics have a life of their own. Relics travel, self-generate, and provide protection to people and kingdoms. An attack on Buddhist images is more than simply violence done to objects. It is an attack on the living sacred. In Buddhism, there are three categories for relics: physical remains of the sacred (*sarira*), items of use by the sacred (*paribhogika*), and items of remembrance of the sacred (*uddesika*).

This chapter first reviews the historical value and importance Buddhist scholars and Buddhist institutions have placed on items of remembrance, namely, Buddha images. It then locates the ways in which Buddhist governments and Buddhist organizations respond to neoliberal uses of the Buddha images. Behind the commercialization of Buddha images and Buddhist protests of blasphemy lies a clash of branding between modern neoliberal and traditional institutional religious treatments of Buddha images.

Blasphemy and the Life of Relics

Too often, Western scholars undervalue the importance of Buddha relics or see them as subordinate to doctrine. In the study of Buddhism, Gregory Schopen (1991) laments Western scholars' tendencies to make archaeology (and material culture) a handmaiden to scriptures.[4] Many scholars of religion attribute this problem to adopting a Protestant gaze that is not delimited to Buddhism but to religion in general. John Hinnells (2005, 10) writes, "Writers have a tendency to think that 'real' Islam is found in the Middle East and in Arabic texts; or 'real' Hinduism is found in Sanskrit texts." While some Buddhist traditions highly venerate scriptures, such as Pure Land Buddhism, other Buddhist traditions view relics *as* doctrine.[5] Throughout religious systems, relics are highly venerated, and Buddhism is no exception. To understand the clash between the neoliberal branding of Buddha images and Buddhist groups' use of Buddha images, it is important first to understand the value Buddhists place on Buddha images as relics.

A rich discourse exists on Buddhist relics and the ways in which they have a life of their own. As mentioned earlier, Buddhists recognize relics (*dhātu*) within a three-part hierarchical structure. The most revered are the relics from the bodily remains of awakened persons (*sarīra*). These bodily remains are enshrined in stupas and pagodas or placed within temples. One such temple is the Sri Dalada Maligawa, a Sri Lankan temple that is home to the tooth relic of the Buddha. Less plentiful than bodily remains are relics from contact with awakened persons (*pāribhogika*), which comprise the second tier. While bodily remains may come from any awakened beings, relics from contact largely pertain to the historical Buddha. The third and last tier, and the most bountiful, consists of relics of representation (*uddesika*), such as images and sculptures. In contemporary times, these fall under the umbrella of Buddha images. Buddhist doctrine identifies severe repercussions for slandering or mistreating relics, regardless of their tier. In his book on Buddhist relics, John Strong proposes that one should see relics as alive, serving as extensions of the Buddha's biographical process:

> It is perhaps possible to think of this as an assertion of the ongoing "presence" of the Buddha, but it is preferable to think of it as the further development of a powerful narrative. . . . The Buddha's relics, as we shall see, do not just recall events from his life, but have adventures of their own. . . . Either way, the relics continue to do things the Buddha did, to fill the roles the Buddha filled; but they also do new things that the Buddha never did. (Strong 2004, 7–8)

Relics have a life of their own. In South and Southeast Asia, Buddhist relics serve as palladia for countries. There are legends of relics with incredible powers that protect cities and its inhabitants, such as Thailand's Emerald Buddha and Laos' Phra Bang. The Emerald Buddha and Phra Bang are not merely protective amulets but guardians ascribed with sentient attributes. Frank Reynolds (1978, 180) writes that the two palladia were "considered to be competitive, antagonistic and prone to cause problems when they were kept together within the confines of a single kingdom."

There are also legends about relics that procreate. Strong (2004, xiv) notes the common assumption that relics can "reproduce themselves, to grow, multiply, or appear miraculously." It is rumored that the great Mauryan Emperor Asoka dispatched 84,000 relics of the Buddha's body across Asia. Beyond the metaphorical spread of Buddhism, many believe that Asoka literally spread thousands of relics. The relics multiplied to serve the needs of the Buddhist doctrine. These beliefs underscore the value that Buddhists place on relics, which includes the veneration of Buddha images.

Blasphemy as a Sin of Immediate Retribution

If, as Strong suggests, Buddhists treat relics as living artifacts, then the destruction of a relic does more than destroy Buddhist material culture. It injures what is most venerated in Buddhism, what we can call the Buddhist sacred. The significance of such an attack is exemplified in the analysis of Buddhism's five sins of immediate retribution (*ānantarya-karma*).

The Buddhist classification lists the five gravest sins as patricide, matricide, killing a fully awakened person (*arhant*), spilling the Buddha's blood, and causing a schism in the Buddhist monastic community. It is believed that the five sins of immediate retribution are so unwholesome that they will interrupt noble attainments in one's current birth. The Theravāda "Parikuppa Sutta" explains:

> There are these five inhabitants of the states of deprivation, inhabitants of hell, who are in agony & incurable. Which five? One who has killed his/her mother, one who has killed his/her father, one who has killed an arahant [fully awakened being], one who—with a corrupted mind—has caused the blood of a Tathagata [Buddha] to flow, and one who has caused a split in the Sangha. These are the five inhabitants of the states of deprivation, inhabitants of hell, who are in agony & incurable. (Thanissaro Bhikkhu 2010)

These heinous crimes are said to affect people throughout their many rebirths. Thanissaro Bhikkhu (2010) writes that one of the Buddha's foremost disciples, Moggallana, had killed his parents many rebirths ago, and the ramifications of such an act followed Moggallana into his final lifetime, when he was beaten to death. One of the more infamous examples is that of the Buddha's cousin Devadatta, who allegedly tried to kill the Buddha and led the Buddha to bleed. This act caused the earth to split open and swallow Devadatta whole.

Buddhists have connected the severity and longevity of these five sins to slandering Buddhism. For instance, the famous Japanese monastic scholar Nichiren argues that disparaging the *Lotus Sutra* is "like the five heinous offenses . . . killing one's father, mother, or an arhat; causing the body of the Buddha to bleed; or fomenting disunity in the saṅgha—in that it leads to the Avīci Hell, or the Hell without Respite . . ." (Stone 2012, 129). Similarly, in the Chinese version of the *Kṣitigarbha Sutra,* the Buddha's mother Maya converses with the bodhisattva Kṣitigarbha (Earth Womb). Kṣitigarbha explains: "Beings who shed the Buddha's blood, slander the Triple Jewel, and do not venerate Sutras will fall into the Relentless Hell where for billions of eons they will seek escape in vain."[6]

An attack on a Buddhist stupa does more than denigrate a Buddhist pilgrimage site, as illustrated earlier, and injuring the Buddha does not pertain only to his physical body. While the historical Buddha died and can no longer bleed, he lives on in his relics. In this vein, an attack on a relic is an attack on and injury to the Buddha.

Scriptures warn about the severe repercussions that come from the blasphemous treatment of relics of representation (*uddesika*). In the Songdian version of the Chinese apocryphal text *The Sutra of the Causes and Effects of Actions,* the Buddha recounts the karmic repercussions for particularly good and bad actions to his disciple Ānanda. Among the vilest acts are maligning stupas, scriptures, the Three Jewels, and Buddha images.[7] For instance, if one places the Buddha image "in that porch where there is smoke, they are reborn black" (MacKenzie 1970, 7). If they forget to venerate the Buddha image and the *sutra,* they are reborn in a dark black hell (15).

Legal, Economic, and Social Media Approaches to Blasphemy

For centuries, Buddhist institutions monitored and supervised the correct treatment of Buddha images and their marketing. Buddhist monks have overseen the dimensions and materials used in the creation of Buddha images. Some Buddha images served to evince a Buddhist institution's importance. There is a myriad of contemporary examples, such as the Leaning Buddha at Wat Pho in Bangkok, Thailand, and the Buddha Memorial Centre at the Fo Guang Shan's Nan Tien Institute.

The method of overseeing the Buddha image changed over the last century. As Buddhists entered the twentieth century, their notions of self and Buddhism changed with regard to the advent of the nation-state paradigm and nationalism. It was during this process that colonial laws were placed upon countries like Myanmar and Sri Lanka and imported to Thailand, stressing neutrality and respect for the nebulous category of religion. For instance, the current Sri Lankan Penal Code that addresses blasphemy, under chapter 15, "Offenses Relating to Religion," states:

> The current Sri Lankan Penal Code includes prohibitions against: injuring or defiling a place of worship with the "intension of thereby insulting" that religion (290); voluntarily disturbing a religious ceremony (291); deliberately wounding the religious feelings of a person with word, sounds, or gestures (291A); maliciously insulting the religious beliefs of another group (291B); and trespassing on burial places in order to offend others (292).

This act derives from the British colonial Penal Code Ordinance No. 2 of 1883 (Schonthal 2016, 141). The previous history of blasphemy in Buddhist texts shows it would be a mistake to consider colonial influences the cause of Sri Lankan views on blasphemy; however, it is clear that colonial laws had a significant effect in the crafting of the current legal language. In addition to this colonial legal framework, the nebulous category of religion has affected the legal treatment of religion and its defamation in, for example, Burmese and Sri Lankan courts.

There is no global consensus on the protocol with regards to religious paraphernalia, commercialization, or public rhetoric. Buddhist governments such as those of Myanmar, Thailand, and Sri Lanka enforce strict regulations on Buddha images and rhetoric about Buddhism. In June 2015, a prominent Burmese writer was imprisoned for criticizing Buddhist monastic views and thus maligning Buddhism (AFP 2015). In August 2015, two women were charged with violating Thailand's Section 13 of the Ancient Monuments, Antiquities, and National Museums Act. They had danced in short red dresses to music inside a Buddhist monastery in Ayutthaya. According to Thai law, the two Thai women's actions caused moral injury and added insult to religion and culture.[8]

Governments and their court systems may recognize and respect general institutionalized religious norms, but the diversity present within religious systems is too vast to implement legally in a manner that protects everyone's traditions.[9] Beyond political and legal processes, Buddhists have engaged in collective protests and taken to social media in order to affect the way the Buddha image is marketed.

Buddhist Collective and Social Media Protests

Buddhists around the world have found success in their protest of the neoliberal marketing and branding of Buddha images. Among these successes is the protest over marketing using Buddha images in the United States. In 2002, the US company Abercrombie & Fitch faced fierce criticism over one of their

Asian-themed T-shirts, which displayed an image of a pudgy Buddha wearing a Hawaiian lei, with the words "Buddha Bash: Get Your Buddha on the Floor." When people called for a boycott, the line was eventually pulled (Shields 2000, 84).

James Mark Shields (2000, 83) locates the reemergence of this concern two years later, when Victoria's Secret launched a bikini with a Buddha image on the left breast. Within weeks, Asian-American and Asian Buddhist leaders protested the swimsuit. Buddhists used the internet to submit complaints worldwide. The mounting criticism began to include non-Asians in the United States as well as people living in Europe. Facing this growing worldwide image problem, Victoria's Secret eventually discontinued the line.

Beyond the jurisdiction of Buddhist judiciaries and economic boycotts, Buddhists have turned to alternative venues, such as online protests. In Russia, for example, Buddhists protested against Buddha bars using social media and journalism. On a Change.org petition against the bars, the petitioner Valeria Sanzhieva (2017) explains:

> We are aware that, "Buddha Bar" night clubs, bars and restaurants are being opened up in Russian cities such as Moscow, Saint Petersburg, Yakutsk, Rostov, Orenburg, Tyumen, Taganrog, Krasnoyarsk, Shakhty and others. There are images and statues of Buddha in these entertainment establishments and people take photographs with them, naked woman perform go-go dancing in front of them and touching them; alcohol drinks are consumed there. These establishments upload their photographs and videos to the Internet, encourage drinking, singing, entertainment, organize slumber parties, parties with alcohol and hookah and various shows. This sort of attitude towards the Buddhist religion and ancient philosophy is rude and inappropriate considering that it infringes on religious people's rights and feeling all across Russia.[10]

As of February 2017, this petition had received over 2,400 signatures.

When discussions of the appropriate use of Buddha images enter global platforms, protests take on more prosaic and less organized means of expressing discontent. In October 2016, Buddhists around the world expressed outrage over an Instagram photo of the Portuguese professional football captain Cristiano Ronaldo placing his foot (the dirtiest part of the body for Buddhists) on a representation of the Buddha—an *uddesika* relic. Sam Street reports for the *Sun,* "Facebook user Shubham Pandey said, in a comment that received over 12,000 likes: 'This is disrespectful. . . . How can he put his leg on Gautam Buddha. . . . I was not expecting this stupidity from Ronaldo. . . . Sir today u lost one of ur fan this is very bad'" (Street 2016).

Unlike country-specific laws, public outrage manifests through transnational efforts and puts global pressure on companies and organizations.

There is a historical legacy of Buddhist responses to harm in the form of slander and disrespect. Buddhist groups such as the Knowing Buddha Organization view such acts as blasphemy. Blasphemy against the Buddhist doctrine, relics, and images provokes condemnations in various forms. The inappropriate use of a Buddha image has led to arrests and deportations in countries including Myanmar, Thailand, and Sri Lanka. There are also international campaigns of protest and a belief in karmic repercussions in the form of violence and numerous rebirths in the hell realm. Some Buddhists, particularly those who do not place a high value on Buddha images, do not necessarily subscribe to such legal actions. However, in the twenty-first century the transnational protests and outcries provide a unified front across various Buddhist traditions to protect and value Buddha images. Contemporary Buddhist organizations like the Knowing Buddha Organization are in the process of marshaling greater global awareness of what they deem the proper treatment of Buddha images and the harm they experience from their mistreatment.

Knowing Buddha Organization

On February 20, 2016, over one thousand people marched down Thailand's famous backpacker and tourist destination, the Khao San Road in Bangkok, as a "Dharma Army" (*kawngtaptham*). It was their third annual march down the road to stand against the disrespect shown to Buddha images. The day after the march, their leader, Master Acharavadee Wongsakon, posted a short reflection, explaining:

> With a campaign of over a thousand people, this army does not possess guns or swords. It has no malice or any hidden ill-intent. We do not [do this] for any personal interests, but in order to tell the world: "Buddhists regret the lack of awareness [shown] to the continued attacks [*yamyī*] and blasphemy [*loblū*] against the symbols of the Lord Buddha."[11]

Although the "army" is nonviolent, their concern is not. The organization behind the march, the Knowing Buddha Organization, views disrespect to Buddha images as a form of blasphemy and violence against Buddhism.

The Knowing Buddha Organization models a collective protest of the neoliberal branding of the Buddha image. They have chosen to promote education, heighten awareness, petition companies, and appeal to consumer bases. Only four years old, KBO membership has grown to over five thousand, a significant increase from two thousand in 2014. Since its foundation, the organization has successfully launched campaigns to protect Buddha images in Thailand and worldwide. On their website, the KBO explains their view of Buddha images:

> When [the] Buddha was still alive he never asked his followers to make statues or worship him in images. Instead he taught us to not have any attachment to anything—not even himself. Buddha said that the best way to worship him was to follow his teachings. And that after he passed away, after his "Nippana" or "Nirvana", his teachings would take his place.
>
> 100 years later some of his followers wondered how Buddha looked. They prayed to an angel who used to meet Buddha. Then the angel appeared in [the] Buddha's image, and so the first Buddha statues were created. Since then Buddha statues have become a key element for most Buddhists around the world [and they] are reminded of his compassion, kindness and his teachings and feel the highest regard for him. (KBO 2015a)

Here, the historical development of Buddhist iconography becomes inconsequential. Although the KBO's explanation may differ from other accounts, their value of the Buddha image remains and is in concert with many scriptural accounts of *uddesika* relics (relics of memory). The KBO founders explain that, though Buddhist doctrine instructs adherents in the *act of* letting go of attachments, this act is not the same as ignoring *harm*—harm such as blasphemy to the Buddha and Buddha images: "Suppose there is a garbage [*sic*] dumped in the middle of the house. If we focus on 'letting go,' we then leave it [to rot] in the house without doing anything. That is what we call 'neglect,' which is not the right understanding" (5000s.org 2015).

Channeling Business Skills into Buddhist Enterprises

The KBO is the brainchild of Acharawadee Wongsakon, a young Thai entrepreneur-turned-meditation master. From KBO's inception, Acharawadee has channeled her entrepreneurial skills and business tactics into artistically powerful productions on the KBO website and Facebook page, LCD displays, and billboards and in DVDs, magazines, and booklets. Her efforts have not gone unrewarded. There is wide and growing support for the KBO in Thailand. In addition to its growing number of members, the organization receives significant contributions from local and national Thai businesses. The KBO is composed largely of educated Thais, the majority of whom are female. Their wide membership also attracts local Thais, who occasionally join in their marches, such as the annual protest down the famous backpacker streets of

Khao San Road. The organization publishes the magazine *5000s.Org: Modern Lifestyle with Buddhist Thought,* dharma books, as well as brochures that appear in the Grand Palace (a favorite tourist site) and warning signs at the Don Muang and Suvarnabhumi airports. It has submitted a video campaign for consideration to Thai Airways.

While Buddhists generally agree that karma addresses blasphemy, instances occur wherein Buddhists feel compelled to take action. The KBO was formed on April 17, 2012, with this very intent. Its genesis occurred in 2011, when Acharawadee visited France. At one point, she came upon a "Buddha Bar" and became greatly distressed. A KBO volunteer recounted,

> [Acharawadee] came to a bar—and filled up [with] tears. She felt pain and felt alone there. And she said, "It is not right. Why put the Buddha in the middle of the bar? It is what the Buddha taught that is not right: to drink, to dance, and everything [are] not the way of the Buddha." She said she could not do anything. She cried at the bar.[12]

While Acharawadee was unable to do anything in 2011, her organization has accomplished a considerable amount since then. During the organization's first year alone it tracked over one hundred cases of disrespect worldwide and has had many companies remove Buddha images from their products.

The KBO's Mobilization

One of the KBO's identified cases of disrespect came from the Disney's Air Buddies film series, which features a dog named Buddha. According to the Disney Wiki website, "He wears a Buddhist collar and usually ends his sentences with 'Namaste.' He is the calmest of the Buddies and almost never loses his temper."[13] The KBO railed against this depiction, claiming that such creative license of a religious founder's name would not lead Disney to name a dog Jesus or Muhammad. During its rally in June 2012, Acharawadee explained she created the Knowing Buddha protest movement after seeing Walt Disney's Buddha dog in January, "when my daughters rented the film from iTunes" (Ehrlich 2012).

The following year, the KBO's infrastructure and mobilization tactics increased. On January 4, 2013, the KBO protested a Los Angeles restaurant called Rock Sugar, which lined the interior and entrance of its restaurant with Buddha statues. The following month, it complained to a French hotel and manufacturer for their use of a Buddha image on toilet seats. And on March 25, 2013, it protested the Italian 21st Living Art Company's use of Buddha heads. Many of the KBO's campaigns have been quite successful. The Buddha images on toilet lids were removed in France; a seductive photo shoot in front of Buddha images in *Maxim* magazine was cancelled. In 2013, the Dutch company Boels created Buddha-image portable toilets in Brunssum, Netherlands. The KBO wrote to the embassy on January 25, 2013, requesting that the government take action. The Netherlands responded immediately; they ordered a removal of the portable toilets and issued an apology letter on February 15, 2013.

On April 17, 2013, its first anniversary, the organization posted online that it had encountered challenges in getting others to recognize the importance of protecting Buddha images but that it would remain steadfast in its efforts to defend the Buddha images. Its perseverance was emphatically declared at the end of its message:

> The first year of the protection of Lord Buddha, the first year of extreme tasks that no one dares to fight for, Knowing Buddha Organization will proceed with full thrust with faith and loyalty to Lord Buddha. We will keep the faith strong and guard Lord Buddha till our last breath and there will be the next and the following years. "We will never stop." —Knowing Buddha Organization *"To Guard Against any Threat and Blasphemy to Buddhism"* (KBO 2015a)

In my conversations with KBO members, it became clear that the majority see their work as profoundly important. Fewer than a dozen of the five thousand members are paid; the rest are volunteers. Each member has graduated from Acharawadee's meditation courses; they explained to me that it is through these meditative practices that they have become acutely sensitive to the disrespect shown to the Buddha and to Buddha images.

One of the KBO's more international acts to protect the Buddha image occurred from May 29 to June 1, 2015, the time of the year during which Thai Buddhists celebrate Visakha Bucha, a holiday that commemorates the Buddha's birth, awakening, and death. On the island of Koh Samui, a full moon festival was also taking place at the Centara Grand Beach Resort Hotel. Hundreds of international tourists attended the party, celebrated Visakha Bucha, and enjoyed the beautiful scenery. With large numbers of international visitors primed to think about Buddhism, it was also an ideal opportunity for the Knowing Buddha Organization (KBO) to launch its most important march of the year.

For the occasion, the KBO prepared its exhibition "Miracle of the Middle Path," with information booths in English detailing the inappropriate use of Buddha images and references to the Buddha. Each day, roughly a hundred visitors learned about the KBO's mission and the disrespectful ways people treat Buddha images. Thai and international visitors to the booths were invited to write postcards to businesses that mistreat Buddha images or use the name "Buddha" in inappropriate ways: the 21st Living Art (Italy), Sugar Buddha Bar (United States), Tien Shui Yueh Hotpot Restaurant (Taiwan), Jim Thompson House (Thailand), and Deny Designs (United States). During her preparations for the event, KBO's art director Apanee Wongsakon not only explained that the exhibition informed people about how to respect Buddha images properly but also said that the exhibition served as a means "for people to become a part of protecting the Buddha image."[14] On the last day of the celebrations, the KBO welcomed people to attend Chaweng Beach, near the Centara Grand Beach Resort. There, the KBO founder gave an eight-minute speech in English about the meaning of Visakha Bucha; this was followed by a short session in which people gathered in silent meditation to pay respect to the Buddha.

KBO Views: Blasphemy as Violence

From the KBO's establishment to its recent efforts in Koh Samui, the organization identifies the protection of Buddhism as its primary purpose. The KBO uses the English term "blasphemy" or the equivalent Thai word *loblū* to describe the mistreatment of the Buddha and Buddha images.[15] The KBO sees such blasphemous behavior as harmful to Buddhists and explains in one of their brochures, "True Buddhists who see a Buddha image placed as objects in inappropriate places will feel very unhappy and may become subject to conflict arising from such situations."

In a conversation with a KBO member, I asked how she felt when she saw people disrespect the Buddha. The member explained that since she has joined the KBO, she has witnessed many cases in which this happens and that she often cries. "For example, I have been in Barcelona a lot of times . . . and [once] I walked past a travel agency. [This one] showed a Buddha head, just the Buddha head, on the ground—yeah, right in front of the street, the window shop, and my hotel is nearby, so I had to walk past it all the time. It—I [didn't] know what to say." The member eventually went into the store and told them but believed she did not have any effect.[16]

Whether it is a Buddha beer, Buddha skateboard, Buddha headphones, or psychedelic art depicting the Buddha, KBO members see these uses of the Buddha image as blasphemous, and they feel harmed.[17] The KBO's secretariat Sayan Chueyuksorn explains that KBO members use peaceful protests and seek civil recourse through the creation of laws in order to protect the Buddha and his images.[18] Thailand has laws with regard to the defamation of religion, but the KBO considers the current language too ambiguous, which leads to a lack of enforcement. In contrast, they look favorably upon the recent actions of Buddhist governments in countries such as Sri Lanka, which has, for example, arrested and deported tourists tattooed with images of the Buddha. During one of the more recent cases, a Sri Lankan police spokesperson stated that the tourist "was arrested for 'hurting others' religious feelings'" (BBC 2014).[19] Sayan was unaware of the recent blasphemy charges in Myanmar, in which a bar owner and manager were imprisoned for using an image of a Buddha wearing headphones in their advertisements.[20] However, when I reviewed the situation with him, Sayan Chueyuksorn replied, "That's what we expect."

The KBO considers many of these problems to be the result of general ignorance about Buddhism. One prominent example is an email the KBO received in 2013. A group of Europeans had inquired about the correct way to create a Buddha-image carpet for the Buddha's birthday. Implicit in their question is a lack of awareness that Buddha images should be placed up high as a sign of respect in Asia; the dirtiest and most impolite parts of the body are the soles of the feet. Although people may intend to show respect, KBO members see practices as paramount to the intention. Sayan Chueyuksorn reflects,

> We [have] had cases [like this] and we discuss [the issue] with them; the majority of [these cases] are from overseas. Half of [the people in these cases] do not understand. And I think this is related to *loblū* [blasphemy]. Because some of them [intend to show] respect, but do not understand the correct way [to show respect] like that.[21]

For Sayan, karma will account for a person's intention, but laws should address the person's practice. He and other members acknowledge that there may be different cultural views and values, but they believe there are correct ways to treat Buddha images regardless of the person's culture and intention.

Over the last three years, the KBO has gained support from other organizations and from the Thai government. In March 2015, Thailand's Office of National Buddhism, which oversees Buddhist activities throughout the country, began to send letters of support on behalf of the KBO. With the government's assistance, the KBO was able to put a stop to a German company that was printing Buddha images on toilets.[22] Currently, the KBO—under their sister organization 5000s.org—has five international petitions against US- and UK-based spa companies, nightclubs, and candy stores that use "the Buddha's name and image with extreme inappropriateness."[23] Rapidly expanding its membership base, international exposure, and media outlets, the KBO is influencing the global treatment of Buddha images.

It would be a mistake to frame the discussion over Buddhism and branding and neglect the Buddhist entrepreneurial dimension. In this volume, Lionel

Obadia rightly points to Buddhist enterprises that draw upon Buddhist concepts and materials. Businesses also target the "Buddhist" consumer, such as the "dharma shoppers." When non-Buddhist companies appeal to a wider consumer base, they may do so in a way that complements Buddhist principles. Inken Prohl's work points to the ways in which commercial branding promotes the positive qualities of Buddhist doctrine. Companies pair the melting of ice cream with the Buddhist notion of impermanence; progressive and organic cosmetics and food companies pair their products with the Buddhist ethics of compassion. However, some commercial enterprises, such as the Funky Buddha Brewery, promote products at odds with Buddhist doctrine.

The Knowing Buddha Organization provides an example of Buddhist protests over the misuse of Buddha images. One may argue that Buddhists' reactions to the defacement of images or relics neglects Buddhist doctrinal principles, such as the avoidance of attachments. However, this approach operates at the expense of respecting alternative Buddhists' views and feelings. Companies like the Funky Buddha Brewery make use of the Buddha image in ways that contradict fundamental Buddhist moral codes. Buddhists, such as those in the KBO, view this appropriation as disrespectful. This neoliberal branding of Buddha images does not simply come from Western companies but Asian ones as well.

The Chinese beer Lucky Beer manufactures bottles in the shape of the Buddha. Their website's tagline is "Get Enlightened," and the beer flavor purportedly "enlightens" the senses. Lucky Beer protects their use of the Buddha image with the argument that the image is cultural and not religious. According to their website,

> The "Laughing Buddha" depicted on Lucky Buddha beer is actually not THE Buddha and therefore not religious but cultural. He is incorporated in Buddhist, Taoist and Shinto traditions. The term buddha means "one who is awake", connoting one who has awakened into enlightenment.[24]

The company correctly sees the Laughing Buddha image as endemic to Chinese Buddhist traditions. While Lucky Beer may espouse the Buddha image as cultural and not religious, their assertion does not remove the potential clash that can occur between their use of the Buddha image and the Buddhist precept against drinking alcohol. As such, the company's assertion does not prevent Buddhists from seeing the image as religious and Lucky Beer's use of the Laughing Buddha as the blasphemous treatment of a Buddhist relic.

The controversy over the use of Buddha images is not new; Buddhist concerns over slandering the doctrine and Buddha images have existed for centuries. Yet, as evidenced through legal actions in Myanmar, Sri Lanka, and

Thailand, contemporary Buddhist reactions to improper treatments of Buddha images continue to transform laws and business practices. As the global market continues to evolve, new complementary and contradictory approaches will surface between neoliberal forms of branding religious images and traditional institutional religious forms of branding their images.

Notes

Portions of this chapter were adapted or taken from Michael Jerryson's *If You Meet the Buddha on the Road: Buddhism, Politics, and Violence* (Oxford: Oxford University Press, 2018).

1 The Funky Buddha Brewery's website and online store is available at https://funkybuddhabrewery.com.

2 In a famous article from the *New York Times Magazine,* Milton Friedman (1970) notes the arguments for social responsibility in neoliberal businesses but dismisses the premises. People may have social responsibilities, but corporations do not. Drawing from his book *Capitalism and Freedom,* Friedman writes: "There is one and only one social responsibility of business—to use its resource and engage in activities designed to increase its profits so long as it stays within the rules of the game, which is to say, engages in open and free competition without deception or fraud."

3 For instance, the British monk Sangharakshita argues that there is no such thing as blasphemy in Buddhism. While he acknowledges Buddhadatta's translation of the Sanskrit term *ariyupavada* as blasphemy (literally, the insulting of a noble, *ariya + upavāda*), Sangharakshita (1978, 9) contends that this is a modern coinage. For a response to Sangharakshita's position and an exploration of scriptural instances of blasphemy, see Crosby (1999).

4 Gregory Schopen (1991, 19) reinforces this point in his call for the inclusion of information beyond texts: "The methodological position frequently taken by modern Buddhist scholars, archaeologists, and historians of religion looks, in fact, uncannily like the position taken by a variety of early Protestant 'reformers'" (Schopen 1991, 19).

5 Buddhist studies scholars mistakenly have paralleled relics and images to the materialist dimension of *rūpakāya* (literally, "material body"), thereby subordinating relics to a lower ontological status than the corollary dimension called the *dhammakāya* (body of the doctrine). Steven Collins (2014, 259) writes, "it has become a stereotype in modern studies of Theravāda to say that the term *rūpakāya* in Pali texts refers to relics and images of the Buddha after his death. This, I try to show, is wrong."

6 This sutra can be found at BuddhaSutra.com, "Sutra of the Past Vows of Earth Store Bodhisattva," at http://www.buddhasutra.com/files/ksitigarbha_sutra.htm.

7 Kate Crosby (1999, 222) underscores that intensity of condemnation in the sutra; if a person destroys or damages a stupa, they are born for multiple lives in hells.

8 Their five-minute clip was posted on YouTube on August 5, 2015. The two women, Thannicha Nampanya and Nitikarn Chotthanapongsathit, surrendered on August 8 (Sunthon Pongpao 2015).

9 For a framing of this argument in the United States, see Sullivan (2007).

10 I would like to thank Kristina Jonutyte for introducing me to the protests and information.

11 Translated by the author from KBO (2016).

12 Personal communication with Natarat Buathong at the KBO School of Life, Bangkok, June 29, 2014.

13 The Disney Wiki's "Buddha" entry can be found at http://disney.wikia.com/wiki/Buddha.

14 Personal communication with Apanee Wongsakon at KBO headquarters, Bangkok, May 20, 2015.

15 The translation of *loblū* as blasphemy has strong etymological support. *Loblū* means "to insult" or "disparage" and is closely aligned with the Greek root *blasphēmia, which means to slander or harm a reputation.*

16 Personal communication with a KBO member at KBO headquarters, Bangkok, May 20, 2015.

17 On their website, they exclaim, "[When] you step on the Buddha Symbol, [many] hearts would be crush[ed] upon your step" (KBO 2015a).

18 Personal communication with Sayan Chueyuksorn at KBO headquarters, Bangkok, May 20, 2015.

19 On the KBO's "News Update" for March 19, 2013, they wrote: "There is serious action in Sri Lanka. What about us?" (KBO 2015b).

20 A New Zealand bar manager and two Burmese were sentenced to two years for denigrating Buddhism. U Ye Lwin, the judge who oversaw the case, explained, "It is clear the act of the bar offended the majority religion in the country" (Moe and Ramzy 2015). For more information on Burmese codes against blasphemy, see Fuller (2016).

21 Personal communication with Sayan Chueyuksorn at KBO headquarters, Bangkok, May 20, 2015.

22 Personal communication with Sayan Chueyuksorn at KBO headquarters, Bangkok, May 20, 2015.

23 The first case is Olive Spa in the United States, which displays a Buddha head at the shop and in its spa rooms. The second is the Las Vegas space Encore, which uses Buddha statues as decorations in their spa. The third case is the British night club, Sugar Buddha Deansgate Locks, which named their bar after the Buddha. The fourth case is the Chicago-based specialty store Sweet Buddha, which sells candy, jewelry, and apparel in the shape of the Buddha. The fifth case is the US brewery Funky Buddha Lounge and Brewery, which decorates its bar with Buddha statues and places Buddha images on its logos and beer taps (5000s.org 2015).

24 This disclaimer can be found at http://www.luckydrinkco.com/luckybeer/index.php?l=0.

8

Economies of Religion, Buddhism and Economy, Buddhist Economics

Challenges and Perspectives

Lionel Obadia

THE RELATIONSHIPS BETWEEN BUDDHISM AND ECONOMY ARE all but new. Since the foundation of Buddhist studies under the influence of Eugène Burnouf in the early nineteenth century, the scholarly interest has been focused on ethics, myths, doctrines, rituals, values, and norms—and not on economic issues. Economic issues have nevertheless occasionally surfaced in research on Buddhism, especially after Weber and the Weberian school of the sociology of religion. Weber's work *Introduction to the Economic Ethics of the World Religions* (2004, first published in 1916) paved the way for understanding the ways in which economic aspects shape religious ethics and, conversely, how religious ideas shape economic practices. The dialogical relationship between economy and religion have therefore been nourished by several empirical works but, until recently, often only at the margins of more authoritative subject matters in Buddhist studies (Sizemore and Swearer 1990). By chance, the current interest of religious studies in economic theories and methods and, in turn, the increased attention on economics in religion have changed the ways scholars think about this topic. Recent research has echoed this work in progress toward a new approach to religious beliefs and practices in different fields of knowledge. Labeled as "economics of religion," this field of research was generated from the study of monotheistic traditions in the West, in particular Christianity in North America (Iannaccone 1998). There are significant and rich contributions to the field of "economics of religion." Nowadays, however, this research interest is expanding to the study of other traditions and diverse geographic and cultural contexts, such as Islam in Asia

(Green 2011). Buddhism is one of the first traditions in history in which economic issues have received theological or philosophical attention. Gustavo Benavides (2005) reopened the debate in the mid-2000s with a decisive chapter on economy as a key concept of Buddhist studies, in which he exposed the specific developments relating to the field of economics and religion. His analysis demonstrated that the time had come to open up the field of Buddhist studies. An update was needed—one that welcomed more modern issues—in relation to the increasing importance of economy in the cultural and religious context of Buddhist countries.

More than two decades later, Brox and Williams-Oerberg (2017) have shown how the topic of economy and economics for Buddhism and Buddhist studies was fecund and relevant: issues regarding economy have gained in surface, depth, and relevance, and conceptual models have been diversified enough to offer a broader range of perspective than previously. This chapter does not aim at restating what these authors have already done. Instead, it attempts to enlarge the scope of the discussion to underscore the broad context in which Buddhist studies are affected by what looks to be a new trend: the "economics of religion." To what extent and under which conditions do reflections that began and developed mainly in the study of monotheistic religions in a Western context apply to Buddhism in Asia? It is time to appraise the promises and perils of such approaches in Buddhist studies, whether the research is focused on Western or Asian contexts, be they ethnographically informed or more focused on scriptural material.

An Emerging Genre or a Trendy Reference?

In the 2000s and 2010s, religious traditions have been active in public debates about globalization, and their voices have been loud in their criticism of the side effects of economic imbalance, poverty, social inequalities, or ecological degradation. Buddhist voices have sounded more strongly than monotheistic ones, since Eastern traditions have gained the reputation of offering sustainable models for the world. Like other traditions, Buddhist organizations put forward alternative solutions and position themselves clearly in debates on the prejudicial effects of globalization. In turn, the semantic resonance and the repertoire of economics in the discourse *of* religions and in the discourse *on* religions have dramatically widened. The lexicon of economics has become commonplace, and expressions such as the "magic of markets," "divine capitalism," "business of religions," "consuming faith," "branding of religious commodities," and the like disseminate quickly (Obadia 2013).

In the ideological background of these lexical developments, economists seem to want to convince themselves (and the rest of the world) that the new mythological or cosmological horizon of modern societies, and perhaps a new hypermodern religion, is made from the market or is the market itself (Dufour 2012). The vogue for economic concepts is new and must be questioned with a critical distance: it is indeed not certain that these models have always fully demonstrated their relevance. It has become fashionable to use economics to explain social, cultural, psychological, and religious facts in new ways. The zeal for such explanations echoes a context of globalization that is mainly interpreted in economic terms or whose economic features are considered more salient than, for example, its cultural and religious aspects (Obadia 2011). Historically speaking, economy and religion used to go hand in hand along the routes of merchants. Religious clergy and merchants used the same circuits, but their coexistence in the same contexts and on the same roads neither meant that these were the same actors nor the same diffusion patterns (Kale 2004). The excessive emphasis upon economy and economics in the understanding of civilizations and religions in history is rather recent and is, for instance, topical in globalization studies (Waters 2001) but has been relativized (Sklair 1999) and somewhat relocated in its "own place" by grounded approaches. Seeing globalization deterministically can otherwise lead to a reduction of the theoretical scope: global economy is often globalization itself, since it is, empirically and conceptually, the new frame for global conditions and global geography—North-South, Center-Periphery. It is also seen as the driving force for the expansion of a global consumer culture (Featherstone 1991). Actually, under the umbrella term "global economy," most scholars and observers are of the opinion that the spread of modern capitalism and the hegemonic position of transnational neoliberalism dominate domestic economies (Appadurai 1990). This is one of the reasons why the debate on economy is rendered complex by the ideological background and the political attitudes toward globalization, dividing the pro- and the antiglobalization camps. When economic factors are used to examine religious changes in the context of modernity, they are evaluated against neoliberal models. Buddhism has logically been affected—like others—by the rise of global forces, and especially by the rapid and massive extension of a modern capitalist system of production and of the corresponding consumer culture. It is uncertain, however, whether Buddhist traditions have been affected by global forces or if it has played a role in the global economy different from other religions. Buddhism seems to take on a specific experience of modern economy and global capitalism. This is why the 2,500-year-old Asian tradition, to a certain extent, has been regarded as modernity friendly and consequently also eco-friendly (Kolm 1982).

Economy: Threat or Chance for Religion?

The relationships between religion and economy are characterized by ambivalence and an ongoing tension between ethics and practices, between ideal models and down-to-earth realities. Pope Francis' harsh critiques against the immorality of the economy in the 2000s are good examples, illustrating the unbroken attitude of a Roman Catholicism torn between the acceptance of the economic system they are leaning on and the rejection of the antisocial feelings created by the possession and use of money. European scholars were prompt to consider that this posture distinguishes Western monotheistic traditions (mainly Christian) from the rest of the world—as if non-Western polytheistic societies were not concerned (or at least not in the same way). Nevertheless, the Fourteenth Dalai Lama's recurrent charges against the outcomes of industrial productivity and the domination of money over culture appear, among other examples, in the typical critiques pointed at the global market economy, which are common among other religions as well. Paradoxically, criticism is counterbalanced by the benefits that Christianity and Buddhism make of modern and global economic circuits and flows: they spread throughout the world, convert new individuals and groups, take root in different countries, and reorganize themselves alongside the new network society described by the sociologist Manuel Castells (2000).

It seems obvious that Buddhism, like other religions, has ambivalent relationships with economy and money: Buddhism is indeed ethically against economic logic but pragmatically needs it (Benavides 2005). Likewise, Gregory Schopen (2004) has recalled that "business" matters for Buddhism—even in the case of ancient forms of scriptural Buddhism in India. Actually, similar to monotheistic traditions, it is rather obvious that the problem for Buddhism is not economy but money, and especially usury. Indeed, most theistic religions, monotheisms in particular, have an ambivalent relationship with money: currency is the media by which wealth circulates and stabilizes the production, exchange, and consumption systems of the economy. Sometimes, predominantly in polytheistic contexts, money is allotted "magical" powers. Traditions like Christianity and Islam have (to a certain extent) considered money, above all, a source of antisocial feelings (for example, greed, envy, and jealousy). Therefore, the practice of usury (lending with interest), though crucial to the balance of economic systems in theistic societies, has been *officially* rejected as a source of impurity but discreetly been maintained, though persecuted (Obadia 2013). Yet, unlike Brahmanism, Buddhism has since its beginnings allegedly been economy friendly, and not only with regard to modernity. Subsequently, one can wonder whether there is really something new or modern in the "Buddhist attitude" toward the economy, even if the logics, circuits, dynamics, and collective representation of the economy have been subjected to significant changes. It is rather easy to demonstrate that in every cultural context, Buddhism relies upon the same system of communication and exchange of symbolic and material goods (San.: *dāna*) and retribution (karma) (da Col 2007). In every Buddhist country, there exists a Buddhist monastic economy responding to the transformations of the broad social, cultural, political, and economic environment, especially for the production of surplus wealth susceptible to injection into monastic communities (see Walsh 2014, in the case of China). Buddhist groups of devotees (except for monks subjected to the prohibition of trade) also engaged in economic activities not against but on the grounds of the legacy of the scriptures and the many evocations of mendicants, wealth, and markets (Lewis 1993). As Todd Lewis recalls: "Buddhist texts often speak the language of the bazaar: the *Mahālamkāra sāstra* compares the dharma to 'a great market where the goods are sold to all'" (140). As we can see, both scriptural and practical ethics of Buddhism contain elements in favor of a sort of "compatibility" between Buddhism and economic activities.

What about Buddhism?

These debates arose and developed far from Buddhist studies and from Asia. They were framed after the historical vicissitudes of monotheisms in "modern" Western societies, especially in the circumstances of the diversification of their religious landscape, in what is labeled, for better or worse, as an "open economy of religious preferences." To what extent do these trends and theories apply outside the cultural and intellectual context in which they have been framed? How do they apply in the context of Buddhism? Scholars of Buddhist studies everywhere seem increasingly interested in issues regarding both economy *and* Buddhism as well as the economy *in* Buddhism. It is common wisdom to recall that Buddhism was born in the context of an emerging monetary economy in Asia and the apparition of specific social forms like guilds (Weber 1958) or in the backgrounds of commercial civilizations (Tehranian 2007). In practice, and not only in context, one of the pillars of Buddhism is the notion of "religious spending" (*dāna*), which is the structural foundation of the *bhikku-upasaka* social and religious model, that is, the monk-to-lay interactions that circulate, in one direction, symbolic items (performances and sacredness from monks to lay followers) and, in reverse, material goods and offerings in a reciprocal exchange (Spiro 1966). These are somewhat classical approaches to economy, and they are hardly affected by the innovative paradigm of the economics of religion, that is, the interpretation of religious beliefs, behaviors, and dynamics in economic terms or models. So, what is the meaning of the term "economics of Buddhism"? A few recent examples demonstrate an opening of the field that offers promising perspectives: one of the most famous studies, conducted in the West and mainly relying upon the conceptual devices of economics of religion, is the study of Soka Gakkai in America by Hammond and Machacek (1999). The two authors apply supply-and-demand theory to explain the appeal and conversion processes that Buddhism has in North America. The economic models used in this and other studies are associated with the economics of religion, yet most of the scholarly work conducted until now continues to focus upon the economy *in* Buddhism rather than the economics *of* Buddhism, even though new perspectives (economics of religion) slowly progress and incite stimulating analytical models. Benavides (2005), for instance, pointed toward the tension between asceticism (associated with an ideal of poverty) and money (the possibility to accumulate wealth, located at the opposite pole of symbolism in Asian traditions). Yet, according to him, both asceticism and money require "transcendental realities" (either truth or value). To connect these developments more directly with the distinction just mentioned, when the focus is placed on the materialistic dimension of economy, or when economy refers to concrete needs of existence (money) and the ways they influence the religious lives of monks or ordinary lay followers, the model is "economy *in* Buddhism." When, however, the analytical emphasis is put on the internal logics of religious life, and when these logics are interpreted in economic terms (though not economic per se), the model is "economy *of* Buddhism."

Ethnographic Experience and Analytical Models

What is beyond the recent and massive emphasis on economy in the study of religions and especially with Buddhism? I assert that it would be an intellectual trap to mix economy with economics. This inclination to see religion through an economic approach is not only a matter of empirical conditions to which religions must adapt, like the extension of global capitalism; it is also a matter of changing perspectives in religious studies and the rise of the economic paradigm in the social sciences and humanities, and by extension in religious studies. The economics of religion in this paradigm is framed after the transformations of monotheistic traditions (mainly Christianity) in a Western (North American) context. The economist Laurence Iannaccone is credited as the founder of the field in the late 1980s and early 1990s, with pioneering works on the market structure and human capital in religious choices and dynamics. Yet some scholars trace the origins of this theoretical framework to an earlier time, to the works of Adam Smith. If we set aside the genealogy of the field for now (see Obadia and Wood 2011a), it is important to note that after Iannaccone, a new generation of scholars are scrutinizing the role of economy in religious dynamics and the role of religion in economic processes (see Sriya Lyer 2015). More recently, they have also examined the market-driven dynamics of religious organizations (Spickard 2008). These studies cover all kinds of methodologies, from microscopic case studies to large-scale quantitative surveys (experimental economics/econometrics). Nowadays, global approaches to religion rely significantly on these models (Kurtz 2007).

A significant shift has occurred when the concepts of economics enters the debate, that is, when scholars study economy (empirically based production of wealth) by adding models and concepts of economics in order to shed a new light on empirical materials, practices, and beliefs. Several models have emerged and have become widespread and relevant: models such as rational choice theory, supply and demand, market theory, spiritual consumerism, religious branding and advertising, commodification and marketization of religion, sacred fetishism of merchandises, cost and benefits in religious preferences, theory of belief as bet, and so forth range among the many conceptual frames that are used nowadays in diverse disciplinary fields (Iannaccone 1998). The risk, however, is the possibility of forcing sacred and spiritual phenomena into interpretations in materialistic and down-to-earth terms. With such an extensive usage, though, the notion of economics is subjected to semantic variations. Likewise, "economics of religion" is not the only analogical model referring to economy/ics. The word is entrenched in a much wider semantic network: a common lexical basis ("eco") gave rise to a complex lexicon with reversible signification. The meaning of expressions such as "moral economies" wavers, for instance, between moral expertise on the market and a market-oriented outlook on morality or ethics. Similarly, the extensive concept of ritual economies can be understood alternatively as economic components of a ritual (economy in rituals) as well as an economy of ritual, in the sense that the ritual produces a rationalized process. We can add to this list the more restricted concept of "cultural economics," which is another way to label the accumulation of prestige, charisma, or knowledge. These examples make obvious the possibility of theorizing economies without economy (or almost), since they allude *to* but not necessarily partake *in* economy. The existence of two parallel conceptual repertoires established on the same lexical roots but aiming at the description of two different realities raises a crucial and complex issue, namely, the epistemological status of economics. Are we discussing economics as analogy or as ontology?

The analogical perspective—the most relevant to this chapter—is not exactly new but is the more intellectually challenging. In *Economy and Society* (1978), Max Weber related religious terminology to concepts like entrepreneurship, monopoly, salvation goods, and competition. He relied upon an analogical approach to cast an economic light on the social and political dynamics of religion. His contemporary, the philosopher Walter Benjamin, applied the same analogy but with a somewhat different conclusion. In his short but much-quoted essay "Capitalism as Religion" (see Löwy 2009), Benjamin portrayed the nineteenth and twentieth centuries' rising global economic system as a cult. Indeed, capitalism itself was grounded on abstractions, values, faith, and loyalty for those who had confidence in it. By comparison, the same features also characterized religious systems, and Benjamin concluded that capitalism was "the most powerful" religion of the time. While Weber's approach remained strictly analogical in aim and scope, Benjamin forcefully extended the analogy to the final point of recreating an ontology, making economy not the metaphor of religion but the substance of it. Subsequent criticisms have addressed the tendency to overstate the economic color or flavor of modern religious life (Bruckner 2002; Csordas 2009).

Adopting an economic perspective on religious behaviors and dynamics is not solely a matter of methodological or epistemological choices. It also relies on the changing economic conditions and lifestyles in Asia and elsewhere around the globe. Buddhist groups and organizations are inevitably implicated and even entangled by the context of capitalistic globalization, and they have to adjust their dynamics, for better or worse, to these conditions. The issue of economics is therefore as governed by empirical evidence as it is impelled by theoretical considerations. To take just one example, Kagyu Tibetan Buddhist traditions in Western countries have embraced the "market": Tibetan Buddhism has become a fashionable item subjected to marketization processes and spiritual consumption. "Buddhism sells," as precisely stated by Inken Prohl (this volume). This slogan can be applied to every Buddhist tradition, in Asia and in the West. What I have learned from my ethnographic exploration of community practices in Europe, Nepal, and the Middle East and from the historical retrospective of Buddhism in the West is that Buddhism is settling in wealthy societies. This settling is happening on the ambiguous grounds that "greed is the poison of modern society" and that Buddhism is the response. However, as Kagyupa followers and converts used to tell me, "monks do not fly in the air" (that is, they need plane tickets), pointing at the contradiction between the somewhat abstract ethical posture and the effective down-to-earth needs of the communities. Douglas Padgett's (2000) punch line (and the title of his scholarly article) "Americans Need Something to Sit On" accurately sums up the material and infrastructural needs of convert Buddhist followers in the West. In other words, the transplantation of Buddhism in the West is not only a matter of relocation and reconstruction of traditions and institutions (Baumann 1995, 1997) but also an issue of reconstructing economic networks and reinstalling material culture at the heart of spiritual life (Padgett 2002).

Can we consider this situation special or unique in the context of "highly developed," "modern" Western societies? This would be a rather limited scope for reflection, in my opinion. Similar to my observations from the rebuilding of the Tibetan Kagyu tradition in the West, economic issues are also prominent in Asian settings. During my ethnographic fieldwork conducted in the early 2000s, I observed how the Tibetan Nyingma tradition in Nepal was significantly involved in economic issues. First, Tibetan exiles and expatriates in Nepal faced harsh living conditions and had to engage in economic activity in a foreign country where they were not citizens. Second, resettled monastic communities were connected with economic circuits, and Tibetans in Nepal were dependent upon foreign and local financial sources (Frechette 2002). Third, the monastery where I conducted investigations, Thupten Choeling Monastery in the northern mountain district of Solukhumbu, constituted (like many others) a nodal position in local and global circuits of spiritual tourism and NGO support and was a place where one could meet a diverse population: Tibetan monks, Nepalese and Tibetan merchants in search of business, Western spiritual seekers in search of sacredness, and Western trekkers attracted by the "exoticism" of local culture. Not only that, but I have also observed for years the flourishing economy of auspicious fortune objects in Bodhanath, in the Valley of Kathmandu, where monks from mountains and cities were buying amulets and liturgical artifacts. Regardless of the geographic and cultural specificity of my ethnographic fieldwork among the Tibetan Kagyu tradition in the West and the Tibetan Nyingma tradition in Nepal, both cases epitomize, in not so different ways, the adaptive strategies of Buddhism to the economic systems they interact with.

Critical Views of Buddhists on Global Economy

To move ahead in the reflection but return to an aforementioned point, the advances of economic-oriented theoretical frameworks in Buddhist studies are counterbalanced by the ethical stances and/or ideological postures of Buddhist intellectuals or leaders. These intellectuals and leaders are also often scholars in Buddhist studies, for example, Preecha Changkhwanyuen or Alfred Bloom (see Obadia 2011). Consequently, they are situated in a position that is blurring the frontier between insider and outsider perspectives on Buddhism (Prebish 1999). This divides Buddhist discussions on economic issues into two separate directions: religious and academic. In fact, while Buddhist individuals, groups, or organizations attempt to adapt to global capitalism, on the one hand, and while Buddhism is regarded through economic lenses, on the other hand, Buddhist political attitudes are ambiguously highly critical of global capitalism. To quote only one example here, the famous Buddhist leader Sulak Sivaraksa (2005, 41) asserted that:

> In the contemporary world, the quest for greater profit ultimately determines the actions of the rich and powerful, taking precedence over other motives. As such, any top-down attempt to redress class or ecological problems is likely to fail; at best it will only be a palliative. The teachings of the Buddha however state that the rich and powerful, especially the rulers, must have only overriding concern, that of upholding the law of dhamma.

How representative is this sentiment, however? I argue that this position is far from isolated—quite the reverse. Which "Buddhist voice" is expressed, then? What kind of economy is it targeting? Indeed, the image of capitalism as immoral, corrupt, and unmoved by ethical values and respect for human beings is widespread. If this is true, to a certain extent, then the modern global economy is also turning (slightly) more "humanistic." It is witnessing a relocation of moral, cultural, and religious issues at the very heart of productive organizations within the broader context of a massive ideological charge against the expansive and hegemonic neoliberal economic and economic program (Banks 2006). Additionally, it is obvious that there is neither such a thing as a single discourse nor a single Buddhist "attitude" toward economy. On the contrary, there are obviously a wide range of Buddhist traditions interacting with different facets of economic systems and processes, and they adopt somewhat different reactions, torn between the opposite poles of conservatism and progressivism (Pryor 1990). Following Daniels (2005), we can even prolong the relativist deconstruction of the economy and Buddhism every so often as essentialist concepts and models and suggest that these "Buddhist voices" against economy only express *a certain idea of Buddhism,* on a *certain idea of what mainstream economy* is supposed to be.

Applications and Uses

If we maintain the discussion within the constricted scope of theoretical relevance or irrelevance of economic approaches to Buddhism, the debate seems obviously limited to an abstract discussion, and we miss the point of possible applications. Several models do indeed cast a new light on the relationships between Buddhism and capitalism, as well as between Buddhism and consumer culture, whose effects on religious behavior have been recorded worldwide. This exposes the reflection to stimulating new fields. First and foremost is the understanding of Buddhism as a "commodity" in the global open economy of religions, and this work in progress partakes in a renewal of the sociology of the religious mobility of ideas, beliefs, and practices. It is true that, in many places, Asian religious practices are directly engaged in the global economy; for instance, meditation practices are "marketized" and "advertised" in the connection between local and global economies.

A second but equally important line of development is the approach of the Buddhist groups as "enterprises" advertising their "products" in a competitive market. Although this is also an innovation, the field of the sociology of religious institutions has long been more inclined to focus on the logics of organized diffusion and conversion. Third, a crucial point in the debate are the "consumers" of Buddhism in a market of spiritual commodities. These consumers have been labeled under different categories, in particular as dharma shoppers (who are also dharma hoppers), as described by Thomas Tweed (1999). This perspective improves the previous approaches by adding to these the sociology of actors. Finally, a last conceptual line calls attention to the sociology of forms or systems, and Buddhism can be seen as a kind of "spiritual capitalism," since it relies upon the accumulation of symbolic capital for rebirth or salvation. Moreover, this inner rationality might be a key (but not the only one) to understanding the success of a supposed "outer-worldly" tradition in the context of economic globalization (Obadia 2011).

From Academic Circles to Society?

These discussions are grounded on empirical evidence, even if they sometimes reach the level of pure abstraction. The ethereal plane of academic circles and the material life of temples, however, are not the only spheres where economic and religious realities encounter and interact. They are also embodied in aspects that are more down to earth, including lay practices relative to the engagement of Buddhism and Buddhists in contemporary economic life and the militant practices and underlying political program, that is, a Buddhist reformation of the economy, in part or in totality. Ernest Schumacher's *Small Is Beautiful* (1973) was a first conceptual attempt to apply Buddhist principles to the (market and industrial) economy with the aim of injecting more humanist values into an already highly criticized materialistic and instrumental capitalist economy. Four decades later, Schumacher's project is still a work in progress and an ambivalent program governed by the opposite posture of a firm rejection of the global economy. In parallel, however, Buddhist groups, institutions, and individuals have massively aligned on the logics of global economy (and benefit from it). Peter L. Daniels (2005, 246) is right to mention that "the notion of 'Buddhist' economics appears as a profound oxymoron." Yet, despite obvious intellectual resistance against the extension of Buddhism as an effective implement *for a* modern economy, and although it is positioned as more or less radically opposed *against* the values of the same economic system, Buddhist ideas and practices have quickly been integrated in the global market economy. Buddhist meditation techniques and ethics have been integrated in the workplace (Goldman Schuyler 2016) and have brought about new conceptions of "humanistic economy," even if they did not actually reach the degree of influence or bring about the ethical revolution they were supposed to. The impact of Buddhism on the modern economy cannot be something other than constrained to specific locations of this system. Johansen and Gopalakrishna (2006, 342) stipulate that "demands of the modern world may make it almost impossible to totally embrace the precepts [of Buddhism]; however, one should make choices that move toward compassion and the reduction of suffering."

Selling in Buddhism, Selling Buddhism

These reflections finally bring the recently framed conceptual slogan "selling Buddhism" to the front of the theoretical agenda, against the background of a wider discussion on the marketization of religion or spirituality, which is more adapted in the case of Buddhism (Carrette and King 2005). But a distinction must be made between two expressions almost similar in form but rather different in content. I call the first distinction "selling *in* Buddhism." It is frequently found in Buddhism, along with other religions, that the problem with antisocial feelings ("poisons") is that they are produced by cravings, such as excessive attraction to money, which is considered a source of impurity. Nonetheless, Buddhist organizations have always been in need of markets and have sometimes even ruled their own markets. This is a fairly different viewpoint offered by the analogical model of "selling Buddhism," treating Buddhism as something that is produced, promoted, and distributed like a commodity. Nowadays, "selling" is a label commonly used in religious studies regardless of the tradition and the context. The slogan "selling Buddhism" is also balanced by the corresponding catchword "consuming Buddhism," referring to the process of absorbing Buddhist ideas, symbols, and practices as if they were commodities (like hamburgers, for instance) (Obadia 2011). Yet again, whatever relevance the analogy brings, these models are limited. Gordon Mathews (2000), whose study on global culture included a chapter on the globalization of Tibetan Buddhism, emphasized the dialectics of truth and value, revisited in the context of the individual appropriation of Buddhist items in "global spiritual supermarkets." This inclination toward an economic design or shaping of religious attitudes and activities is not only a Western, modern habit or trend but also a pattern in Asia, where economic elites also "consume" Buddhism (Kent 2006). The similarity of processes cannot otherwise lead us to conclude that the Asian context of economic and religious modernization is a replication of the Western one (Antlöv 1999). On the other hand, the effects of religious economies in Buddhist Asia offer substantial similarities with what has been defined as "prosperity religions" elsewhere, and especially in South America, where evangelical religious organizations also use economic strategies and circuits and the appeal to wealth to spread and convert (García-Ruiz and Michel 2012). In Asia, the emergence of these new economic patterns and dynamics in the religious sphere entailed a disjunction in traditional relationships between politics and state. Nonetheless, the state, in modern China for instance, can still affect new trends or tendencies in a monastic economy grounded on a cultural capital and reframe the relations between religion, economy, and the state (Ji and Liddell 2004). Peter Jackson has also pointed out that in modern Asia, domestic economies have undertaken significant changes, in which both prosperity religions and economies of the occult have flourished. In Jackson's view, the marketization of spirituality is associated with religious populism as an expression of popular religion, which is mainly oriented toward worldly affairs. He also underscores that in Asia, like elsewhere, the existence of a market of religion and the presence of religion in the marketplace illustrate a highly criticized process of commodification of religion. For Jackson, though, "the current controversies about commercialized Buddha emerge from nothing more than scattered perceptions and unsystematic anecdotes, not from actual figures of rate growth (or more recently of contraction) in the religious sector of economy" (1999b, 257). Jackson is keen to pinpoint that the impact of global capitalism is not only on established, normative, and ascetic Buddhism but that it also has an effect on more popular and spiritual Buddhism or Buddhist supernaturalism in the context of commodification of individuals, the worship of charismatic masters, and the selling and buying of amulets and all the other objects related to devotion in Buddhist Asian popular culture. Jackson (1999b) notes that this pattern of economic and symbolic accumulation facilitates the economic and religious nexus and their reciprocal integration.

Epistemological and Ideological Issues

The continuous and parallel reference to economy *in* and economics *of* religion in the study of Buddhism is calling, at this point, for rigorous epistemological expertise. Indeed, this dichotomy resembles another famous dichotomy: the map and the territory. Indeed, what are we discussing when looking at economies, realities or models of realities? There is no unequivocal response. A simple solution resides in terminological choices: *economy* refers to real production and exchange of wealth, whereas *economics* stands for conceptual representations of realities. Further problems arise when reflections touch upon the background of economic models of religion, which have been framed after North American experiences (Iannaccone 1998). To what extent are they relevant outside the Christian United States and secular Europe and instead to nonmonotheistic systems and non-Western cultural conditions in Asia? These models are far from being free of cultural concretions. Some scholars, like Stephen R. Warner (1993), judge that the paradigm of secularization is going out of fashion and leaves room for the rising paradigm of religious economics, regardless of any cultural background. Obviously, and on purely theoretical grounds, the former has not been replaced by the latter, and referring to one rather than the other is a matter of personal choice and of surrounding conditions. Micklethwait and Wooldridge (2009) have pointed at the difference between an economic-oriented viewpoint on religious behaviors and dynamics (relating to the American experience) and a politically oriented standpoint (the European experience). Furthermore, the issue is far from neutral or free from criticism. The adoption of this new perspective on religious behavior, that is, their qualification as "economic," is also rooted in a highly criticized global consumer culture. Hannah Arendt (1983) is among the first Western scholars to deplore the marketization of culture in the mid-twentieth century. Half a century later, critics point to a reversed process, the sacralization of the market (Dufour 2012) and, in the latticework, the idea that we live in a world dominated by a purely instrumental relationship to the sacred (Bruckner 2002). In the context of an expansive capitalist economy, the American anthropologist Thomas Csordas (2009) accuses scholars of believing that everything can be interpreted in economic terms, even if the topic is not related at all to economic issues. In the context of highly modern societies, the historian Eric Hobsbawm (2000) prophesized that "the idolatry of the market will not last," for political and historical reasons. As for Buddhism, it is officially and allegedly promoting values in contrast to global capitalism (such as fairness and economic and social equality), but it is spreading thanks to those very same global forces, opposing humanistic values to economic values—a contradiction in both logic and ideals.

Beyond the expected critics, this rather new focus on economics is an opportunity to recast a light on unknown aspects of the monastic economy itself (Ji and Liddell 2004; Walsh 2007).[1] Under such conditions, what is the degree of dependence on the surrounding conditions? Has Buddhism really turned into an "economic" religion? Buddhism seems to adapt to the deep impact of consumer culture: meditation is being advertised, which certainly makes Buddhism directly "connected with consumerism and the business of tourism" (Schedneck 2014, 107). This commodification can be the hallmark of the expanding modern global capitalism, but it can also be regarded as the prolongation of ancient forms of trade in objects and amulets (Tambiah 1984). Are "Buddhism-to-economy" relationships characterized by continuity or rupture, then? Considering that the issue is still being discussed, it is difficult to answer this question.

Similarly, and furthermore, is the "economic turn" mainly a change of theoretical focus or the result of changing empirical realities under global conditions (Obadia 2017)? In his book *Authentic Fakes,* David Chidester (2005) discussed the rise of a genuine hybridization of popular (American) consumer culture and new religiosities and illustrated his views with the emerging religiosities explicitly sanctifying money. This optimistic stance is counterbalanced by James Taylor's (2007) much more critical idea of simulacra and consumer culture in Dhammakaya's modern Thailand. Additionally, Chidester locates these processes in the wider context of recent waves of globalization. However, retrospectively, "clientelism" (in performative exchanges) already existed in orthodox monasticism and supernaturalism in Buddhism. One can wonder to what extent Buddhism is instrumental—or always has been—but in a new form. Benjamin Wood (2013, 41) recalls that there is nothing new in the relationships between religious/ascetic (monastic) life and economic matters—quite the reverse. It is commonly accepted that monks were formally engaged in an economic life with "products and donations, paying at fees and wages in either currency and goods, or setting up and contributing to trust funds."

All these reflections raise one question, *en passant,* which is not apparently directly linked to the issue of Buddhist studies. Modern religious traditions, including Buddhist ones, seem to feel "compelled" to adapt to the dynamics and logics of neoliberal values and models. How deeply are religions affected by the global "new spirit of capitalism" (Boltanski and Chiapello 2005), considering that, far beyond Buddhist traditions, many other religions are jumping on the train of rejecting consumerism but are aligning on marketization processes? Pointing at Buddhists "selling Buddhism" denotes the existence of a spirit of entrepreneurship, which nowadays is widespread, especially in expansive missionary movements like Pentecostalism, the Protestant global movement. This example might suggest the need to recall and revisit Obeyesekere and Gombrich's "Protestant Buddhism" (from an orthodox institution to an "evangelical" one [Berger 1997]) under the influence of more economically rather than politically driven forces.

After this rather general overview of the paths taken and remaining to be taken in the economics of religion, one last question must be addressed within the economics of religion in general and for the application to the field of Buddhist studies in particular: is this a real theoretical and methodological "revolution," or is it only being referred to more extensively in the social sciences, humanities, and religious studies because it has gained popularity given the background of a globalization of modern capitalism? This "economic turn" might be a fashionable approach made of reversible slogans, abstracted models, and ideological charges against globalization, but it is still a relevant perspective that sheds new light on religious dynamics and behaviors. Engaging in the debate means taking into account the difference between *economies* as reality and *economics* as abstractions of realities, two facets of the same discussion. Beyond the "map and territory" issue, other epistemological issues are at stake, such as analogy for an ontology (when models of religious economics highlight the reality of economic changes in religion) or from analogy to ontology (when economic-inspired models of religion influence religions to turn more "economic"). Despite significant advances in theory, the economic paradigm is under fire from critics. As a final conclusion on Buddhism and its "economic turn" (if there is one), crucial questions should be raised on the relevance of economic models in the search for understanding religion. The ontology of phenomena (are religious "things" turning into economic ones?) and the heuristics of concepts, namely, the market, consumption, rationality, and value, are also ideas that need to be looked into. But as Brox and Williams-Oerberg (2017) have demonstrated, economic approaches to Buddhism are not reduced to recent issues in religious commodification or to the economic backgrounds of Buddhist life in Asia or elsewhere. Between what are considered to be "classical" approaches to Buddhism and economy and more fresh and topical issues in the "economics of Buddhism," there is a place for both.

Note

1 To deepen the exploration of the cultural impacts of the Buddhist economy of merit and fortune on religion, see Lewis (1993) and da Col (2007), and for the impact of the monastic economy on society, see Gernet (1956) and Wood (2013). Conversely, for the adaptive strategies of "commodification" of Buddhism in the context of mass tourism and the market economy, especially in the promotion of meditation targeting a foreign audience, see Scott (2009) and Schedneck (2014).

Works Cited

5000s.org. 2015. "5 Disrespectful International Cases." http://www.5000s.org/campaign/index/id/1. Accessed on June 4, 2015.

5000s.org. "Why." http://www.5000s.org/why. Accessed on June 4, 2015.

Abramson, Paul R., and Ronald F. Inglehart. 1995. *Value Change in Global Perspective*. Ann Arbor: University of Michigan Press.

Adams, Vincanne. 1996. "Karaoke as Modern Lhasa, Tibet: Western Encounters with Cultural Politics." *Cultural Anthropology* 11, no. 4: 510–546.

AFP. 2015. "Myanmar Jails Writer for 2 Years for 'Insulting Religion': Lawyer Sentenced after Promoting Religious Freedom." *Express Tribune*. June 2. http://tribune.com.pk/story/896369/myanmar-jails-writer-for-2-years-for-insulting-religion-lawyer/.

Agency for Cultural Affairs. 2017. *Shūkyō nenkan*. Tokyo: Agency for Cultural Affairs. http://www.bunka.go.jp/tokei_hakusho_shuppan/hakusho_nenjihokokusho/shukyo_nenkan/pdf/h29nenkan.pdf. Simplified English version: http://www.bunka.go.jp/english/policy/religious_institutions/index.html.

Ahmed, Sara. 2004a. "Affective Economies." *Social Text* 79, vol. 22, no. 2: 117–139.

——. 2004b. "Collective Feelings: Or, the Impressions Left by Others." *Theory, Culture, and Society* 21, no. 2 (April 2004): 25–42. doi:10.1177/0263276404042133.

Alexandrin, Glen. 1993. "Elements of Buddhist Economics." *International Journal of Social Economics* 20 (2): 3–11.

Almond, Philip C. 1988. *The British Discovery of Buddhism*. Cambridge: Cambridge University Press.

Amstutz, Galen. 2012. "Materiality and Spiritual Economies in Premodern Japanese Buddhism: A Problem in Historical Change." *Journal of Religion in Japan* 1 (2): 142–167.

Andree, Martin. 2010. *Medien machen Marken—Eine Medientheorie des Marketing und des Konsums*. Frankfurt: Campus.

Antlöv, Hans. 1999. "The New Rich and Cultural Tensions in Rural Indonesia." In *Culture and Privilege in Capitalist Asia*, edited by Michael Pinches, 189–208. London: Routledge.

Appadurai, Arjun. 1990. "Disjuncture and Difference in the Global Cultural Economy." *Theory, Culture, and Society* 7: 295–310.

Arat, Alp. 2017. "What It Means to Be Truly Human: The Postsecular Hack of Mindfulness." *Social Compass* 64, no. 2: 167–179.

Arendt, Hannah. 1983. *La condition de l'homme moderne*. Paris: Éditions du Seuil.

Ariyaratne, A. T. 1999. *Buddhist Economics in Practice in the Sarvodaya Shramadana Movement of Sri Lanka*. New York: Sarvodaya Support Group.

Arvidsson, Adam. 2006. *Brands: Meaning and Value in Media Culture*. London: Routledge.

Asad, Talal. 2003. *Formations of the Secular: Christianity, Islam, and Modernity*. Stanford, CA: Stanford University Press.

Asayama Taichi. 2017. *Uchigawa kara miru Sōka gakkai to Kōmeitō*. Tokyo: Discover Twenty-One.

Astley, Trevor. 1995. "The Transformation of a Recent Japanese New Religion: Ōkawa Ryūhō and Kōfuku no Kagaku." *Japanese Journal of Religious Studies* 22, nos. 3–4: 343–380.

Atkin, Douglas. 2004. *The Culting of Brands: Turn Your Customers into True Believers*. New York: Portfolio.

Badiner, Aallan Hunt, ed. 2002. *Mindfulness in the Marketplace: Compassionate Response to Consumerism*. Berkeley, CA: Parallax.

Baffelli, Erica. 2011. "Charismatic Blogger? Authority and New Religions on the Web 2.0." In *Japanese Religions on the Internet: Innovation, Representation and Authority*, edited by Erica Baffelli, Ian Reader, and Birgit Staemmler, 118–135. New York: Routledge.

Bailey, Greg, and Ian Mabbett. 2003. *The Sociology of Early Buddhism*. Cambridge: Cambridge University Press.

Banks, Mark. 2006. "Moral Economy and Cultural Work." *Sociology* 40, no. 3: 455–472.

Bao, Jiemen. 2005. "Merit-Making Capitalism: Re-territorializing Thai Buddhism in Silicon Valley, California." *Journal of Asian American Studies* 8, no. 2: 115–142.

Barnett, Robert. 2001. "Violated Specialness: Western Political Representations of Tibet." In *Imagining Tibet: Perceptions, Projections, and Fantasies*, edited by Thierry Dodin and Heinz Räther, 269–316. Boston: Wisdom Publications.

——. 2006. "Beyond the Collaborator-Martyr Model: Strategies of Compliance, Opportunism, and Opposition within Tibet." In *Contemporary Tibet: Politics, Development, and Society in a Disputed Region*, edited by B. Sautman and J. T. Dreyer, 25–66. Armonk, NY: M. E. Sharpe.

Barnett, Robert, and Ronald Schwartz, eds. 2008. *Tibetan Modernities: Notes from the Field on Cultural and Social Change*. Leiden: Brill.

Baumann, Martin. 1995. "Creating a European Path to Nirvana: Historical and Contemporary Developments of Buddhism in Europe." *Journal of Contemporary Religion* 10, no. 1: 55–70.

——. 1997. "The Dharma Has Come West: A Survey of Recent Studies and Sources." *Critical Review of Books in Religion* 10: 1–14.

BBC. 1999. "Anger over Murdoch's Tibet comments." BBC. September 7, 1999. http://news.bbc.co.uk/1/hi/world/asia-pacific/440899.stm.

——. 2014. "Sri Lanka to Deport Buddha Tattoo British Woman." BBC. April 22, 2014. http://www.bbc.com/news/world-asia-27107857.

Beck, Ulrich. 2002. "Sociology in the Second Age of Modernity." In *Conceiving Cosmopolitanism: Theory, Context, and Practice*, edited by Steven Vertovec and Robin Cohen, 61–85. Oxford: Oxford University Press.

Benavides, Gustavo. 2004. "Economics." In *Encyclopedia of Buddhism*, edited by Robert E. Buswell Jr., 1:243–246. New York: Macmillan Reference USA.

——. 2005. "Economy." In *Critical Terms for the Study of Buddhism*, edited by Donald S. Lopez Jr., 77–102. Chicago: University of Chicago Press.

Berger, Peter. 1997. "Four Faces of Global Culture." *National Interest*, Fall 1997, 23–29.

——. 2012. "Further Thoughts on Religion and Modernity." *Society* 49, no. 4: 313–316.

Berlant, Lauren Gail. 2011. *Cruel Optimism*. Durham, NC: Duke University Press.

Blackman, Lisa. 2012. *Immaterial Bodies: Affect, Embodiment, Mediation*. London: Sage.

Boltanski, Luc, and Eve Chiapello. 2005. *The New Spirit of Capitalism*. London: Verso.

Borchert, Thomas. 2005. "Of Temples and Tourists: The Effects of the Tourist Political Economy on a Minority Buddhist Community in Southwest China." In *State, Market, and Religions in Chinese Socieites*, edited by Yang Fenggang and Joseph B. Tamney, 87–111. Leiden: Brill.

Borup, Jørn. 2004. "Zen and the Art of Inverting Orientalism: Buddhisms, Religious Studies, and Interrelated Networks." In *New Approaches to the Study of Religion,* vol. 1: *Regional, Critical, and Historical Approaches,* edited by Peter Antes, Armin W. Geertz, and Randi R. Warne, 451–487. Berlin: Walter de Gruyter.

——. 2015. "Who Are These Buddhists and How Many of Them Are There? Theoretical and Methodological Challenges in Counting Immigrant Buddhists: A Danish Case Study." *Journal of Contemporary Religion* 31, no. 1: 85–100.

——. 2016a. "Branding Buddha: Mediatized and Commodified Buddhism as Cultural Narrative." *Journal of Global Buddhism* 17: 41–55.

——. 2016b. "Mindfulness as a Booming, Diverse, and (Non-)Religious Phenomenon: Mapping and Analyzing Mindfulness in the City of Aarhus." *Religion i Danmark* 7, no. 2: 1–16.

——. 2016c. "Propagation, Accommodation, and Negotiating Social Capital: Jodo Shinshu Responses to Contemporary Crises." *Japanese Religions* 40, nos. 1–2 (Spring and Fall): 85–107.

——. 2018. "Prosperous Buddhism, Prosperity Buddhism, and Religious Capital." *Numen* 65, nos. 2–3: 256–288.

——. 2019. "Spiritual Capital and Religious Evolution. Buddhist Values and Transactions in Historical and Contemporary Perspective." *Journal of Global Buddhism* 20, special issue: "Theoretical and Conceptual Approaches to the Burgeoning Field of Buddhism and Economics" edited by Elizabeth Williams-Oerberg and Trine Brox, 49–68.

Borup, Jørn, et al. 2015. "Mindfulness i Aarhus. En Kortlægning." Center for Contemporary Religion (CSR), Aarhus. http://samtidsreligion.au.dk/oevrige-projekter/mindfulness-i-aarhus/.

Bovbjerg, Kirsten M., Jakob Krause-Jensen, Susan Wright, Grethe Brorholt, and Leif Moos. 2011. "Nye Ledelsesrationaler i Offentlige Organisationer." In *Motivation og Mismod: Det Nye Arbejdslivs Dilemmaer,* edited by K. M. Bovbjerg, 17–42. Copenhagen: Aarhus Universitetsforlag.

Bowler, Kate. 2013. *Blessed: A History of the American Prosperity Gospel.* Oxford: Oxford University Press.

Bowman, Marion. 2013. "Valuing Spirituality: Commodification, Consumption, and Community in Glastonbury." In *Religion in Consumer Society: Brands, Consumers, and Markets,* edited by François Gauthier and Tuomas Martikainen, 207–224. Farnham: Ashgate.

Brox, Trine. 2019. "The Aura of Buddhist Material Objects in the Age of Mass-Production." *Journal of Global Buddhism* 20: 105–125.

Brox, Trine, and Elizabeth Williams-Oerberg. 2017. "Buddhism, Business, and Economics." In *The Oxford Handbook of Contemporary Buddhism,* edited by Michael Jerryson, 504–517. Oxford: Oxford University Press.

Bruckner, Pascal. 2002. *Misère de la prospérité: la religion marchande et ses ennemis.* Paris: Grasset.

Bubandt, Nils, and Martijn van Beek. 2012. "Varieties of Secularism—in Asia and in Theory." In *Varieties of Secularism in Asia: Anthropological Explorations of Religion, Politics, and the Spiritual,* edited by Nils Bubandt and Martijn van Beek, 1–27. London: Routledge.

Bubna-Litic, David. 2000. "Buddhism Returns to the Market-Place." In *Contemporary Buddhist Ethics,* edited by Damien Keown, 183–212. Richmond: Curzon.

BuddhaSutra.com. "Sutra of the Past Vows of Earth Store Bodhisattva." http://www.buddhasutra.com/files/ksitigarbha_sutra.htm.

Caple, Jane. 2015. "Faith, Generosity, Knowledge, and the Buddhist Gift: Moral Discourses on Chinese Patronage of Tibetan Buddhist Monasteries." *Religion Compass* 9: 462–482. https://doi.org/10.1111/rec3.12181.

——. 2017. "The Ethics of Collective Sponsorship: Virtuous Action and Obligation in Contemporary Tibet." *Religion and Society* 8: 145–157. https://doi.org/10.3167/arrs.2017.080109.

——. 2019. *Morality and Monastic Revival in Post-Mao Tibet.* Honolulu: University of Hawai'i Press.

Caring-Lobel, Alex. 2016. "Corporate Mindfulness and the Pathologization of Workplace Stress." In *Handbook of Mindfulness,* edited by Ronald E. Purser, David Forbes, and Adam Burke, 195–215. Cham: Springer.

Carlson, Matthew. 2014. "Kōmeitō, Sōka Gakkai, and Money in Japanese Politics." In *Kōmeitō: Politics and Religion in Japan,* edited by George Ehrhardt, Axel Klein, Levi McLaughlin, and Steven R. Reed, 163–186. Berkeley: University of California Press.

Carrette, Jeremy, and Richard King. 2005. *Selling Spirituality: The Silent Takeover of Religion.* London: Routledge.

Casanova, José. 2006. "Secularization Revisited: A Reply to Talal Asad." In *Powers of the Secular Modern: Talal Asad and His Interlocuters,* edited by David Scott and Charles Hirschkind, 12–30. Stanford, CA: Stanford University Press.

Castells, Manuel. 2000. *The Information Age: Economy, Society, and Culture.* 2nd ed. Malden: Blackwell.

Cederström, Carl, and André Spicer. 2015. *The Wellness Syndrome.* Malden: Polity.

Ceremony Japan. http://ceremonyjapan.jp/en/.

Chandler, Daniel, and Rod Munday. 2011. *A Dictionary of Media and Communication.* Oxford University Press.

Chapman, David. 2015. "'Ethics' Is Advertising." *David Chapman at Wordpress* (blog). https://vividness.live/2015/10/05/buddhist-ethics-is-advertising/.

Chaskalson, Michael. 2011. *The Mindful Workplace: Developing Resilient Individuals and Resonant Organizations with MBSR.* Somerset: Wiley.

Chidester, David. 2005. *Authentic Fakes: Religion and American Popular Culture.* Berkeley: University of California Press.

Chiesa, Alberto. 2013. "The Difficulty of Defining Mindfulness: Current Thought and Critical Issues." *Mindfulness* 4, no. 3: 255–268.

Clarke, Graham E. 1989. "Merit (bsod-nams), Virtue (dge-ba), Blessing (byin-rlabs), and Material Prosperity (rten-'brel) in Popular Thought." *Acta Orientalia Academiae Scientiarum Hungaricae* 43 (2–3): 223–242.

Collins, Randall. 1997. "An Asian Route to Capitalism: Religious Economy and the Origins of Self-Transforming Growth in Japan." *American Sociological Review* 62, no. 6: 843–865.

Collins, Steven. 2014. "Reflections on the Dichotomy *Rūpakāya/Dhammakāya.*" *Contemporary Buddhism* 15, no. 2: 259–273.

Cook, Joanna. 2016. "Mindful in Westminster. The Politics of Meditation and the Limits of Neoliberal Critique." *Hau: Journal of Ethnographic Theory* 6, no. 1: 141–161.

——. 2017. "'Mind the Gap': Appearance and Reality in Mindfulness-Based Cognitive Therapy." In *Meditation, Buddhism, and Science,* edited by David McMahan and Erik Braun, 114–132. Oxford: Oxford University Press.

Covell, Stephen G. 2005. *Japanese Temple Buddhism: Worldliness in a Religion of Renunciation.* Honolulu: University of Hawai'i Press.

——. 2012. "Money and the Temple: Law, Taxes, and the Image of Buddhism." In *Handbook of Contemporary Japanese Religions,* edited by Inken Prohl and John Nelson, 159–176. Leiden: Brill.

Crispin, Shawn W. 2003. "Money and Monks." *Far Eastern Economic Review* 166, no. 42: 54–56.

Crosby, Kate. 1999. "Blasphemie und Sakrileg im Buddhismus in Geschichte und Gegenwart mit besonderer Berücksichtigung des Verses *Bodhicarayāvatāra* 6.64."

In *Buddhismus in Geschichte und Gegenwart Band III Śāntidevas "Eintritt in das Leben zur Erleuchtung,"* 207–227. Hamburg: Universität Hamburg.

Csordas, Thomas. 2009. "Modalities of Transnational Transcendence." In *Transnational Transcendence: Essays on Religion and Globalization,* edited by Thomas Csordas, 1–29. Berkeley: University of California Press.

da Col, Giovanni. 2007. "The View from Somewhen: Events, Bodies, and the Perspective of Fortune around Khawa Karpo, a Tibetan Sacred Mountain in Yunnan Province." *Inner Asia* 9, no. 2: 215–235.

——. 2012. "The Elementary Economies of Dechenwa Life." *Social Analysis* 56, no. 1: 74–98. https://doi.org/10.3167/sa.2012.560106.

Daniels, Peter L. 2005. "Economic Systems and the Buddhist World View: The Twenty-First Century Nexus." *Journal of Socio-Economics* 34, no. 2: 245–268.

Dawson, Andrew. 2013. "Entangled Modernity and Commodified Religion: Alternative Spirituality and the 'New Middle Class.'" In *Religion in Consumer Society,* edited by Francois Gauthier and Tuomas Martikainen, 127–142. London: Ashgate.

Deal, William E., and Brian Ruppert. 2015. *A Cultural History of Japanese Buddhism.* New York: John Wiley & Sons.

Dhondup, Yangdon, Ulrich Pagel, and Geoffrey Samuel, eds. 2013. *Monastic and Lay Traditions in North-Eastern Tibet.* Leiden: Brill.

Digance, Justine. 2006. "Religious and Secular Pilgrimage." In *Tourism, Religion, and Spiritual Journeys,* edited by Dallen J. Timothy and Daniel H. Olsen, 36–48. New York: Routledge.

Dobbelaere, Karel. 2001. *Soka Gakkai—From Lay Movement to Religion.* Salt Lake City, UT: Signature.

Dodin, Thierry, and Heinz Räther, eds. 2001. *Imagining Tibet: Perceptions, Projections, and Fantasies.* Boston: Wisdom Publications.

Dorzhi. 2016a. "Buddhist Wisdom and Corporate Management." http://people.tibetcul.com/mrzf/201601/37351.html. Accessed on July 13, 2017.

——. 2016b. "How to Invoke Yellow Dzambhala [wealth god] for Wealth." http://rufodao.qq.com/a/20160906/041296.htm.

Douglas, Mary, and Baron Isherwood. 1979. *The World of Goods: Towards an Anthropology of Consumption.* London: Allen Lane.

Drinck, Barbara, and Eva Kreienkamp. 2006. "Reactions to the Gender and Queer Perspective: Market Research Is Empowered by Accepting Gender and Sexual Orientation as Consumer Categories." In *Gender and Consumer Behavior,* edited by Lorna Stevens and Janet Borgerson, 8:83–93. Edinburgh: Association for Consumer Research.

Dufour, Dany-Robert. 2012. *Le divin marché: la révolution culturelle libérale.* Paris: Gallimard/Folio.

Durkheim, Emile. 1915. *The Elementary Forms of the Religious Life.* New York: Free Press.

Ehrhardt, George, Axel Klein, Levi McLaughlin, and Steven R. Reed, eds. 2014. *Kōmeitō: Politics and Religion in Japan.* Institute of East Asian Studies, University of California, Berkeley.

Ehrlich, Richard S. 2012. "Thailand Tourists, Disney Asked to Show Buddha Some Respect." CNN, July 9. http://travel.cnn.com/bangkok/visit/bangkok-tourists-disney-asked-show-buddha-some-respect-290393.

Einstein, Mara. 2017. *Advertising. What Everyone Needs to Know.* New York: Oxford University Press.

Eklöf, Jenny. 2016. "Saving the World: Personalized Communication of Mindfulness Neuroscience." In *Handbook of Mindfulness,* edited by Ronald E. Purser, David Forbes, and Adam Burke, 323–335. Cham: Springer.

Elsass, Peter, and Karma Lhundup. 2011. *Buddhas Veje.* Copenhagen: Dansk Psykologisk Forlag.

Elwes, R. H. trans. 1900. *The Ethics* [of Spinoza]. In *The Rationalists: Descartes, Spinoza, Leibniz.* New York: Anchor.

Emling, Sebastian, and Katja Rakow. 2014. *Moderne religiöse Erlebniswelten in den USA: "Have Fun and Prepare to Believe!"* Transformierte Religionen. Berlin: Dietrich Reimer Verlag.

Featherstone, Mike. 1991. *Consumer Culture and Postmodernism.* London: Sage.

Ferrier, Morwenna. 2017. "Buddha Branding Is Everywhere—but What Do Buddhists Think?" *Guardian,* January 8. https://www.theguardian.com/lifeandstyle/shortcuts/2017/jan/08/buddha-branding-buddhists-religion-philosophy-year-anxious.

Fischer, Andrew M. 2008. "The Muslim Cook, the Tibetan Client, His Lama, and Their Boycott: Modern Religious Discourses of Anti-Muslim Economic Activism in Amdo." In *Conflict and Social Order in Tibet and Inner Asia,* edited by Fernanda Pirie and Toni Huber, 159–192. Leiden: Brill.

Fjorbacke, Lone. 2016. "5 grunde til at vi skal træne vores mentale sundhed." *Politiken,* August 2. https://politiken.dk/debat/art5631845/5-grunde-til-at-vi-skal-tr%C3%A6ne-vores-mentale-sundhed.

Foxeus, Niklas. 2017. "Possessed for Success: Prosperity Buddhism and the Cult of the Guardians of the Treasure Trove in Upper Burma." *Contemporary Buddhism* 18, no. 1: 108–139. doi:10.1080/14639947.2017.1301033.

Frechette, Ann. 2002. *Tibetans in Nepal: The Dynamics of International Assistance among a Community in Exile.* Oxford: Berghahn.

Friedman, Milton. 1970. "The Social Responsibility of Business Is to Increase Its Profits." *New York Times Magazine.* September 13. http://umich.edu/~thecore/doc/Friedman.pdf.

Fuller, Paul. 2016. "The Idea of 'Blasphemy' in the Pali Canon and Modern Myanmar." *Journal of Religion and Violence* 4, no. 2: 159–181.

García Ruiz, Jesus, and Patrick Michel. 2012. *Et Dieu sous-traita le salut au marché.* Paris: Armand Colin.

Gauthier, Francois, Linda Woodhead, and Tuomas Martikainen. 2013. "Introduction: Consumerism as the Ethos of Consumer Society." In *Religion in Consumer Society: Brands, Consumers, and Markets,* edited by Francois Gauthier and Tuomas Martikainen, 1–26. Surrey: Ashgate.

Gayley, Holly. 2017. "The Compassionate Treatment of Animals: A Contemporary Buddhist Approach in Eastern Tibet." *Journal of Religious Ethics* 45, no. 1: 29–57.

Gekken Jūshoku. 2017 (February). *Shūkyō yosan no wakaru dentō.*

Germano, David. 1998. "Re-membering the Dismembered Body of Tibet: Contemporary Tibetan Visionary Movements in the People's Republic of China." In *Buddhism in Contemporary Tibet: Religious Revival and Cultural Identity,* edited by Melvyn C. Goldstein and Matthew T. Kapstein, 53–94. Berkeley: University of California Press.

Germano, David, and Nicolas Tournadre. 2003. "THL Simplified Phonetic Transcription of Standard Tibetan." *The Tibetan and Himalayan Library.* https://www.thlib.org/reference/transliteration/#!essay=/thl/phonetics/.

Gernet, Jacques. 1956. *Les aspects économiques du bouddhisme dans la société chinoise du Ve au Xe siècle.* Saigon (Hô Chi Minh-Ville, Vietnman) Publications de l'Ecole Française d'Extrême-Orient.

——. 1995. *Buddhism in Chinese Society: An Economic History from the Fifth to the Tenth Centuries.* New York: Columbia University Press.

Geron, Tomio. 2012. "YY.com: China's Unique Real-Time Voice and Video Service with a Virtual Goods Twist." *Forbes,* June 11. https://www.forbes.com/sites/tomiogeron/2012/06/11/yy-com-chinas-unique-real-time-voice-and-video-service-with-a-virtual-goods-twist.

Giddens, Anthony. 1991. *Modernity and Self-Identity: Self and Society in the Late Modern Age*. Cambridge: Polity.

Gobé, Marc. 2009. *Emotional Branding: The New Paradigm for Connecting Brands to People*. New York: Allworth.

Goldman Schuyler, Katherine. 2016. "Mindfulness as Waking Up: Musings about How to Be Optimally Alive." *Journal of Corporate Citizenship* 62: 59–75.

Goldstein, Melvyn C. 1989. *A History of Modern Tibet, 1913–1951: The Demise of the Lamaist State*. Berkeley: University of California Press.

Goldstein, Melvyn C., and Matthew T. Kapstein, eds. 1998. *Buddhism in Contemporary Tibet: Religious Revival and Cultural Identity*. Berkeley: University of California Press.

Gombrich, Richard, and Gananath Obeyesekere. 1988. *Buddhism Transformed: Religious Change in Sri Lanka*. Princeton, NJ: Princeton University Press.

Good, Darren J., Christopher J. Lyddy, Theresa M. Glomb, Joyce E. Bono, Kirk Warren Brown, Michelle K. Duffy, Ruth A. Baer, Judson A. Brewer, and Sara W. Lazar. 2016. "Contemplating Mindfulness at Work: An Integrative Review." *Journal of Management* 42, no. 1: 114–142.

Goodwin, Janet R. 1994. *Alms and Vagabonds: Buddhist Temples and Popular Patronage in Medieval Japan*. Honolulu: University of Hawai'i Press.

Goossaert, Vincent, and David A. Palmer. 2007. *The Religious Question in Modern China*. Chicago: University of Chicago Press.

Graburn, Nelson H. 2004. "The Kyoto Tax Strike: Buddhism, Shinto, and Tourism in Japan." In *Intersecting Journeys: The Anthropology of Pilgrimage and Tourism*, edited by Ellen Badone and Sharon R. Roseman, 125–139. Urbana: University of Illinois Press.

Grant, John. 2000. *The New Marketing Manifesto: The Twelve Rules for Building Successful Brands in the Twenty-First Century*. London: Texere.

Green, Nile. 2011. *Bombay Islam: The Religious Economy of the West Indian Ocean, 1840–1915*. New York: Cambridge University Press.

Grieve, Gregory Price, and Daniel Veidlinger. 2017. "Buddhism and Media Technologies." In *The Oxford Handbook of Contemporary Buddhism*, edited by Michael Jerryson, 469–486. Oxford: Oxford University Press.

Gutschow, Kim. 2004. *Being a Buddhist Nun: The Struggle for Enlightenment in the Himalayas*. Cambridge, MA: Harvard University Press.

Gyatso, Janet. 2008 [2007]. "One Plus One Makes Three: Buddhist Gender, Monasticism, and the Law of the Non-Excluded Middle." In *Defining Buddhism(s): A Reader*, edited by Karen Derris and Natalie Gummer, 281–205. London: Routledge.

Hallisey, Charles. 1995. "Roads Taken and Not Taken in the Study of Theravada Buddhism." In *Curators of the Buddha*, edited by Donald S. Lopez, 31–61. Chicago: University of Chicago Press.

Hammond, Philip E., and David W. Machacek. 1999. *Soka Gakkai in America: Accommodation and Conversion*. New York: Oxford University Press.

Hanh, Thich Nhat. 2008. "Be Free Where You Are." Talk given at the Maryland Correctional Institute. Published online by ReadHowYouWant. https://www.readhowyouwant.com/books/search/Be%20Free%20Where%20You%20Are.

Hansen, Valerie. 1998. "The Path of Buddhism into China: The View from Turfan." *Asia Major*, third series, 11, no. 2: 37–66.

Hanson, Rick. 2013. *Hardwiring Happiness: The New Brain Science of Contentment, Calm, and Confidence*. New York: Harmony Books.

Happy Science. N.d. "Shoshinkan and Shojas: Main Temples." https://happy-science.org/activities/main-temples/.

——. 2014. *Shōja e ikō*. Tokyo: Happy Science.

——. 2015. *Group Profile 2015*. http://www.happyscience.org.my/images/2015groupprofile.pdf.

Hardacre, Helen. 1984. *Lay Buddhism in Contemporary Japan: Reiyūkai Kyōdan.* Princeton, NH: Princeton University Press.
Harvey, Peter. 2000. "Economic Ethics." In *An Introduction to Buddhist Ethics, Foundations, Values, and Issues,* 187–238. Cambridge: Cambridge University Press.
Heim, Maria. 2004. *Theories of the Gift in South Asia: Hindu, Buddhist, and Jain Reflections on Dāna.* New York: Routledge.
Higuma Takenori. 1971. *Toda Jōsei: Sōka gakkai.* Tokyo: Shinjinbutsu Ōraisha.
Hinnells, John R. 2005. "Why Study Religions?" In *The Routledge Companion to the Study of Religion,* edited by John R. Hinnells, 5–20. New York: Routledge.
Hobsbawm, Eric. 2000. *On the Edge of the New Century: Eric Hobsbawm in Conversation with Antonio Polito.* New York: New Press.
Hochschild, A. Russell. 2012 [1979]. *The Managed Heart: Commercialization of Human Feeling.* Berkeley: University of California Press.
Hoover, Stewart. 2006. *Religion in the Media Age.* London: Routledge.
Horii, Mitsutoshi. 2018. *The Category of "Religion" in Contemporary Japan.* Palgrave Macmillan.
Hsing Yun. 2011. "Prayers for Wealth." Fo Guang Shan Tsunglin University Facebook. https://zh-tw.facebook.com/notes/%E4%BD%9B%E5%85%89%E5%B1%B1%E5%8F%A2%E6%9E%97%E5%AD%B8%E9%99%A2/%E6%98%9F%E9%9B%B2%E5%A4%A7%E5%B8%AB%E6%B1%82%E8%B2%A1%E5%AF%8C%E7%A5%88%E9%A1%98%E6%96%87/10150097506802140/.
Hua, Shiping. 1995. *Scientism and Humanism: Two Cultures in Post-Mao China (1978–1989).* Albany: State University of New York Press.
Hyatt, Susan Brin, Boone W. Shear, and Susan Wright. 2015. *Learning under Neoliberalism: Ethnographies of Governance in Higher Education.* New York: Berghahn.
Iannaccone, Lawrence. 1998. "Introduction to the Economics of Religion." *Journal of Economic Literature* 36, no. 3: 1465–1495.
Illouz, Eva. 2008. *Saving the Modern Soul: Therapy, Emotions, and the Culture of Self-Help.* Berkeley: University of California Press.
——. 2009. "Emotions, Imagination, and Consumption: A New Research Agenda." *Journal of Consumer Culture* 9: 377–413.
Inglehart, Ronald. 1999. "Globalization and Postmodern Values." *Washington Quarterly* 23, no. 1: 215–228.
Irizarry, Joshua A. 2015. "Putting a Price on Zen: The Business of Redefining Religion for Global Consumption." *Journal of Global Buddhism* 16, special issue: "Zen and Popular Culture," edited by Martin Baumann and Cristina Rocha, 51–69.
Ivy, M. 2005. "Modernity." In *Critical Terms for the Study of Buddhism,* edited by D. Lopez Jr., 311–332. Chicago: University of Chicago Press.
Jackson, Peter A. 1999a. "Royal Spirits, Chinese Gods, and Magic Monks: Thailand's Boomtime Religions of Prosperity." *South East Asia Research* 7, no. 3: 245–320.
——. 1999b. "The Enchanting Spirit of Thai Capitalism: The Cult of Luang Phor Khoon and the Post-Modernization of Thai Buddhism." *Southeast Asian Research* 7, no. 1: 5–60.
Jansen, Berthe. 2014. "The Monastery Rules: Buddhist Monastic Organization in Premodern Tibet." PhD diss., University of Leiden.
Japan National Tourism Organization. https://www.seejapan.co.uk.
Jenkins, Stephen. 2016. "Debate, Magic, and Massacre: The High Stakes and Ethical Dynamics of Battling Slanderers of the Dharma in Indian Narrative and Ethical Theory." *Journal of Religion and Violence* 4, no. 2: 129–157.
Jerryson, Michael K. 2007. *Mongolian Buddhism: Rise and Fall of the Sangha.* Chaing Mai: Silkworm.
Ji, Zhe, and Philip Liddell. 2004. "Buddhism and the State: A New Relationship: Increasing Numbers of Believers Bring Great Changes to the Monastic Economy in China." *China Perspectives* 55: 2–10.

Jiqun Fashi. 2010. *Buddhist Perspective of Wealth* [Fojiao de caifu guan]. http://www.jiqun.com/dispdir.php?class=0050#.

Johansen, Barry-Craig and D. Gopalakrishna. 2006. "A Buddhist View of Adult Learning in the Workplace." *Advances in Developing Human Resources* 8, no. 3: 337–345.

Jones, Alison Denton. 2010. "A Modern Religion? The State, the People, and the Remaking of Buddhism in Urban China Today." PhD diss., Department of Sociology, Harvard University.

Kabat-Zinn, Jon. 1994. *Wherever You Go There You Are: Mindfulness Meditation in Everyday Life*. New York: Hyperion.

——. 2005. *Coming to Your Senses: Healing Ourselves and the World through Mindfulness*. New York: Hyperion.

——. 2011. "Some Reflections on the Origins of MBSR, Skillful Means, and the Trouble with Maps." *Contemporary Buddhism: An Interdisciplinary Journal* 12, no. 1: 281–306.

——. 2013. *Full Catastrophe Living: Using the Wisdom of Your Body and Mind to Face Stress, Pain, and Illness*. Rev. ed. New York: Bantam.

Kale, Sudhir. 2004. "Spirituality, Religion, and Globalization." *Journal of Macromarketing* 24, no. 2: 92–107.

Kapstein, Matthew. 2009. "Introduction: Mediations and Margins." In *Buddhism between Tibet and China,* edited by M. Kapstein, 1–20. Boston: Wisdom Publications.

Kelso, Anthony. 2006. "Advertising." In *Encyclopedia of Religion, Communication, and Media,* edited by Daniel A. Stout, 1–5. New York: Routledge.

Kemper, Steven. 1990. "Wealth and Reformation in Sinhalese Buddhist Monasticism." In *Ethics, Wealth, and Salvation: A Study in Buddhist Social Ethics,* edited by Russell F. Sizemore and Donald K. Swearer, 152–169. Columbia: University of South Carolina Press.

Kent, Alexandra. 2006. "Reconfiguring Security: Buddhism and Moral Legitimacy in Cambodia." *Security Dialogue* 37, no. 3: 343–361.

King, Matthew. 2016. "Buddhist Economic: Scales of Value in Global Exchange." Oxford Handbooks Online. http://www.oxfordhandbooks.com/view/10.1093/oxfordhb/9780199935420.001.0001/oxfordhb-9780199935420-e-64.

Kitiarsa, Pattana. 2010. "Buddha-izing a Global City-State: Transnational Religious Mobilities, Spiritual Marketplace, and Thai Migrant Monks in Singapore." *Mobilities* 5, no. 2: 257–275.

Klein, Axel. 2012. "Twice Bitten, Once Shy: Religious Organizations and Politics after the Aum Attack." *Japanese Journal of Religious Studies* 39, no. 1: 77–98.

Knowing Buddha Organization. N.d. "Dos and Don'ts on Buddha." https://www.knowingbuddha.org/dos-and-donts.

——. 2015a. "Inspiring Stories." http://www.knowingbuddha.org/inspiring/. Accessed on June 4, 2015.

——. 2015b. "News Update." http://www.knowingbuddha.org/news/. Accessed on June 4, 2015.

——. 2016. "gōngthapthāmkungphutthakān" [Dharma Army in the middle of the Buddha's era]. February 21. http://www.knowingbuddha.org/#!%E0%B8%81%E0%B8%AD%E0%B8%87%E0%B8%97%E0%B8%B1%E0%B8%9E%E0%B8%98%E0%B8%A3%E0%B8%A3%E0%B8%A1%E0%B8%81%E0%B8%B6%E0%B9%88%E0%B8%87%E0%B8%9E%E0%B8%B8%E0%B8%97%E0%B8%98%E0%B8%81%E0%B8%B2%E0%B8%A5/cjds/56cb16910cf2836ff5d4e9ae.

Koch, Anne. 2016. "Economy." In *The Oxford Handbook of the Study of Religion,* edited by Michael Stausberg and Steven Engler, 355–365. Oxford: Oxford University Press.

Kolm, Serge-Christophe. 1982. *Le bonheur-liberté: bouddhisme profond et modernité*. Paris: PUF.

Kuitert, Wybe. 2002. *Themes in the History of Japanese Garden Art*. Honolulu: University of Hawai'i Press.

Kurtz, Lester R. 2007. *Gods in the Global Village: The World's Religions in Sociological Perspective*. 2nd ed. Thousand Oaks, CA: Pine Forge.

Laird, Pamela Walker. 1998. *Advertising Progress: American Business and the Rise of Consumer Marketing*. Baltimore, MD: John Hopkins University Press.

Lengzhi Duojie. 2014. "Domé Gelukpé göndé riknékyi gyurdokla chepa: Palung [Ch. Hualong] Dzong Ditsa Gönpa zhirzungpa" [mdo smad dge lugs pa'i dgon sde'i rig gnas kyi 'gyur ldog la dpyad pa: dpa' lung rdzong dhi tsha dgon pa gzhir bzung pa]. PhD diss., Xibei Minzu Daxue.

Lennerfors, Thomas Taro. 2015. "A Buddhist Future for Capitalism? Revising Buddhist Economics for the Era of Light Capitalism." *Futures* 68, suppl. C: 67–75. doi:https://doi.org/10.1016/j.futures.2014.09.003.

Levine, Gregory P. A. 2017. "Zen Sells Zen Things: Meditation Supply, Right Livelihood, and Buddhist Retail." In *Zen and Material Culture,* edited by Pamela D. Winfield and Steven Heine, 257–288. New York: Oxford University Press.

Li, Huawei. 2011. "A Critique of the Ecology of Religion." In *Annual of Religious Studies in China,* edited by Cao Zhongjian. Beijing: Religion and Culture Press.

Li, Jin. N.d. "Buried Past and Excavated Hope: Larung and Buddhist Interactions between Tibet and China Today." https://case.edu/affil/tibet/tibetanMonks/documents/Buried_Past_and_Excavated_Hope.pdf.

Li, Xiangping. 2010. "The State Imagination of Religious Beliefs: Critiquing the 'Ecology of Religion' Perspective." *China Ethno-News,* July 27.

Lincoln, Bruce. 2012. "Theses on Comparison." In *Gods and Demons, Priests and Scholars: Critical Explorations in the History of Religions,* 121–130. Chicago: University of Chicago Press.

Lindstrom, Martin. 2010. *Brand Sense: Sensory Secrets behind the Stuff We Buy*. New York: Free Press.

Lorentz, Todd. 2001. "The Dharma and the West: Can Buddhism Survive Consumerism?" *Contemporary Buddhism: An Interdisciplinary Journal* 2, no. 2: 191–199.

Löwy, Michael. 2009. "Capitalism as Religion: Walter Benjamin and Max Weber." *Historical Materialism* 17: 60–73.

Lyer, Sriya. 2015. "The New Economics of Religion." IZA Discussion Paper 9320, August. ftp://repec.iza.org/RePEc/Discussionpaper/dp9320.pdf.

MacKenzie, D. N., trans. 1970. *The "Sūtra of the Causes and Effects of Actions" in Sogdian*. London: Oxford University Press.

Magnuson, Joel. 2016. *From Greed to Wellbeing: A Buddhist Approach to Resolving Our Economic and Financial Crises*. Chicago: Bristol University Press, Policy Press.

Makley, Charlene. 2005. "The Body of a Nun: Nunhood and Gender in Contemporary Amdo." In *Women in Tibet,* edited by Janet Gyatso and Hanna Havnevik, 259–284. New York: Columbia University Press.

——. 2007. *The Violence of Liberation: Gender and Tibetan Buddhist Revival in Post-Mao China*. Berkeley: University of California Press.

Malkki, Lisa. 2015. *The Need to Help: The Domestic Arts of International Humanitarianism*. Durham, NC: Duke University Press.

Martikainen, Tuomas, and Francois Gauthier. 2013. *Religion in the Neoliberal Age: Political Economy and Modes of Governance*. Burlington, VT: Ashgate.

Martin, Craig. 2014. *Capitalizing Religion: Ideology and the Opiate of the Bourgeoisie*. London: Bloomsbury.

Martin, Emily. 2000. "Flexible Survivors." *Cultural Values* 4 (4): 512–517.

——. 2007. *Bipolar Expeditions: Mania and Depression in American Culture*. Princeton, NJ: Princeton University Press.

Mathews, Gordon. 2000. *Global Culture/Individual Identity: Searching for Home in the Cultural Supermarket*. London: Routledge.

Mauss, Marcel. 1990 [1950]. *The Gift: Forms and Functions of Exchange in Archaic Societies*. New York: Norton.
Mazzarella, William. 2009. "Affect: What Is It Good For?" In *Enchantments of Modernity, Empire, Nation, Globalization*, edited by Saurabh Dube, 291–309. London: Routledge.
McKenzie, John S. 2013. "Buddha for Sale! The Commoditization of Tibetan Buddhism in Scotland." In *Religion in Consumer Society: Brands, Consumers, and Markets,* edited by François Gauthier and Tuomas Martikainen, 159–173. Burlington, VT: Ashgate.
McLaughlin, Levi. 2009. "Sōka Gakkai in Japan." PhD. diss., Princeton University.
——. 2012. "Sōka Gakkai in Japan." In *Handbook of Contemporary Japanese Religions,* edited by Inken Prohl and John Nelson, 269–308. Leiden: Brill.
——. 2015. "Komeito's Soka Gakkai Protesters and Supporters: Religious Motivations for Political Activism in Contemporary Japan." *Asia-Pacific Journal* 13, no. 40. http://apjjf.org/-Levi-McLaughlin/4386.
——. 2019. *Soka Gakkai's Human Revolution: The Rise of a Mimetic Nation in Modern Japan*. Honolulu: University of Hawaiʻi Press.
McMahan, David L. 2004. "Modernity and the Early Discourse of Scientific Buddhism." *Journal of the American Academy of Religion* 72, no. 4: 897–933.
——. 2008. *The Making of Buddhist Modernism*. Oxford: Oxford University Press.
McMahan, David, and Erik Braun. 2017. *Meditation, Buddhism, and Science*. Oxford: Oxford University Press.
Meyer, Birgit. 2006. "Religious Sensations: Why Media, Aesthetics, and Power Matter in the Study of Contemporary Religion." Inaugural speech, Universiteit Amsterdam.
Micklethwait, John, and Adrian Wooldridge. 2009. *God Is Back: How the Global Revival of Faith Is Changing the World*. London: Allen Lane.
Miller, Geoffrey. 2009. *Spent: Sex, Evolution, and Consumer Behavior*. New York: Penguin.
Mills, Martin A. 2003. *Identity, Ritual, and State in Tibetan Buddhism: The Foundations of Authority in Geluk Monasticism*. London: RoutledgeCurzon.
Mitchell, Scott. 2012. "Buddhism, Media, and Popular Culture." In *Buddhism in the Modern World,* edited by David McMahan, 305–323. London: Routledge.
Moe, Wai, and Austin Ramzy. 2015. "Myanmar Sentences 3 to Prison for Depicting Buddha Wearing Headphones." *New York Times,* March 17.
Moore, Rick Clifton. 2005. "Spirituality That Sells: Religious Imagery in Magazine Advertising." *Advertising and Society Review* 6, no. 1.
Moran, Peter. 2004. *Buddhism Observed: Travelers, Exiles, and Tibetan Dharma in Kathmandu*. London: RoutledgeCurzon.
Morgan, David, ed. 2008. *Key Words in Religion, Media, and Culture*. New York: Routledge.
——. 2013. "Religion and Media: A Critical Review of Recent Developments." *Critical Research on Religion* 3, no. 1: 347–356.
Muehlebach, Andrea. 2014. *The Moral Neoliberal: Welfare and Citizenship in Italy*. Chicago Studies in Practices of Meaning. Chicago: University of Chicago Press.
Müehlhof, Rainer, and Jan Slaby. 2018. "Immersion at Work: Affect and Power in the Post-Fordist Work Cultures." In *Affect in Relation: Families, Places, Technologies. Essays on Affectivity and Subject Formation in the Twenty-First Century,* edited by Birgitt Röttger-Rössler and Jan Slaby, 155–174. New York: Routledge.
Nelson, John K. 2013. *Experimental Buddhism: Innovation and Activism in Contemporary Japan*. Honolulu: University of Hawaiʻi Press.
Nippon Foundation. N.d. "Iroha Nihon—Experience the Soul of Japan." https://www.nippon-foundation.or.jp/en/what/projects/iroha-nihon.
Nishino Tatsukichi. 1985. *Denki Toda Jōsei*. Tokyo: Daisan Bunmei.

Norberg-Hodge, Helena. 2002. “Buddhism in the Global Economy.” In *Mindfulness in the Marketplace: Compassionate Response to Consumerism,* edited by Allan Hunt Badiner, 15–27. Berkeley: Parallax.

Obadia, Lionel. 2011. “Is Buddhism Like a Hamburger? Buddhism and the Market Economy in a Globalized World.” *Research in Economic Anthropology* 31: 99–120.

——. 2013. *La marchandisation de Dieu: economies religieuses.* Paris: CNRS Editions.

——. 2017. “Marchés, business et consumérisme en religion: vers un «tournant économique» en sciences des religions?” *Mélanges de l’École française de Rome—Italie et Méditerranée modernes et contemporaines* 129, no. 1. http://journals.openedition.org/mefrim/3475.

Obadia, Lionel, and Donald C. Wood. 2011a. “Economics and Religion, Economics in Religion, Economics of Religion: Reopening the Grounds for Anthropology?” *Research in Economic Anthropology* 31, no. 1: xiii–xxxvii.

——, eds. 2011b. *The Economics of Religion: Anthropological Approaches.* Bingley: Emerald.

Obeyesekere, Gananath. 1970. “Religious Symbolism and Political Change in Ceylon.” *Modern Ceylon Studies* 1: 43–63.

Ohnuma, Reiko. 2005. “Gift.” In *Critical Terms for the Study of Buddhism,* edited by Donald S. Lopez, 103–123. Chicago: University of Chicago Press.

——. 2006. *Head, Eyes, Flesh, Blood: Giving Away the Body in Indian Buddhist Literature.* New York: Columbia University Press.

Oldmeadow, Peter. 2001. “Tibetan Buddhism and Globalization.” In *The End of Religion? Religion in an Age of Globalization,* edited by Carole M. Cusack and Peter Oldmeadow, 266–279. Sydney: Department of Studies in Religion, University of Sydney.

Ornatowski, Gregory K. 1996. “Continuity and Change in the Economic Ethics of Buddhism: Evidence from the History of Buddhism in India, China, and Japan.” *Journal of Buddhist Ethics* 3: 198–240.

Ostrowski, Ally. 2006. “Buddha Browsing: American Buddhism and the Internet.” *Contemporary Buddhism* 7, no. 1: 91–103.

Padget, Doug. 2002. “The Translating Temple: Diasporic Buddhism in Florida.” In *Westward Dharma: Buddhism beyond Asia,* edited by Martin Baumann and Charles S. Prebish, 201–217. Berkeley: University of California Press.

Padgett, David M. 2000. “‘Americans Need Something to Sit on,’ or Zen Meditation Materials and Buddhist Diversity in America.” *Journal of Global Buddhism* 1, no. 1: 61–81.

Paine, Jeffrey. 2004. *Re-Enchantment: Tibetan Buddhism Comes to the West.* New York: Norton.

Payutto, Prayudh Aryankura. 1998. *Buddhist Economics: A Middle Way for the Market Place.* Bangkok: Buddhadhamma Foundation.

Pickert, Kate. 2014. “The Mindful Revolution.” *Time* 3: 34–48.

Pitman, Don. 2001. *Toward a Modern Chinese Buddhism: Taixu’s Reforms.* Honolulu: University of Hawai‘i Press.

Plate, S. Brent, ed. 2015. *Key Terms in Material Religion.* New York: Bloomsbury.

Polanyi, Karl. 1944. *The Great Transformation: The Political and Economic Origins of Our Time.* Boston: Beacon.

Powers, John. 1995. *Introduction to Tibetan Buddhism.* Ithaca, NY: Snow Lion.

Prebish, Charles. 1999. “The Academic Study of Buddhism in America: A Silent Sangha.” In *American Buddhism, Methods and Findings in Recent Scholarship,* Curzon Critical Studies in Buddhism, edited by Duncan Ryuken Williams and Christopher S. Queen, 183–214. Richmond: Curzon.

Prebish, Charles S., and Damien Keown. 2010. *Introducing Buddhism.* London: Routledge.

Prohl, Inken. 2009. "In Stein gemeißelte Erleuchtung. Überlegungen zur hermeneutischen Flexibilität des Symbolbegriffs am Beispiel der sogenannten Zen-Gärten in Japan." In *Sprachen ohne Worte,* edited by Thomas Pfeiffer and Stephan Frings, 69–90. Studium Generale. Heidelberg: Universitätsverlag Winter Heidelberg.

——. 2017. "Same Forms, Same Sensations? The Practice of Sitting Still in Traditional Japanese and Contemporary Urban Settings." In *Eastspirit: Transnational Spirituality and Religious Circulation in East and West,* edited by Jørn Borup and Marianne Qvortrup Fibinger, 100–119. Leiden: Brill.

Prohl, Inken, and Katja Rakow. 2008. "Transformationen Buddhistisch Inspirierter Vorstellungen und Praktiken. Eine Empirische Studie im Raum Berlin." *Transformierte Buddhismen* 1, no. 1: 3–27.

Pryor, Frederic L. 1990. "A Buddhist Economic System—in Principle." *American Journal of Economics and Sociology* 49, no. 3: 339–349.

Purser, Ronald E. 2018. "Critical Perspectives on Corporate Mindfulness." *Journal of Management, Spirituality, and Religion* 15, no. 2: 105–108. doi:10.1080/14766086.2018.1438038.

Purser, Ronald E., David Forbes, and Adam Burke, eds. 2016. *Handbook of Mindfulness: Mindfulness in Behavioral Health.* Cham: Springer.

Rambelli, Fabio. 2017. "Materiality, Labor, and Signification of Sacred Objects in Japanese Buddhism." *Journal of Religion in Japan* 6, no. 1: 1–26.

Reader, Ian, and George J. Tanabe Jr. 1998. *Practically Religious: Worldly Benefits and the Common Religion of Japan.* Honolulu: University of Hawai'i Press.

Real Estate Japan. N.d. "What Is the Average Salary in Japan by Occupation and Age?" https://resources.realestate.co.jp/living/average-salary-japan-occupation-age/.

Reynolds, Frank E. 1978. "The Holy Emerald Jewel: Some Aspects of Buddhist Symbolism and Political Legitimation in Thailand and Laos." In *Religion and Legitimation of Power in Thailand, Laos, and Burma,* edited by Bardwell L. Smith, 175–193. Chambersburg: Anima.

Rimke, Heidi Marie. 2000. "Governing Citizens through Self-Help Literature." *Cultural Studies* 14, no. 1: 61–78.

Rindfleisch, Jennifer. 2005. "Consuming the Self: New Age Spirituality as 'Social Product' in Consumer Society." *Consumption, Market, Culture* 8, no. 4: 343–360.

Ritzer, George. 1999. *Enchanting a Disenchanted World: Revolutionizing the Means of Consumption.* Thousand Oaks, CA: Pine Forge.

Robson, James. 2010. "Neither Too Far, nor Too Near: The Historical and Cultural Contexts of Buddhist Monasteries in Medieval China and Japan." In *Buddhist Monasticism in East Asia: Places of Practice,* edited by James A. Benn, Lori Meeks, and James Robson, 1–17. London: Routledge.

Roche, Gerald. 2018. "Does Ideological Clarification Help Language Maintenance? Exploring the Revitalization Paradox through the Case of Manegacha, a Tibetan Minority Language." *Anthropological Linguistics* 60 (4): 1–21.

Rose, Nikolas S. 1996. *Inventing Our Selves: Psychology, Power, and Personhood.* Cambridge: University of Cambridge Press.

Rotman, Andrew. 2009. "Marketing Morality: The Economy of Faith in Early Indian Buddhism." In *Srīnidhih: Professor Shrikant Shankar Bahulkar's Gratitude Volume,* edited by G. B. Shripad, S. Shilpa, and V. K. Ambarish, 253–290. Pune: Samvidya Institute of Cultural Studies.

Rozenberg, Guillame. 2004. "How Giving Sanctifies: The Birthday of Thamanya Hsayadaw in Burma." *Journal of the Royal Anthropological Institute* 10: 495–515. https://doi.org/10.1111/j.1467-9655.2004.00199.x.

Rudnyckyj, Daromir, and Filippo Osella. 2017. *Religion and the Morality of the Market.* Cambridge: Cambridge University Press.

Sa mtsho skyid and Gerald Roche. 2011. "Purity and Fortune in Phug sde Tibetan Village Rituals." *Asian Highlands Perspectives* 10: 231–284.

Sakurai Yoshihide. 2011. "New Religions—Economic Aspects." In *Establishing the Revolutionary,* edited by Birgit Staemmler and Ulrich Dehn. Hamburg: LIT Stalker.

Salamon, Karen L. 2002. "Prophets of a Cultural Capitalism: An Ethnography of Romantic Spiritualism in Business Management." *Folk* 44, no. 4: 89–115.

Samuel, Geoffrey. 1993. *Civilized Shamans: Buddhism in Tibetan Societies*. Washington, DC: Smithsonian Institution Press.

Samuels, Jeffrey. 2010. *Attracting the Heart: Social Relations and the Aesthetics of Emotion in Sri Lankan Monastic Culture*. Honolulu: University of Hawai'i Press.

Sanger, David E. 1989. "Japan Finds Latest Scandal in a Dump." *New York Times,* July 20.

Sangharakshita (D. P. E. Lingwood). 1978. *Buddhism and Blasphemy: Buddhist Reflections on the 1977 Blasphemy Trial*. London: Windhorse.

Sanzhieva, Valeria. 2017. "Prohibit Buddha Bars All over Russia!" *Change.org,* https://www.change.org/p/%D0%B7%D0%B0%D0%BF%D1%80%D0%B5%D1%82%D0%B8%D1%82%D0%B5-%D0%B1%D1%83%D0%B4%D0%B4%D0%B0-%D0%B1%D0%B0%D1%80%D1%8B-%D0%BF%D0%BE-%D0%B2%D1%81%D0%B5%D0%B9-%D1%80%D0%BE%D1%81%D1%81%D0%B8%D0%B8.

Schaefer, Donovan O. 2015. *Religious Affects: Animality, Evolution, and Power*. Durham, NC: Duke University Press.

Schedneck, Brooke. 2014. "Meditation for Tourists in Thailand: Commodifying a Universal and National Symbol." *Journal of Contemporary Religion* 29, no. 3: 439–456.

Scheper-Hughes, Nancy, and M. Lock. 1987. "The Mindful Body: A Prolegomenon to Future Work in Medical Anthropology." *Medical Anthropology Quarterly* 1: 6–41.

Schober, Juliane. 1989. "Paths to Enlightenment: Theravāda Buddhism in Upper Burma." PhD diss., University of Illinois at Urbana-Champaign.

Schofield Clark, Lynn. 2007. "Why Study Popular Culture? Or, How to Build a Case for Your Thesis in a Religious Studies or Theology Department." In *Between Sacred and Profane: Researching Religion and Popular Culture,* edited by Gordon Lynch, 5–33. London: I. B. Tauris.

Schonthal, Benjamin. 2016. "Environments of Law: Islam, Buddhism, and the State in Contemporary Sri Lanka." *Journal of Asian Studies* 75, no. 1 (February): 137–156.

Schopen, Gregory. 1991. "Archaeology and Protestant Presuppositions in the Study of Indian Buddhism." *History of Religions* 31 (1): 1–23.

———. 1999. "The Bones of a Buddha and the Business of a Monk: Conservative Monastic Values in an Early Mahāyāna Polemical Tract." *Journal of Indian Philosophy* 27: 279–324.

———. 2004. *Buddhist Monks and Business Matters: Still More Papers on Monastic Buddhism in India*. Honolulu: University of Hawai'i Press.

Schumacher, Ernest F. 1973. *Small Is Beautiful*. London: Abacus.

Schwartz, Ronald. 1994. *Circle of Protest: Political Ritual in the Tibetan Uprising, 1987–1992*. New York: Columbia University Press.

Scott, Rachelle M. 2009. *Nirvana for Sale? Buddhism, Wealth, and the Dhammakāya Temple in Contemporary Thailand*. Albany, NY: SUNY Press.

Shichiri Wajō. 2000. *Ikeda Daisaku gensō no yabō: shōsetsu* ningen kakumei *hihan*. Tokyo: Shin Nippon Shuppansha.

Shields, James Mark. 2000. "Sexuality, Blasphemy, and Iconoclasm in the Media Age: The Strange Case of the Buddha Bikini." In *God in the Details: American Religion in Popular Culture,* 2nd ed., edited by Eric Michael Mazur and Kate McCarthy, 80–101. New York: Routledge.

——. 2015. "Buddhism: The Conversion of Captain America: Buddhism and Postwar US Popular Culture." In *The Routledge Companion to Religion and Popular Culture,* edited by John C. Lyden and Eric Michael Mazur, 401–418. London: Routledge.

Shimada Hiromi. 2004. *Sōka Gakkai*. Tokyo: Shinchō Shinsho.

——. 2008. *Shin shūkyō "bijinesu."* Tokyo: Kodansha.

——. 2013. *Shinshūkyō mōke no karakuri*. Tokyo: Takarajimasha.

Shūkan daiyamondo. July/August 2004; June 25, 2016.

Shūkan daiyamondo. 週刊ダイヤモンド 2016. Special feature: Sōka Gakkai. June.

Shūyō shūkan tōyō. 週刊東洋経済. 2018. Special feature: *Shūkyō kane to kenryoku* 宗教と権力. September.

Sihlé, Nicolas. 2013. "Money, Butter, and Religion: Remarks on Participation in the Large-Scale Collective Rituals of the Rep kong Tantrists." In *Monastic and Lay Traditions in North-Eastern Tibet,* edited by Yangdon Dhondup, Ulrich Pagel, and Geoffrey Samuel, 165–186. Leiden: Brill.

——. 2015. "Towards a Comparative Anthropology of the Buddhist Gift and Other Transfers." *Religion Compass* 9: 462–482. https://doi.org/10.1111/rec3.12185.

——. 2017. "Ritual Virtuosity, Large-Scale Priest-Patron Networks, and the Ethics of Remunerated Ritual Services." Paper presented at the workshop "Sangha Economies: Temple Organisation and Exchanges in Contemporary Buddhism," Max Planck Institute for Social Anthropology, Halle, September 21–22, 2017.

Silk, Jonathan A. 2007. "Good and Evil in Indian Buddhism: The Five Sins of Immediate Retribution." *Journal of Indian Philosophy* 35: 253–286.

Simmer-Brown, J. 2002. "Remedying Globalization and Consumerism: Joining the Inner and Outer Journeys in 'Perfect Balance.'" *Buddhist-Christian Studies* 22: 31–46.

Sivaraksa, Sulak. 2005. *Conflict, Culture, Change: Engaged Buddhism in a Globalizing World*. Somerville, MA: Wisdom Publications.

——. 2011. *The Wisdom of Sustainability: Buddhist Economics for the Twenty-First Century*. United Kingdom: Souvenir.

Sizemore, Russell, and Donald Swearer, eds. 1990. *Ethics, Wealth, and Salvation: A Study in Buddhist Social Ethics*. Columbia: University of South Carolina Press.

Sklair, Leslie. 1999. "Competing Conceptions of Globalization." *Journal of World-Systems Research* 5, no. 2: 143–164.

Slater, Don. 2005. "The Sociology of Consumption and Lifestyle." In *The Sage Handbook of Sociology,* edited by Craig Calhoun, Chris Rojek, and Bryan Turner, 174–187. London: Sage.

Smart, Tom. 2016. "If You Want to Practice Mindfulness, the Garden Is the Place to Be." *Guardian*, September 1. https://www.theguardian.com/lifeandstyle/gardening-blog/2016/sep/01/if-you-want-to-practice-mindfulness-the-garden-is-the-place-to-be.

Smyer Yü, Dan. 2006. "Genuine Charisma and Its Transmissibility: The Inner Landscape of Tibetan Tulkus in Kham and Golok." *Tibet Journal* 31, no. 4: 57–78.

——. 2008. "Living Buddhas, Netizens, and the Price of Religious Freedom." In *Privatizing China: Socialism from Afar,* edited by In Li Zhang and Aihwa Ong, 197–213. Ithaca, NY: Cornell University Press.

——. 2011. *The Spread of Tibetan Buddhism in China: Charisma, Money, Enlightenment*. London: Routledge.

——. 2015a. "Apologetics of Religion and Science: Conversion Projects in Contemporary China." In *Atheist Secularism and Its Discontents: A Comparative Study of Religion and Communism in Eurasia,* edited by N. Tam and J. Quijada, 155–172. New York: Palgrave.

——. 2015b. "Ensouling the Nation through Fiction: Liang Qichao's Applied Buddhism." *Review of Religion and Chinese Society* 2: 5–20.

——. 2015c. *Mindscaping the Landscape of Tibet: Place, Memorability, and Ecoaesthetics*. Berlin: De Gruyter.

Sodargye. 2000. "A Scientific Treatise on Buddhism." In *A Treasure House of Buddhist Faith*, 145–302. Hong Kong: Chinese Culture Press.

——. 2002. *The Whitecaps on the Ocean of Wisdom*. Hong Kong: Chinese Culture Press.

——. 2012a. *Accomplishing by Doing: A Shower of Blessings from Khenpo*. Lanzhou, Gansu: Gansu People's Art Press.

——. 2012b. *Living with Suffering: Khenpo Teaches You How to Stand Your Ground*. Lanzhou, Gansu: Gansu People's Art Press.

——. 2012c. "Zen and Wealth Management" (lecture transcript). Wisdom and Compassion Buddhist Web. http://www.zhibeifw.com/dxyj/yj_list.php?id=11358.

——. 2013. "Buddhist Cultural Values." http://blog.sina.com.cn/s/blog_5e1e2d280102eabl.html.

——. 2015a. *There's Nothing We Can't Let Go*. Beijing: China Planning Press.

——. 2015b. *What Can't You Part With?* Beijing: China Planning Press.

——. 2017 "The Seven Kinds of Wealth a Practitioner Should Seek." http://www.wanfo.org/thread-83861-1-1.html.

Sodargye, Khenpo, and Dan Smyer Yü. 2017. "Revisioning Buddhism as a Science of the Mind in a Secularized China: A Tibetan Perspective." *Journal of Global Buddhism* 18: 1–23.

Sōka Gakkai Kōhōshitsu. 2016. 2016 年活動報告 [2016 *nen katsudō hōkoku*].

Soka Gakkai Yonjūshūnen Hensan Iinkai, ed. 1970. *Sōka gakkai yonjūnenshi*. Tokyo: Soka Gakkai.

Speck, Simon. 2013. "Religion, Individualisation, and Consumerism: Constructions of Religiosity in 'Liquid' and 'Reflexive' Modernity." In *Religion in Consumer Society: Brands, Consumers, and Markets*, edited by François Gauthier and Tuomas Martikainen, 27–42. Burlington, VT: Ashgate.

Spickard, James V. 2008. "Organizational Transformations in Global Religions: Rethinking the Relationships between Organization, Culture, and Market." *New Religions and Globalization: Empirical, Theoretical, and Methodological Perspectives*, edited by Armin W. Geertz and Margit Warburg, 109–127. Aarhus: Aarhus University Press.

Spinoza, Benedict de. 1990. [1677] *The Ethics*. Translated by R. H. Elwes. In *The Rationalists. Descartes, Spinoza, Leibniz*. New York: Anchor.

Spiro, Melford. 1966. "Religion: Problems of Definition and Explanation." In *Anthropological Approaches to the Study of Religion*, edited by Michael Banton, 85–126. London: Tavistock.

——. 1982. *Buddhism and Society: A Great Tradition and Its Burmese Vicissitudes*. Berkeley: University of California Press.

Stanley, Steven. 2014. "Sila and Sati: An Exploration of Ethics and Mindfulness in Pali Buddhism and Their Implications for Secular Mindfulness-Based Applications." In *Buddhist Foundations of Mindfulness*, edited by E. Shonin et al., 89–113. Cham: Springer.

Stanley, Steven, and Charlotte Longden. 2016. "Constructing the Mindful Subject: Reformulating Experience through Affective-Discursive Practice in Mindfulness-Based Stress Reduction." In *Handbook of Mindfulness*, edited by Ronald E. Purser, David Forbes, and Adam Burke, 305–321. Zurich: Springer.

Stark, Rodney. 1999. "Secularization, RIP." *Sociology of Religion* 60, no. 3: 249–273.

Stolow, Jeremy. 2005. "Religion and/as Media." *Theory, Culture, and Society* 22, no. 4:119–145.

Stone, Jacqueline I. 2012. "The Sin of 'Slandering the True Dharma' in Nichiren's Thought." In *Sins and Sinners: Perspectives from Asian Religions*, edited by Phyllis Granoff and Koichi Shinohara, 111–152. Leiden: Brill.

Street, Sam. 2016. "Cristiano Ronaldo Causes Outrage among Buddhists with Latest Instagram Photo." *Sun,* October 21. https://www.thesun.co.uk/sport/2018934/cristiano-ronaldo-causes-outrage-among-buddhists-with-latest-instagram-photo/.

Strong, John. 2004. *Relics of the Buddha.* Princeton, NJ: Princeton University Press.

Suh, Sharon. 2015. *Silver Screen Buddha: Buddhism in Asian and Western Film.* London: Bloomsbury.

Sullivan, Brenton. 2013. "The Mother of All Monasteries: Gönlung Jampa Ling and the Rise of Mega Monasteries in Northeastern Tibet." PhD diss., University of Virginia.

Sullivan, Winnifred. 2007. *The Impossibility of Religious Freedom.* Princeton, NJ: Princeton University Press.

Sunthon Pongpao. 2015. "Racy Temple Dancers Surrender." *Bangkok Post.* August 8. http://www.bangkokpost.com/news/general/648836/racy-temple-dancers-surrender.

Taixu. 1995a. "An Explanation of Life-Buddhism: Speech at the Virtues of Frugality and Saving Conference in Shanghai, 1928." In *Taixu Collection,* edited by Huang Xianian, 228–231. Beijing: China Academy of Social Sciences Press.

——. 1995b. "Origin of Buddhism and Its New Movements." In *Taixu Collection,* edited by Huang Xianian, 378–390. Beijing: China Academy of Social Sciences Press.

——. 2005. "How to Construct Humanistic Buddhism." In *Writings of Master Taixu,* 47:431–456. Beijing: Religion and Culture Press.

Tamano Kazushi. 2008. *Sōka gakkai no kenkyū.* Tokyo: Kōdansha.

Tambiah, Stanley J. 1970. *Buddhism and the Spirit Cults in North-East Thailand.* Cambridge: Cambridge University Press.

——. 1984. *The Buddhist Saints of the Forest and the Cult of Amulets.* Cambridge: Cambridge University Press.

Taylor, Charles. 2007. *A Secular Age.* Cambridge, MA: Belknap.

Taylor, Jim. 2007. "Buddhism, Copying, and the Art of the Imagination in Thailand." *Journal of Global Buddhism* 8: 1–19.

——. 2008. *Buddhism and Postmodern Imaginings in Thailand: The Religiosity of Urban Space.* Aldershot: Ashgate.

Tehranian, Majid. 2007. "Globalization and Religious Resurgence: An Historical Perspective." *Muslim World* 97 (July): 385–394.

Tenzin Jinba. 2014. *In the Land of the Eastern Queendom: The Politics of Gender and Ethnicity on the Sino-Tibetan Border.* Seattle: University of Washington Press.

Thanissaro Bhikkhu. 2010. "Parikuppa Sutta: In Agony" (AN 5.129). *Access to Insight (Legacy Edition).* July 3. http://www.accesstoinsight.org/tipitaka/an/an05/an05.129.than.html.

Thomas, Jolyon Baraka. 2015. "The Buddhist Virtues of Raging Lust and Crass Materialism in Contemporary Japan." *Material Religion* 11, no. 4: 485–506.

Tibet Policy Institute. 2017. *Cultural Genocide in Tibet: A Report.* Dharamsala: Central Tibet Administration.

Tideman, Sander G. 2011. "Gross National Happiness." In *Ethical Principles and Economic Transformation—A Buddhist Approach,* edited by László Zsolnai, 133–153. Springer.

Todd Lewis, L. 1993. "Newar-Tibetan Trade and the Domestication of 'Siṃhala sārthabāhu Avadāna.'" *History of Religions* 33, no. 2: 136–160.

Travis, Daryl. 2013. *How Does It Make You Feel? Why Emotion Wins the Battle of Brands.* Chicago: Brandtrust.

Tsing, Anna Lowenhaupt. 2015. *The Mushroom at the End of the World: On the Possibility of Life in Capitalist Ruins.* Princeton, NJ: Princeton University Press.

Tsukada Hotaka. 2015. *Shūkyō to seiji no tentetsuten: hoshu gōdō to seikyō itchi no shūkyō shakaigaku.* Tokyo: Kadensha.

Tuttle, Gary. 2005. *Tibetan Buddhists in the Making of Modern China.* New York: Columbia University Press.

Tweed, Thomas. 1999. "Night-Stand Buddhists and Other Creatures: Sympathizers, Adherents, and the Study of Religion." In *American Buddhism, Methods and Findings in Recent Scholarship,* Curzon Critical Studies in Buddhism, edited by Duncan Ryuken Williams and Christopher S. Queen, 71–90. Richmond: Curzon.

——. 2008. "Why Are Buddhists So Nice? Media Representations of Buddhism and Islam in the United States since 1945." *Material Religion: The Journal of Objects* 4, no. 1: 91–93.

Twitchell, James A. 1996. *Adcult USA: The Triumph of Advertising in American Culture.* New York: Columbia University Press.

Uprety, Prem R. 1996. "The Economics of Buddhism: An Alternative Model for Community Development." *Contributions to Nepalese Studies* 23, no. 1: 119–124.

Usunier, Jean-Claude. 2014. "'9591': The Global Commoditization of Religions through GATS, WTO, and Marketing Practices." In *Religions as Brands: New Perspectives on the Marketization of Religion and Spirituality,* edited by Jean-Claude Usunier and Jorg Stölz, 27–43. Farnham: Ashgate.

Walsh, Michael J. 2007. "The Economics of Salvation: Toward a Theory of Exchange in Chinese Buddhism." *Journal of the American Academy of Religion* 75, no. 2: 353–382.

——. 2010. *Sacred Economies: Buddhist Monasticism and Territoriality in Medieval China.* New York: Columbia University Press.

——. 2014. "The Buddhist Monastic Economy." In *Modern Chinese Religion,* part 1: *Song-Liao-Jin-Yuan (960–1368),* Handbook of Oriental Studies, Section Four: China, edited by John Lagerwey and Pierre Marsonne, 1268–1301. Leiden: Brill.

Warner, Stephen R. 1993. "Work in Progress toward a New Paradigm for the Sociological Study of Religion in the United States." *American Journal of Sociology* 98: 1044–1093.

Watanabe Takesato. 2000. *Seikyō shinbun no yomikata: Sōka gakkai kikanshi no enerugī-gen o saguru.* Tokyo: Sangokan.

Waters, Malcolm. 2001. *Globalization.* 2nd ed. London: Routledge.

Watts, Jonathan, and Masazumi Okano. 2012. "Reconstructing Priestly Identity and Roles and the Development of Socially Engaged Buddhism in Contemporary Japan." In *Handbook of Contemporary Japanese Religions,* 345–372. Leiden: Brill.

Weber, Max. 1958. *The Religion of India: The Sociology of Buddhism and Hinduism.* Glencloe, IL: Free Press.

——. 1978 [1922]. *Economy and Society.* 2 vols. Berkeley: University of California Press.

——. 2004. "Introduction to the Economic Ethics of the World Religions." In *The Essential Weber: A Reader*, edited by Sam Whimster, 55–80. London: Routledge.

Weber, Thomas. 1999. "Gandhi, Deep Ecology, Peace Research, and Buddhist Economics." *Journal of Peace Research* 36, no. 3: 349–361.

Wieczorek, Iris. 2002. *Neue religiöse Bewegungen in Japan: Eine empirische Studie zum gesellschaftspolitischen Engagement in der japanischen Bevölkerung.* Hamburg: Institut für Asienkunde.

Williams, Duncan R. 2005. *The Other Side of Zen: A Social History of Sōtō Zen.* Princeton, NJ: Princeton University Press.

Williams-Oerberg, Elizabeth. 2020. "Buddhism: A Unique Selling Point in Ladakh." In *Buddhist Tourism in Asia: Global Networks within Sacred Sites,* edited by Courtney Bruntz and Brooke Schedneck. Honolulu: University of Hawai'i Press.

Wilson, Jeff. 2019. "Buddhism Without Merit: Theorizing Buddhist Religio-Economic Activity in the Contemporary World." *Journal of Global Buddhism* 20, special issue: "Theoretical and Conceptual Approaches to the Burgeoning Field of Buddhism and Economics," edited by Elizabeth Williams-Oerberg and Trine Brox, 87–104.

Winter, Franz. 2016. "When Tibetan Buddhism Goes West." *Religious Studies Review* 42 (March 1): 15–18.

Wisdom and Compassion Buddhist Web. 2012. "30% of the 500 Nouveau Riche Believe in Buddhism." http://www.zhibeifw.com/wap/r.php?id=7231.

Wood, Benjamin. 2013. "The Scrupulous Use of Gifts for the Sangha: Self-Ennoblement through the Ledger in Tibetan Autobiography." *Revue d'Etudes Tibétaines* 26 (April): 35–55.

Woodhouse, Emily. 2012. *The Role of Tibetan Buddhism in Environmental Conservation under Changing Socio-Economic Conditions in China.* Centre for Environmental Policy and the Department of Life Sciences, Imperial College, London.

Wuthnow, Robert, and Wendy Cadge. 2004. "Buddhists and Buddhism in the United States: The Scope of Influence." *Journal for the Scientific Study of Religion* 43, no. 3: 363–380.

Xu, Hongdi. 1992. "The Origin of the Relationship between Merchants and Buddhism in Ancient India." *Journal of Shanxi Normal University* 1: 72–76.

Xu Xiao. 2014. "Khenpo Sodargye: Descending from the Mountains and Gentle Diligence." *Portrait Magazine* no. 1: 118–121.

Yang, Fenggang. 2006. "Red, Black, and Gray Markets of Religion in China." *Sociological Quarterly* 47: 93–122.

Yang, Mayfair. 2008. *Chinese Religiosities: Afflictions of Modernity and State Formation.* Berkeley: University of California Press.

Yano Economic Research Institute. "Research on Funeral Business Market." https://www.yano.co.jp/press-release/show/press_id/1765.

Yeh, Emily. 2013. *Taming Tibet: Landscape Transformation and the Gift of Chinese Development.* Ithaca, NY: Cornell University Press.

Yinshun. 2010. *Buddha in the Human World.* Beijing: Zhonghua Book Company.

Yui, Monami. 2015. "Try Before You Buy a Coffin: Death Business Thrives in Japan." *Bloomberg.com.* https://www.bloomberg.com/news/articles/2015-12-15/try-a-coffin-for-size-the-death-business-is-thriving-in-japan.

Zhang, Yinong. 2014. "Between Nation and Religion: The Sino-Tibetan Buddhist Network in Post-Reform China." *Chinese Sociological Review* 45, no. 1: 55–69. https://doi.org/10.2753/CSA2162-0555450103.

Zsolnai, László. 2007. "Western Economics versus Buddhist Economics." *Society and Economy* 29, no. 2: 145–153.

——, ed. 2011. *Spirituality and Ethics in Management.* Springer.

Zsolnai, László, and Knut Johannessen Ims, eds. 2006. *Business within Limits: Deep Ecology and Buddhist Economics.* Vol. 1. Bern: Peter Lang.

Contributors

Jørn Borup is associate professor in the Department of the Study of Religion at Aarhus University. He has conducted research on Japanese Buddhism, Buddhism in the West, religious diversity, spirituality and religion, and migration. Besides articles for journals and publications in Danish, he is the author of *Japanese Rinzai Zen Buddhism: Myōshinji, a Living Religion* (2008) and coeditor of *Eastspirit: Transnational Spirituality and Religious Circulation in East and West* (2017) and *The Critical Analysis of Religious Diversity* (2018).

Trine Brox is associate professor of modern Tibetan studies and the director of the Center for Contemporary Buddhist Studies in the Department of Cross-Cultural and Regional Studies, University of Copenhagen. Brox is the PI of the international collaborative research project Buddhism, Business, and Believers and one of the founders of the research community Object Lessons from Tibet and the Himalayas. Brox has written extensively about contemporaneous issues in Tibet and the Tibetan exile, including the monograph *Tibetan Democracy: Governance, Leadership, and Conflict in Exile* (2016). She has also coedited the book *On the Fringes of the Harmonious Society: Tibetans and Uyghurs in Socialist China* (2014, with Ildikó Bellér-Hann).

Jane Caple is a Marie Skłodowska-Curie Fellow at the University of Copenhagen. Her primary research interests are in religion, economy, and morality. She is the author of *Morality and Monastic Revival in Post-Mao Tibet* (2019) as well as a number of journal articles on Buddhism, economy, and society in late-twentieth- and early-twenty-first-century Amdo/northeastern Tibet.

Marianne Viftrup Hedegaard is an anthropologist and PhD fellow in the Department of Cross-Cultural and Regional Studies at the University of Copenhagen. In her PhD project "Burnout and Bliss—Mindfulness at Work," she deals with the influx of mindfulness interventions and contemplative practices in Danish workplaces, focusing on the entanglements of working bodies, economy, and religion.

Michael Jerryson is professor of religious studies at Youngstown State University. His research interests pertain to religion and identity, particularly with regard to gender, race, and class. He is the author of *Buddhist Fury: Religion and Violence in Southern Thailand* (2011), and he has coedited the *Oxford Handbook of Religion and Violence* (2013) and *Buddhist Warfare* (2010). His latest publication is *If You Meet the Buddha on the Road: Buddhism, Politics, and Violence* (2018), and he is working on a forthcoming edited volume tentatively entitled *Buddhist-Muslim Relations in a Theravada World.*

Levi McLaughlin is associate professor in the Department of Philosophy and Religious Studies at North Carolina State University. He received his PhD from Princeton University after previous study at the University of Tokyo, and he holds a BA and MA in East Asian studies from the University of Toronto. Levi is coauthor and coeditor of *Kōmeitō: Politics and Religion in Japan* (2014) and the special issue "Salvage and Salvation: Religion and Disaster Relief in Asia" (*Asian Ethnology,* June 2016). He is the author of *Soka Gakkai's Human Revolution: The Rise of a Mimetic Nation in Modern Japan* (2019).

Lionel Obadia is full professor of anthropology at the University of Lyon, France, and at other French universities (EHESS, EPHE, SciencePo). He specializes in the anthropology of religion, Asian religions, and globalization. He has conducted fieldwork in France, Europe (on Buddhism in the West), Nepal (on Buddhism and shamanism), and South India. He has published ten books and more than 150 papers (journal articles and book chapters). He now heads the department of Social Sciences and Humanities at the French Agency for Research (ANR).

Inken Prohl is professor of religious studies at the Universität Heidelberg since 2006. For several years she has been conducting fieldwork in Japan and Germany. Her research interests focus on modern transformations of Buddhism, new approaches of "Material Religion," and religion and branding. Together with John Nelson she published the *Handbook of Contemporary Japanese Religions* (2012). Her publications also include *Religiöse Innovationen: Die Shinto-Organisation World Mate in Japan* (2005), *Zen für Dummies* (2010), and "Buddhism in Contemporary Europe" (2014; in Mario Poceski, ed., *The Wiley Blackwell Companion to East and Inner Asian Buddhism*).

Dan Smyer Yü is Kuige Professor of Ethnology, School of Ethnology and Sociology, and founding director of the Center for Trans-Himalayan Studies, at Yunnan University. Before his current faculty appointment, he was a senior researcher and a research group leader at the Max Planck Institute for the Study of Religious and Ethnic Diversity in Göttingen, Germany. He is the author of *The Spread of Tibetan Buddhism in China: Charisma, Money, Enlightenment* (2011) and *Mindscaping the Landscape of Tibet: Place, Memorability, Ecoaesthetics* (2015). His research interests are religion and ecology, environmental humanities, and comparative studies of Eurasian secularisms.

Elizabeth Williams-Oerberg is assistant professor and codirector of the Center for Contemporary Buddhist Studies in the Department of Cross-Cultural and Regional Studies, University of Copenhagen. As part of the Buddhism, Business, and Believers collaborative project, her research currently focuses on Buddhism and tourism in Ladakh, India. She is coeditor of the *Journal of Global Buddhism*'s special issue "Theoretical and Conceptual Approaches to the Burgeoning Field of Buddhism and Economics" (2019). She is working on a forthcoming special issue and edited volume on the topic of "Buddhism and Youth" and a book monograph based on her PhD, entitled *Young Buddhism.*

Index